Rug Hooking In Maine

1838-1940

Mildred Cole Péladeau

4880 Lower Valley Road Atglen, Pennsylvania 19310

Dedicated to
Alice "Ma" Peasley and "Aunt" Minnie Light
I Wish I Had Known Them

Designed by John P. Cheek
Cover design by Bruce Waters
Type set in Zurich BT

ISBN: 978-0-7643-2882-4
Printed in China

Schiffer Books are available at special discounts for
bulk purchases for sales promotions or premiums.
Special editions, including personalized covers, corporate imprints, and excerpts can be created in large
quantities for special needs. For more information
contact the publisher:

Published by Schiffer Publishing Ltd.
4880 Lower Valley Road
Atglen, PA 19310
Phone: (610) 593-1777; Fax: (610) 593-2002
E-mail: Info@schifferbooks.com

For the largest selection of fine reference books on
this and related subjects, please visit our web site at
www.schifferbooks.com
We are always looking for people to write books on
new and related subjects. If you have an idea for a
book please contact us at the above address.

This book may be purchased from the publisher.
Include $3.95 for shipping.
Please try your bookstore first.
You may write for a free catalog.

In Europe, Schiffer books are distributed by
Bushwood Books
6 Marksbury Ave.
Kew Gardens
Surrey TW9 4JF England
Phone: 44 (0) 20 8392-8585; Fax: 44 (0) 20 8392-9876
E-mail: info@bushwoodbooks.co.uk
Website: www.bushwoodbooks.co.uk
Free postage in the U.K., Europe; air mail at cost.

Contents

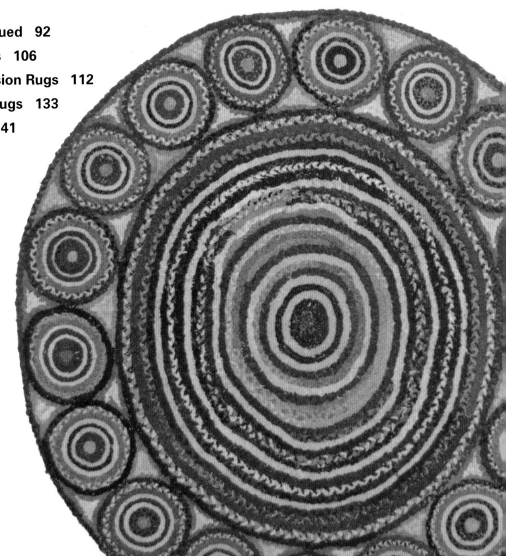

Foreword

What if everyone was able to find their passion and share it such as Mildred Cole Péladeau has done? How much richer the world would be! And, as Péladeau has said in her Introduction, "What a wondrous thing!"

Péladeau has acted on her passion and the result of her staggering amount of research is a wonderful book unrivalled in depth and scope. Not since Kate and Joel Kopp's *American Hooked Rugs: Folk Art Underfoot* has the subject of hooked rugs been explored so credibly. Originally made to warm cold floors and add cheer to a dreary day, hooked rugs have been elevated to an art form. Rug hooking has been a critical means of expression in the United States and Canada and, although historically largely based on need, has given us some of the most exciting examples of folk art. Péladeau's rich, informative text and accompanying photographs clearly illustrate this point.

Through twenty years of research, Péladeau has unearthed a wealth of new, convincing, and defining information that will reorganize current knowledge.

While hooking was mainly a creative outlet for women, Péladeau's book explores how the important craft came to be and how its progression into mainstream commerce was perpetuated by a select group of men who obviously knew a great idea when they saw one. As the craft gained popularity, it is interesting to note the amount of time, energy and financial resources being spent on "women's work" by men. Her research into Waldoboro rugs versus the "Acadian" rugs is groundbreaking and convincingly clarifies previous confusion.

Péladeau left no stone unturned. Her unbridled enthusiasm for the subject is evident on every page. Passion has dictated her research and her ability to share it clearly and convincingly is a tremendous contribution to the scholarship of rug hooking and folk art. Read every word, learn and enjoy – then, share your passion.

Paul Laverty
Author, *Silk Stocking Mats: Hooked Mats of the Grenfell Mission.*

Introduction

I can remember as a small child interrupting play to dash into the house shouting "Rag man's coming. Rag man's coming." Slowly emerging over the brow of the hill was a horse and wagon (the age of mechanized travel had arrived, but some traditions lingered), the driver endlessly chanting "Rags to bags. Rags to bags" in an attempt to solicit old rags from neighborhood homes. Mother scurried into the shed gathering up the pile of rags that had been accumulating. While I raced out to stop the ragman, she dragged forth her treasure. The ragman weighed the rags and paid my mother a paltry sum which I believe was a penny a pound. I did not know then that the rags were being gathered for use in the making of paper, thus explaining the ragman's chant, "Rags to (paper) bags." What a wondrous thing!

Many years later I learned of the rugs that "grew" from just such rags under the influence of crafts people who refused to give up their rags to the ragman. What a wondrous thing! It was the late Roberta Hansen of Yarmouth, Maine, who many collectors and dealers throughout the Northeast will remember as a connoisseur of hooked rugs and all things antique, who introduced me to the value of hooked rugs as folk art.

Long intrigued with Maine's extremely rich history in the field of rug hooking, I have been appalled at how little that heritage has been appreciated and how sparsely it has been preserved within the state. Rug hooking is Maine's premiere handicraft, more prolific even than quilt-making. Many believe it originated in this state and tradition suggests that the craft started in Maine or Nova Scotia.

Our museums are brimming with quilts and samplers, and rightfully so. However, early quilts, to a large extent, are not original forms of folk art. The vast majority show excellent craftsmanship in putting together someone else's design. They are beautiful, but most follow a standard pattern devised by some one person who deserves the single honor of being the true folk artist. There is the Drunkard's Path, the Star of Bethlehem, the Pine Tree, the Schoolhouse, the Log Cabin, the Double Wedding Ring and endless others, all delightfully enchanting, but they are not original designs. There are exceptions, of course, including the wonderful embroidered crazy quilts and certainly the so-called "Baltimore Album quilts." I heartily applaud today's quilters who have taken on the art of self-design to create some true "works of art."

Equally as charming in their own right are the schoolgirl samplers, all of which follow a rather strict formula, but they are made through careful guidance and instruction in technique, following a pre-set concept.

Early rugs, on the other hand, are true examples of folk art, each one individually made, usually by some isolated rural housewife who had no access to pre-designed patterns. She sat in front of the fireplace with a piece of charcoal and let her imagination dictate the character of her rug as she sketched out her design on a piece of linen or a burlap bag. What a wondrous thing! The result may have been really bad, but they created some gems as well, most of which have left the state to be preserved in other museums and collections.

And so, I took upon myself the task of trying to research and preserve at least some of this vast history. To compile the entire history in a single volume would be impossible, so there are omissions; neither does this book delve into contemporary hooking. The book studies the early non-woven rugs through the various stages of that history, until the history — as the adage predicts — begins "to repeat itself." Accumulating appropriate historical photographs and illustrations has resulted in images that are not always up to today's standards, but a book of this type is forced to make use of what was available at the time. The important thing is to preserve the images and make them accessible to others through publication.

Rug Hooking in Maine: 1838-1940 spans the period from 1838 to the 1940s, a period dealing with the inception of rug-making as a craft form in this country to the attempts to turn it into a fine art. It includes the first documented record of rug-making in the United States, the rise of the famous Waldoboro hooked rug, the growth of the pre-printed patterns, the Arts & Crafts period rugs, the "Folk Art Period' and the attempts to use rug hooking as a medium for fine art.

For the first time, the interrelationship of E.S. Frost & Company, Ebenezer Ross and Alvin Gibbs is unraveled and a fourth entity (The American Rug Pattern Company) is revealed as playing a vital role in what became a tangled quadrangle.

The cycle which follows the growth of three significant Maine "cottage" industries ends the century around the onset of World War II when the history begins to repeat itself. There was a renewed interest in the Arts & Crafts Movement, the continued adoration of folk art rugs and the exploration by contemporary hookers in creating rugs as fine art. That history will undoubtedly continue to evolve and grow in centuries to come, but its roots will always be a vital part of Maine's history.

Mildred Cole Péladeau
Readfield, Maine
2007

Acknowledgments

Along the way, many people have been extremely helpful in the development of this book. First and foremost, I must thank my husband, Marius. The book never would have happened without his help and guidance, the endless trips to photograph rugs, the endless hours of reading and editing the text, the numerous meals prepared to give me more time at the computer, and for tolerating the endless frustrations when things went awry.

Although he wishes to remain anonymous, I must thank a very special friend who provided his expertise on photography and computer technology.

The staff at the Maine State Library must be singled out for the heroic effort they were always willing to put forth to search the world for some needed item or information — the sincere appreciation of this author!

Many others along the way contributed so very much. Even the unexpected delivery of some homemade fiddlehead doughnuts at a period when frustration was rampant, inched the book a little further along its way to completion.

I also would like to thank the following people for sharing their expertise and encouragement and kindly granting permission to use copyrighted material:

Marianne Barnicle, Archivist, Maine Sea Coast Mission; Beverly BaRoss; Nancy W. Brown, President, Appleton Historical Society; Lora Urbanelli, Director, and Bethany Engstrom, Assistant Registrar, Farnsworth Art Museum; Deanna Bonner-Ganter, Curator of Photography, Art and Archives, Maine State Museum; Dennis Bouley, Computer Technician; Neil Brittman, Pond-Ekberg Press; Dr. Charles E. Burden; Joseph Caputo; Roberta Chandler; Pat Christiansen; Sarah Clemons; Nancy Curtis, Librarian, Fogler Library, University of Maine; David Dearborn, Research Assistant, Maine Maritime Museum; Gary DeLong, Maine Sea Coast Mission; Down East Books; Florence Drake; Dwight B. Demeritt; Fred and Maureen Fenton; Peter Hastings Falk; Jeff and Suzanne Good; Pamela Grossman; Nan Gurley and Peter Mavris.

Also, Emily Guthrie, Assistant Librarian, Winterthur Library; Christopher G. Hall, Registrar, Maine Maritime Museum; Charles Ipcar; Dahlov Ipcar; Robert Ipcar; Thomas Jordan, President, Waldoborough Historical Society; Muriel Kenoyer; Bruce Komusin, Great Cranberry Island Historical Society; Laurie LaBar, Curator, Maine State Museum; Pamela C. LaBonte; C. Gardner Lane Jr.; Paula Laverty, author, *Silk Stocking Mats: Hooked Mats of the Grenfell Mission;* Sally Leahey, Assistant Director, McArthur Library; Christine LeBlond, Tuttle Publishing Company; Nathan Lipfert, Librarian, Maine Maritime Museum; Lovell Historical Society; Townsend Ludington; Sharon and Jeffrey Lipton; Kenneth Martin; John Mayer, Curator, Maine Historical Society; John McDade, Museum Technician, National Park Service; Sam Pennington, Publisher, Maine Antique Digest; Pamela Quick, MIT Press; Robert T. Pyle, Librarian, Northeast Harbor Library; Nancy E. Randolph, Publisher Just Write Books; Scott Robson, Curator, Art Gallery of Nova Scotia; Ann Seaver; Beverly Slye, former President, Waldoborough Historical Society; Earle Shettleworth, Director, Maine Historic Preservation Commission; Patricia Stauble; Lionel N. and Gerry Sterling; Janet Szatkowski, Harry M. Fraser Company; Rosalind G. Tufts; Ellie Vuilleumier, Registrar, Portland Museum of Art; Connie Wiberg, Deer Isle-Stonington Historical Society; and Mrs. Peggy Zorach.

Thanks also goes to the photographers who played a vital role in the production of the book: Elmer R. Grossman, M.D., Charles Ipcar, Robert Ipcar, Bruce Komusin, Dr. Jeffrey Lipton, John Mayer, Neal Scott, Ann Seaver, Nathanial Zorach. All rugs credited to *MCP Collection* belong to the author and the photography was done by her husband.

Chapter I

The Beginning

"Sumptuous palaces" were being constructed on the hearth, in front of which were the "sodded lawns and artfully concealed pewter basins representing duck ponds, in which cork ducks and geese paddled about and seemed almost to quack and hiss." This was not just child's play. It was an educational exercise for Mary Steele of Boston in an early eighteenth century summer. She was learning to properly decorate the hearth, an important consideration for the well brought-up young lady, necessary for becoming a suitable housewife. Years later, childhood reminiscences of these early lessons would be incorporated into an unfinished novel, *The Bay Boy*, written by her son, Royall Tyler (1757-1826), an early American dramatist.[1]

Eventually, the "sumptuous palaces" became far less humble dwellings, and the "sodded lawn" turned into a floral spray or urn of flowers, earnestly reproduced in the form of a hearth rug, probably yarn-sewn or shirred. It was an elaborate undertaking, foreshadowing what may have been the most basic reason for the development of the rug-making craft.

The significance of the hearth as the center of family life should not be underestimated. The cheerfully blazing fireplace, cherished as a source of warmth and well-being, was a natural gathering place for friends and family. While it still remained the gathering place, during the summer months it lost its most basic appeal. The fire, needed for cooking, had been moved to the summer kitchen, leaving a hearth barren of its blazing fire, black with soot and dust. It needed a new attention-getter. This may well explain the "why" of developing yarn-sewn and shirred rugs which were much too delicate to withstand the wear of normal foot traffic. The sometimes crude, but always sincere attempt to come up with a new attraction for fireside dwellers satisfied the need for color and creativity. Certainly a preponderance of the very early rugs was cited as being "hearth rugs."

One can readily surmise that friendly competition among neighbors must have developed to determine who could come up with the most inter-esting hearth adornment. This likely provided the impetus to create ever more elaborate rugs, stimulating a craft form unique to this country.

The craft grew in stages from yarn-sewn and shirred to hooked, the latter still being widely practiced today. Scholars suggest that hooking likely originated in either Maine or the Maritime Provinces of Canada, but a more precise, documented origin is elusive. Who can say what woman (or man) was the first to draw a piece of fabric through a linen or jute foundation? Lack of any early sophisticated rug-making tools certainly is a significant factor supporting the origins as being North American. Had hooking been practiced in other countries, immigrants would have brought the tools with them. This was not a handicap for the hookers were ingenious in devising suitable implements.

Whatever the genesis, five of the most significant developments in America's rug hooking history all had their origins in Maine, a state that has, for more than a century-and-a-half, maintained a leadership role:

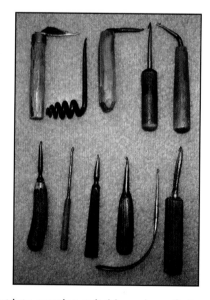

A great deal of effort went into creating suitable and comfortable tools for the hooking process. Generally they consisted of a whittled round wooden handle with a filed nail hook inserted into one end. The implement at the upper left seems to have been made from a jackknife blade filed to dull a sharp edge. Second from the upper left looks like a converted stove lid-lifter. Fairly common was the use of eating utensils such as bone-handled forks with the tine ends removed and the remaining metal rod filed into a hook as seen at the lower left. While artistically made, the hand-forged steel hook, second from the right in the lower row, would have been impossible to work with, the hard edges quickly creating blisters. Early hooks are a special field of collecting. *MCP collection.*

1. The first published record of the rug-making craft appeared in a Maine newspaper.

2. The development and rise to fame of the Waldoboro rug would set standards for technique and artistry still envied today.

3. Edward Sands Frost, a resident of Biddeford, Maine, would forever change the craft by introducing his pre-stamped patterns, with the resultant development of Biddeford as the early Mecca for the manufacture of stamped patterns.

4. Frost's successor, James A. Strout, would initiate the search for and, in cooperation with Ebenezer Ross of Ohio, develop the punch needle machine that would add another entirely new dimension to rug-making.

5. William Winthrop Kent, a Bangor native, would, despite some erroneous conclusions, exert a major influence on hooked rug scholarship through his three books emphasizing the history and social importance of rugs, as well as their artistic significance. These books, even now, demand premium prices and are eagerly sought by contemporary collectors. Kent continues to be quoted, despite some known errors.[2]

The first publication acknowledging the craft of rug making was the pamphlet listing the exhibitors at the *First Exhibition and Fair* sponsored by the Maine Charitable Mechanic Association in 1838 at the Portland, Maine, City Hall.[3] This brochure may well be the most significant document in the entire study of hooking. Its importance cannot be overestimated, for it provides a documentary peg upon which the whole history of American non-woven rugs can be hung.

Any earlier history defiantly resists efforts by the most determined scholars to unearth specific, documented origins. The booklet listing the Fair's prize winners provides a wealth of information as well as a compendium of confusion for what it fails to say.

A quick glance at the booklet immediately questions the separation of "rugs made of yarn" and "rugs made of rags." Those made of yarn were what is known today as "yarn-sewn," so-called to distinguish them from the later punch-needle versions or even rugs hooked with yarn.

A yarn-sewn rug is exactly what its name indicates. A needle was threaded with a homespun wool yarn and "sewn," using a running stitch, through the foundation, usually linen, pulling the stitch snug on the reverse, but leaving a loose loop on the surface, thus creating a pile. The upper surface was usually sheared or clipped resulting in a soft, velvety nap.

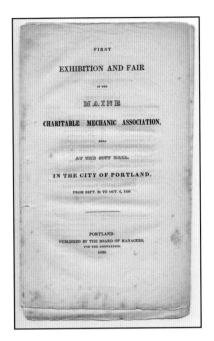

This unique publication is undoubtedly the most important document in the history of American rug-making. While agricultural fairs were held prior to the date of this booklet, it marks the first fair in this country which included craft exhibits. Sponsored by the Maine Charitable Mechanic Association, it was held at Portland (Maine) City Hall from September 24 to October 6, 1838, and provides a valuable list of crafts people exhibiting both yarn and rag rugs. *Maine Historical Society Collections.*

The only way to identify a yarn-sewn is through an examination of the reverse. Unlike a hooked rug, which shows the hooked material in a continuous line, the yarn-sewn has a space between each stitch in a dot and dash pattern.

A second type of yarn-sewn rug is the reed stitch in which a reed or perhaps a knitting needle, is laid upon the foundation surface and the yarn sewn over and over the reed. At the end of the reed it could be slipped out or the yarn could be cut through the center of the loop, thus freeing the reed. Since these loops would all be an even height it was not necessary to shear the rug, thereby saving considerable yarn wasted in the earlier yarn-sewn rug. Since the stitches are made over and over the reed, they will appear lined up side by side on the back of this type of rug, as opposed to the continuous line of one stitch following another in the general yarn-sewn.

Leonard F. Burbank seems to have initiated the term "reed stitch" for it has not been found prior to his article, "Little-Known Masterpieces VII, Reed-Stitch: A Relative of the Hooked Rug," which appeared in *The Magazine Antiques* in 1922. Not only was the stitch used in yarn-sewn rugs, but in the earlier bed rugs, in which it was termed the "stroke stitch." In the catalog accompanying the *Bed Ruggs/1722-1833* exhibition presented by the Wadsworth Atheneum in 1972, the stroke stitch was defined as "short parallel stitches, straight or slightly oblique, forming parallel diagonal stitches on the surface." It does not mention the use of a reed.[4]

Because of the historical significance of the 1838 Fair, the complete list of exhibitors in both yarn and rag categories is being included here. Hopefully it will engender further study and discussion. Not only does the list describe the geographic distribution of the hookers, but it is a study of the scope of the craft, including other auxiliary pieces:

Rugs Made of Yarn

Misses *Hatch*, Kennebunk. Two domestic Rugs, wrought without patterns; many of the colors are specimens of domestic dyeing. They deserve the first attention, being very superior. A Silver Medal.

Miss *Almena Stevens*, Westbrook, aged 15. One Hearth Rug; second best.

The colors are tastefully arranged and the work beautifully executed. A Diploma.

Miss *Sparrow*, Portland. One Rug; good imitation of imported rugs. Third Best, A Diploma.

Mrs. *Barnard*, Waldoboro'. One Rug; handsome and well made. A Diploma.

Miss *Belford*, Portland. One Rug; very handsome.

Miss *B. Stevens*, Westbrook. One Rug; well made and tastefully arranged. A Diploma.

Mrs. *Dunham*, Westbrook. One Rug; very handsome. A Diploma.

Miss *Dean*, Biddeford. One Rug; yarn spun by herself; work good. A Diploma.

Miss *Bradbury*, Portland. One Rug.

Miss *Lucy Stevens*, Portland. One Hearth Rug. A Diploma.

Mrs. *Lowell*, Standish. One Hearth Rug.

Miss *Marr*, Scarboro'. Three Hearth Rugs.

Miss *How*, Portland. One Rug.

Mrs. *Stevens*, Portland. One Rug; excellent work.

Mrs. *Woodman*, Portland. One Rug. A Diploma.

In the yarn-sewn group, Mrs. Barnard of Waldoboro was a significant entry for it helps define the origin of the famous Waldoboro rug discussed in the following chapter. Miss Dean of Biddeford did "one Rug; yarn spun by herself; good work."[5] This goes against tradition in its implication that the other women, as early as 1838, did not spin their own yarns. Seven of the exhibitors were awarded diplomas while five entries received no awards.

The winning entry pointedly states that "many" of the colors were examples of domestic dyeing, suggesting that this was unusual enough to be mentioned and that they were considered "very superior." The fact that these rugs were "wrought without patterns" certainly implies that others may have used patterns. It is doubtful that specific patterns were available, but the "patterns" most likely indicated a design copied from a piece of china, perhaps an embroidery design or other decorative motif available in the various households at that time.

These descriptions are in sharp contrast to the generally established image of early rug-makers spinning their own yarns, gathering berries, barks and greens to create their own dyes to tint their own hand-woven materials. It is plausible to assume that women likely to submit their works for consideration at the Portland Fair were of a more affluent class and could afford to purchase materials already dyed or woven, while the poorer rural lady was doing it the hard way and had little time to be concerned about entries in competitive fairs. In following decades rug-makers would continue or revert to the time-tested do-it-yourself tradition. The pamphlet also carries this listing:

Rugs Made of Rags.

Mrs. *Edgecomb*, Gardiner. One rug; A Diploma.

Mrs. *Joseph Thaxter*, Portland. One Rug; second best. A Diploma.

Mrs. *Waite*, Portland. One Rug; design and colors good; work excellent. A Diploma.

Mrs. *A. Beckett*, Portland. One Rug; Handsome and well made. A Diploma.

Miss *Sewall*, Kennebunk One Rug; handsome. A Diploma.

Mrs. *J. Rolf*, Portland. Hearth Rug; handsome.

Mrs. *Carter*, Orono. A Rug; handsome.

Miss *Hanson*, Portland. One Rug; made of seventy-nine pieces of Carpeting; neatly sewed.

Miss *Cleaves*, Portland. One Rug; well made.

Miss *Noyes*, Portland. One Rug.

Mrs. *E. Thomas*, Portland. One Rug; work good.

Miss *How*, Portland. Two hearth rugs.

Miss *Stevens*, Portland, One Mat.

Miss *Sawyer*, Portland. Four Hearth Rugs.

Miss *Little*, Danville. One Rug; handsome and well made. A Diploma.

Mrs. *Lewis*, Portland. One Rug; Handsome and well made. A Diploma.

Miss ——, Scarboro'. One Rug.

Miss *Lefavor*, Portland. One Rug.

Miss *Huse*, (aged 8,) Portland. One Rug; very well made.

Miss *Woodman*, Portland. Two rugs.

Miss *Ricker*, Parsonsfield. A Mat and Rug; excellent taste and work. A Diploma.

Miss *L. Sawyer*, Portland. One Hearth Rug.

Miss *Soule*, Portland. One Hearth Rug.

Mrs. *Hay*, Portland, an aged lady. A Rug; well made and arranged.

The first rug ever awarded a first prize at a craft fair in this country was one of two yarn-sewn rugs submitted by the Misses Hatch at the exhibition held in 1838 at Portland City Hall. The basket and fruit design shows a surprising artistic sophistication. A cluster of fruits anchors each corner, while a frame of flowers and fruit defines the frame. The yarn fringe is a frequent element in early yarn-sewn rugs. Its current whereabouts is unknown. c.1838. Presumed to be homespun yarn on a handwoven linen base. William Winthrop Kent, *Rare Hooked Rugs,* p. 134, plate 165.

Miss *Whittier,* Portland. A Mat and Rug, made of the head ends of Broadcloth; flowers very neatly worked on. A Diploma.

Miss *Purinton,* Portland. One Rug.

Miss *H. Roberts,* Portland, (aged 54.) Two Rugs made of thrumbs; work good.

Miss *Mary Emery,* Portland. One Hearth Rug.

Miss *S. Going,* Portland. One Hearth Rug.

Miss *Mary C. Herrick,* Portland. One Hearth Rug.

Miss *Butler,* Portland, A Small Rug.

Miss *H. Russell,* Portland. One Hearth Rug.

Miss *Louisa Bradbury,* Portland. One Hearth Rug.

Name unknown. One Hearth Rug.

Mrs. Betsey Lee, Portland. Carpeting made of small braided mats, neatly sewed together; evincing much industry.

The list of "Rugs made of Rags" is sadly lacking in any terms that would identify the technique involved. Woven rag rugs are a possibility, but that does not explain the number of hearth rugs included in this category. Certainly hearth rugs demanded a more sophisticated "art form." Braided and thrummed or pegged can be eliminated for examples of these two

forms have been cited as such in the list. Yarn-sewn has to be eliminated for there was a separate list for this category.

The real gem in this category is the rug exhibited by Miss Whittier of Portland: "A Mat and Rug, made of the head ends of Broadcloth; flowers very neatly worked on." A casual look at a shirred rug might well give the impression that it was made of the "head ends" of broadcloth. The identification of "flowers very neatly worked on," certainly eliminates the possibility of it being a woven rag rug. Obviously it was not a yarn-sewn. Is this the first documented evidence of the shirred technique? Or was it another type of experimental rug?

If it was the latter, the hearth rugs could have been shirred without a descriptive term to identify them as such. There exists still another possibility. Could they have been hooked? The dating of hooked rugs has been linked to the availability of burlap with the 1850s generally accepted as the onset of hooking. And yet, there are numerous examples of rugs hooked on linen — early Waldoboros for example. The early Waldoboro rug seen in the next chapter is hooked of hand-woven woolen materials on a base of hand-woven linen with all vegetable dyes. Certainly hooking implements can readily be found that could well have been made in the 1838 time period.

The Fair list suggests that it was a period of experimentation. For example, Miss Hanson exhibited "One Rug, made of seventy-nine pieces of Carpeting, neatly sewed." Where would Miss Hanson have come up with 79 pieces of carpeting? Could this have been a shirred rug, such as the one seen later in this chapter, in which the rug was worked in sections which were then attached to the linen base?

Mrs. Betsey Lee exhibited "Carpeting made of small braided mats, neatly sewed together; evincing much industry." And perhaps the one made of the head ends of broadcloth was experimental in the shirring technique establishing a positive date for that specialty.

There are three basic types of shirred rugs: bias, caterpillar, and penny or button shirred. The bias shirred rugs are made by cutting, on the bias, a strip of fabric about two inches wide, folding it in half lengthwise and sewing the folded edge to the background fabric. This process is repeated, sewing the second strip so close to the first that it forces the initial strip to stand up, forming the pile. Subsequent rows are made in the same way. Cutting fabric "on the bias" or diagonally from one selvage edge to the other gives the fabric a quality of stretch resulting in slightly undulating edges when folded in half.

The caterpillar is basically the same only the strips are sewn down the middle in a running stitch. When the end of the strip is reached, the thread is drawn taut, creating a puckered "caterpillar" which is then attached to the background fabric. The differences between the two can be seen in the photographs at the close of this chapter.

The penny or button shirring is done by cutting the fabric (usually felt) into circles, folding the circle into quarters and attaching the resultant point to the background fabric. Attaching the circles to the backing close together forces them to stand up creating the pile. All shirred rugs are identified by examining the reverse. No nap fabric is seen on the back, only the stitches made with the cotton or linen sewing thread.

The technique of "pegged" or "brodded" rugs can be ruled out as the source of the hearth rugs since the list separately references "Two rugs made of thrumbs." Thrums or thrumbs were the short ends of weaving leftovers which were poked through the foundation from the reverse, leaving the ends protruding on the front of the rug. A bodkin (awl-like tool) or peg was used in a technique that dates back to ancient times. It is this specific type of craft that caused Kent to mistakenly claim that hooked rugs could be traced back to "Coptic times."[6] He erroneously assumed pegged rugs were hooked.

In addition to the immediate Portland area, entrants in the Maine Charitable Mechanic Association Fair were from Kennebunk, Waldoboro, Biddeford, Standish, Scarborough, Gardiner, Danville, Orono and Parsonsfield. The number of entries and the geographic distribution easily proves that rug-making had become well established by 1838.

A correspondent for the *Boston Mercantile Journal* reviewed the Fair and an excerpt was reprinted in the Portland *Eastern Argus.*[7] The profusion of needlework was considered the "most beautiful part of the whole," and featured "numerous specimens of tufted hearth rugs [i.e., yarn-sewn rugs], many of which, for richness of colors and firmness of make, would vie successfully with the more costly of Wilton Rugs." Only one, a yarn-sewn, was singled out for special mention: Miss Sparrow's rug carried the description: "made it from the wool, doing the carding, dyeing, spinning and tufting all herself."

The newspaper's final report praised the Fair:

The Mechanic's Fair closed last evening [October 5, 1838], after a continuation of eleven days. It has been handsomely sustained – and the question has been settled that such exhibitions at suitable periods, will be supported. The Mechanic Association, we are assured, will be enabled, under the patronage they have received, to defray the very heavy expenses incurred in getting up the Fair, so that their fund, for charitable purposes, will not be diminished by this generous but hazardous enterprise.[8]

In a subsequent Portland Fair, in September 1854, only hearth rugs were exhibited, the one by Mrs. Greenlief Thorn of Westbrook being judged the best. Others were made by Mrs. A. Edgar, Mrs. S. Morris, Mrs. Roberts, M. H. Stevens and Miss Nancy Hanson. The lack of a feminine title for M. H. Stevens strongly suggests this to be the first man exhibiting a homemade hearth rug.[9]

Four years later, at the 1859 Maine Charitable Mechanic Fair, only three rugs were exhibited: Ellen Johnson of Gorham – Best Yarn Rug; Mrs. Ezra Thomes of Gorham – Second Best Yarn Rug; and Mrs. William Todd of Portland – Best Rag Rug.[10] It is clear that interest in rugs had waned somewhat (and was centered in the Portland area) in favor of numerous other crafts, including quilts and counterpanes, beadwork, pressed flowers, shell frame and shell box work, cone baskets, even a "Ladies' Elbow Cushion, neatly made."

Examining fair entries in the rural areas, by 1874 entries in the Bristol, Maine, Farmers Festival, show that the "rag" or "shirred" rugs had totally disap-

The urn or spray of flowers was the most popular design for early hearth rugs. It is seen in this yarn-sewn version and again in the shirred rug pictured later. A comparison of the two designs is a study of the personalities of the two makers. In the shirred rug, the central theme, while generously expansive, is framed with a tightly controlled outline of leaves and flowers. This yarn-sewn on the other hand has a much less elaborate central theme and a much more fluid frame of fantasy flowers and leaves. Interestingly, although yarn-sewn, the maker chose the shirring technique to define the leaf veins. c.1820. Yarn-sewn, shirred and reed-stitched with handspun wool and vegetable dyes on a hand-woven linen foundation, 36" x 63". *Courtesy Jeff and Suzanne Good.*

peared from the list of entries under "Household Manufacturers."[11] Hooked rugs had taken over, but were still being made to both decorate the hearth as well as now becoming "scatter" rugs.

In support of the premise that early rugs were created primarily as decorations for the hearth, Tyler pointedly claimed his mother was taught the craft of hearth decorating. The pivotal word here is "taught." This implies that the decoration of the hearth, like all other skills taught to young girls, was not merely for childhood amusement but was "taught" along with the many other lessons "then deemed necessary to qualify a young lady to adorn the first circles of society."[12]

She also learned to cut paper for "fly cages," diamond nets to preserve the gilt furniture from "this slattern insect," fringes for candlesticks and sconces and "pretty devices for watch cases." She learned to paint on glass and she labored over the "famous sampler where all letters of the alphabet, capitals and small letters, German text and Italian, shown resplendent with all sorts of angles and all the colors of the rainbow." Finally, as noted above, she was "taught" to decorate the hearth, a pastime that would play a future role in the development of yarn sewn and shirred rugs.

The sampler "was framed, glazed and hung over the parlor chimney-place and was for several years the pride and delight of my grandfather and grandmother and the admiration of many polite visitors."[13] It was hung in the most significant spot in the house, the obvious place for a family's most prized possession where everyone entering the house would be sure to see it. Would not the hearth then, likewise, become the place to display the intricately detailed and prized yarn-sewn or shirred rug?

The hearth was closed off during the warm summer months and cooking duties were moved to the "summer" kitchen, to "air condition" the main house. To soften the subsequent barren appearance of the fireplace, various devices were called into play to spruce it up. This might have included a fireboard ornately painted with some scene or faux floral arrangement. These painted images were never intended to be "fine art," but simple ornamentation that would one day "grow up" to become highly coveted folk art in the twentieth century. The evidence supports the premise that early hearth rugs obviously served the same purpose. They were perhaps an adjunct or counterpoint during the summertime to the fireboards, an urn of flowers or other hearth ornamentation.

Written reports indicate these rugs were used to absorb any sparks that might otherwise damage the expensive Oriental carpet. Obviously any person using these rugs to catch sparks never spent long winter nights hooking or shirring a rug. To believe that rug-makers would spend the necessary hours designing and creating a very special rug simply to catch sparks surely is fallacy. That would have been like creating a delicate embroidery on fine linen and then employing it as a dust cloth. It is known that rugs were used as table covers, again as a source for displaying a treasured object.

Early paintings show hearth rugs as an enhancement to other ornamentation within the well of the fireplace, but without a fire. A study by the author of many, many rugs through the years has yielded only one example showing signs of having been charred or burned from flying sparks and that could have been accidental. While there may have been such things as "fire rugs," it is doubtful that the more desirable hearth rugs into which so much effort had been expended would have been made specifically for that purpose.

Today these hearth rugs have been "elevated" to a much higher position, both physically and artistically. Strongly admired as pure folk art they are deemed artistic enough to be hung on the walls with an enthusiasm equal to that of hanging the greatest piece of fine art. Collectors are willing to pay many thousands of dollars for prime examples. A yarn-sewn, priced at what many would consider the staggering sum of $125,000, was seen at a New York antiques show in the spring of 2005.

While yarn-sewn and shirred rugs were still being made, at least by some of the more elite, the last half of the nineteenth century is the period when "hooking" became the paramount technique. As stoves became more prevalent in the first half of the nineteenth century, the primacy of the fireplace would wane. It was a time when burlap became available and hooking came into vogue. The rug — now hooked and much sturdier — would become "scattered" throughout the house.

Most farmwives had access to burlap bags, the open weave ideal for the hooking process, dyes could be easily obtained from readily available barks, berries, and vegetables, and aniline dyes would soon enter the market. Hooking had become a craft open to everyone regardless of financial considerations.

The would-be rug-maker could even fashion her own tool by inserting a nail into a scrap of wood, then bending the nail and filing the end into a hook. A collection of early hooking tools gives emphasis to the indigenous designation that the craft originated in North America. Otherwise the immigrants would have brought the tools with them. Forced to improvise, the settlers were often as inventive and ingenious in developing tools as they were in creating the rugs.

It was a craft developed to fill a deep-seated need for self-expression. No specialized training was required nor was it necessary to purchase any esoteric materials. By hooking a rug the most lowly farmwife could now become an artist. And she did!

A close study of an unfinished reed stitch rug shows the surface loops lined up side by side, having been sewn repeatedly over and over a reed. At the end of the reed it was removed by sliding it out of the row of stitches, as in this rug, or by slitting the stitches down the center. The latter creates a softer more velvety pile. By using a reed, the loops were all of the same height negating the need for shearing. The rug was found in a trunk purchased at a Maine auction many years ago. c. 1850. Wool yarn on a linen foundation, 35" diameter. *Courtesy Muriel Kenoyer.*

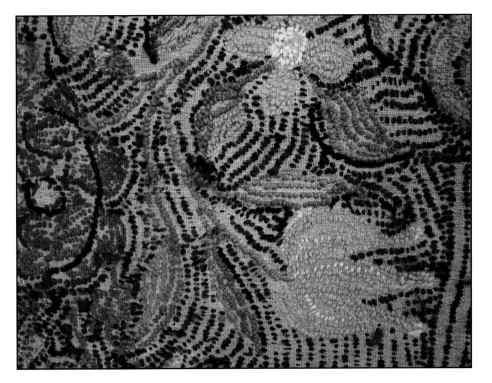

A look at the reverse of the reed stitch rug clearly shows the stitches lined up side-by-side as opposed to an interrupted straight or random line of running stitches in the usual yarn-sewn rug.

15

The wavy lines mark this rug as bias shirred. Cutting the strips of fabric on the bias (diagonally) causes the fabric to become stretchy as opposed to the sharp edges when cut with the weave, thus allowing the strips to undulate to a certain degree when they are attached to the base. The reverse of all shirred rugs will show only the linen or cotton threads used to sew the strips to the backing. This design is marked by its simplicity which is enhanced with wonderful motion, not only in the central theme, but in the fan corners and in the background itself. Slight hints of indigo are an added plus. c.1830-40. Wool on homespun linen, 28.25" x 40.50". *Courtesy Jeff and Suzanne Good.*

A caterpillar shirred rug, in contrast to the bias shirring, has rows of tightly gathered fabric "caterpillars" which are made separately and then attached to the base, again, with needle and thread so all that is seen on the reverse is the thread stitches. In this rug, the drama is provided through the use of color in a very busy design. The central quadrangle is enclosed in a pair of double curve motifs often employed by Native American tribes in the Maine-Maritime region. The design is repeated, in reverse, at each side and framed with an inner row of colorful diamonds and three simple edged borders, c.1830-40. Wool on homespun linen, 27.50" x 40.50". *Courtesy Jeff and Suzanne Good.*

The elongated shape and one-way design immediately identifies this as a traditional hearth rug made to bring a note of color and adornment to a fireplace barren of its fire during the summer. The earliest hearth rugs pre-date the hooking process using instead, a yarn-sewn, or shirring process. This one is comprised of bias shirred woolen strips on a homespun linen background. To overcome the bulk of working the rug in one piece it was made in sections, each section then attached to the homespun linen foundation. Would this technique explain the carpet "made of 79 pieces neatly sewed together," listed in the 1838 Maine fair? A rose with two buds anchors each corner of the leafy border interspersed with cosmos-like flowers framing a central well-balanced spray of the same flowers. c.1830. All vegetable dyes, 32" x 68". *Courtesy Joseph Caputo.*

The penny or button shirred rug consists of small circles that have been folded into quarters and the resultant center point attached to the foundation. Placing them close together keeps them upright just as in the bias or caterpillar shirred. Vivid red brings the white diamonds into sharp focus set against a variety of background fabrics. It is unusual to see a multi-colored border only on the two ends, which are fringed. c. 1880. Hooked with wool through two layers of homespun linen and burlap, 19" x 34" (19" x 38" with fringe). *Courtesy Lionel N. and Gerry Sterling.*

A nineteenth century fireboard clearly exhibits the similarity of design with what would be a very typical pattern for a hearth rug. The basic pot or urn of flowers with its branching stalks of flowers is framed with a repetitive circular motif. This evolution of hearth decoration is too obvious to disregard. Nineteenth Century. Painted wood. 39" x 44". *Cyr Auction.*

17

Chapter II

The Waldoboro Rug

Hooked rug artistry has never been more fully developed than in the small town of Waldoboro, in mid-coast Maine.[1] Descendants of the early German settlers created rugs with such exquisite floral designs as to challenge all others. They are credited with devising a technique of "sculpting" the flowers to more accurately display and accentuate the three-dimensional quality for which they strived, setting their products apart from more traditional hooked rugs. The resultant rugs were so revered and coveted by collectors that in a 1930 auction held by the American Art Association at the Anderson Galleries, Inc., in New York City, a pair of Waldoboro rugs brought a stunning $1,550.[2]

And that was the first year of the Great Depression!

The first indication of rug-making in Waldoboro is in the 1838 Maine Charitable Mechanic Association Fair document outlined in Chapter I, in which Mrs. John Barnard of Waldoboro was awarded a diploma for her yarn-sewn rug described as "handsome and well made.[3] Obviously the "Waldoboro" Mrs. Barnard made lacked the sophistication at that time to walk off with top honors, but Waldoboro hookers, aided by a little publicity and a local antiques dealer would later achieve great fame and come to dominate the market financially. It would, however, take a full century to achieve such well-deserved notoriety.

According to Jasper Stahl, a local historian, the period when Mrs. Barnard exhibited her rug occurred in the "great days" of Waldoboro's history, falling between 1830 and 1860.

The growth and prosperity of the town in its great days was founded on shipbuilding and its related industries. In this respect, as well as in wealth, in its social life, in size and growth, it was one of the half-dozen most rapidly developing and prospering towns in the state . . . The great days in the history of Waldoboro fall between 1830 and 1860. In this period the town reached the peak of development in activity, business and population, and in the wealth and caliber of its citizens. It was a time of bold and unrestrained action in shipbuilding and supporting industries, a time of able and dynamic leadership, and of the building of stately homes which were furnished with the treasures of distant lands, brought back by roving Waldoboro captains from the great trading centers of the world.[4]

But the Waldoboro Rug did not achieve any significant notoriety until long after the period outlined by Stahl. One of the earliest references to the "Waldoboro Rug" appeared in August 1929 when *The Antiquarian* reported:

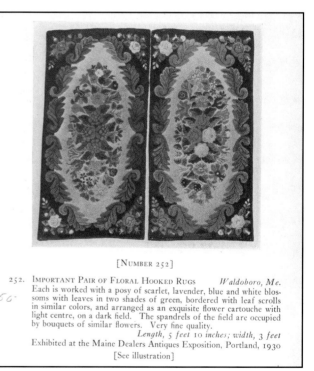

[NUMBER 252]

252. IMPORTANT PAIR OF FLORAL HOOKED RUGS   *Waldoboro, Me.*
Each is worked with a posy of scarlet, lavender, blue and white blossoms with leaves in two shades of green, bordered with leaf scrolls in similar colors, and arranged as an exquisite flower cartouche with light centre, on a dark field. The spandrels of the field are occupied by bouquets of similar flowers. Very fine quality.
Length, 5 feet 10 inches; width, 3 feet
Exhibited at the Maine Dealers Antiques Exposition, Portland, 1930
[See illustration]

At a New York City auction in 1930 offering articles consigned by Warren Weston Creamer, the Waldoboro antiques dealer, this pair of early Waldoboro rugs brought a stunning $1,550 in the first year of the Great Depression! This may have been the single event that catapulted the Waldoboro rug into the consciousness of the American public. Putting it into perspective, at the same auction a Hepplewhite inlaid mahogany card table, c. 1790, sold for $80. From: *Early American Furniture. . . Including Many Heirlooms of the Reed Family*, p. 54.

Of the rugs done on homespun backgrounds, some of the finest examples known have been found in the small towns of Maine. Descendants of the original German settlers in this section of the country developed an unusually good type of rug that has deserved and received the honor of a special title, 'Waldoboro' rug. [Apparently the "Waldoboro" appellation was already established at this time and was not a title initiated by *The Antiquarian.* An article in the same magazine four years earlier, in 1925, mentions the use of "raising" portions of a design for emphasis, but there was no mention of Waldoboro rugs. This raises the probability that Waldoboro rugs were recognized as such sometime between 1925 and 1929. As will be seen in Chapter III, it also is the exact period when the so-called "Acadian" rugs came into existence.][5] The Acadian rugs were said to have been "worked through closely woven homespun, so carefully and so evenly that the resulting texture is a marvel of velvety softness. These rugs are nearly always small in size, and the floral centers are notable for the delicate shading of tones of leaf and blossom."[6]

While the later *Antiquarian* article does not mention the sculpting, it went on to say:

> These rugs were always clipped or sheared, that is the tops of the rug loops were cut across after the rug was completed. Sheared rugs age to a smoother, more velvety texture than those in which the loop remains unsheared, or "tight-hooked rugs" as they were often called.[7]

The sculpting process was more than a simple elevation of the hooked loops shaped to the desired form. They were sculpted in progress, starting the first row of raised hooking at the lowest point and making each subsequent row a little higher until the desired effect was achieved. The design was then refined through careful trimming.

Waldoboro hookers did gain local recognition through friendly competition. The likeliest place of choice to display their projects and win prize money would have been the neighboring Bristol, Maine, Farmer's Festival, held in a community a few miles southwest of Waldoboro. A report of the festival in the *Lincoln County News* of October 9, 1874, identifies those displaying "a great variety of hooked rugs and yarn carpets." Yarn-sewn rugs apparently were still being made but there is no mention of the shirred-type of rugs. Entrants were Mrs. Samuel Hastings, Mrs. Orrin Carter, Ruth E. Small, Mrs. David E. Day, Emma H. Fossett, Mrs. Sylvanus Curtis, M.

A. Blunt and Lila Palmer. Mrs. Harvey Gaul had the "best stair carpet" and Mrs. Willard Sproul, a "very fine carpet."[8]

A more dramatic evolution was unveiled at the Bristol festival three years later, on October 11, 1877, when, for the very first time, rugs appear with a "raised" design. This could pinpoint a three-year span during which the process of sculpting rugs in the Waldoboro manner came into being and it lends credence to the very strong probability that such sculpting was a "Waldoboro" technique. This is reinforced by the fact that among the total of sixteen rugs on display at this Fair, only two featured raised designs. The technique had obviously not yet come into widespread usage.

Mrs. Rachie Morton was awarded First Premium for her hooked rug with "raised work," and Josephine Dow was the second contributor of a sculpted rug. Of the 16 entries, three were yarn-sewn; Mrs. Mary A. Mears earning the blue ribbon; Nettie Fossett, second place, and Miss Lydia Crocker, third premium. There were no shirred rugs.[9]

Mrs. John Webber took a blue ribbon for her hooked rug "beautifully pressed, sheared and shaded." The pressing would have helped smooth out any errant loops that were "unruly," a practice in common use today. While wear would accomplish the same result makers were anxious to achieve the much admired "smooth" look without waiting.[10]

The Fair premium list proves that the "pegged" or "brodded" method was still around, only now called "punched." Ralph O. Stevens, a seven-year-old-boy, was awarded first premium for his "punched rug." It was described as "wonderful for a boy. He must be kept in the house doing fancy work."[11]

In the 1877 *Lincoln County News* account, the 86 entries under "Household Manufactures" included sixteen rugs and thirteen quilts. Several of the women exhibited both. While quilts have today developed as a major craft form eagerly collected by individuals, museums and historical organizations throughout the country, hooked rugs in 1877 were equal to or exceeded quilts in popularity. Despite these numbers, rugs have not attained comparable desirability in the collecting practices of most current museums.

Many of the exhibited quilt patterns were identified [Double Irish Chain, Double Saw Tooth, Lover's Knot, Log Cabin and Star Patch], so the accolades and awards in these entries were strictly for technique and craftsmanship and not for originality.[12] On the other hand, each of the hooked rug patterns was an original design, thus they can be categorized as true folk art. They provide a unique and rare insight into the thoughts and personalities of women in the particular period when the rugs were made.

Both crafts spawned compatible social activities in the form of "bees." A 1941 article in the *Lewiston* [Maine] *Evening Journal*, described "hooking bees." At these bees the women gathered to help the hostess with her rug. Some bees were merely afternoon get-togethers and were held mostly in the rural villages. Outside these settlements, where neighbors were separated by considerable distances, the bees usually lasted through the afternoon and evening. During the afternoon the women worked on the rug. A bountiful supper was served at night with the menfolk all present. The evening was passed socially with plenty of apples and cider to help in making merry.[13]

While the Waldoboro rug was already appreciated at the local fairs in the third quarter of the nineteenth century, Warren Weston Creamer, a local antiques dealer, although a little slow on the uptake, would soon help spread the fame of the Waldoboro rug beyond the borders of Maine. A descendant of the early Waldoboro Creamer family, he lived and conducted his antiques business in Waldoboro, and was obviously situated in exactly the right spot and at the right time to help create a market for the local handicraft. In *The Magazine Antiques* of 1923 he advertised "a great variety of furniture, looking glasses, blue printed ware, china, glass, earthen and stone ware, brass andirons and warming pans, castors, tea trays etc., all of which may be had for cash or approved credit." No hooked rugs were mentioned.[14]

Accentuating the relative anonymity of the Waldoboro rug at that time, Creamer's next *Antiques* advertisement, two years later, in May 1925 did include hooked rugs. He invited visitors to "browse around as long as they wish among the old *Furniture, Prints, Hooked Rugs, Glass, Pewter, Books, etc*, which belonged to the early settlers of this town." Obviously these rugs would have been Waldoboros, but his failure to mention them as such indicates he had not developed an appreciation or awareness of their artistic and monetary value.[15]

Apparently thinking about retirement, Creamer scheduled an auction of his antiques on May 9-10, 1930, at the American Art Association Galleries in New York City. The second day of the auction featured "HOOKED RUGS, Including Fine Specimens of Waldoboro, ME, Workmanship, Which Have the Reputation of Being the Best Obtainable." All the items were "Sold by Order of Warren Weston Creamer of the Old Reed Mansion, Waldoboro, Maine."[16] Creamer had finally recognized the value of the Waldoboro rug, a product readily available in his own back yard these many years. Local towns-

Retrieval from a Waldoboro attic gives this rug provenance, and the bright, bold design stamps it as the product of a dramatic personality. A very early Waldoboro rug, it precedes the sculpting or modeling technique, but it exhibits characteristics that would be further developed in coming decades. The vivid red roses, the use of several shades of green on the leaves and the leaves themselves seem to foreshadow the inception of the scrolls which later became so highly developed. c.1840-50. Wool on linen, sheared, all vegetable dyes, 31.50" x 64.50". *MCP Collection.*

people, eager for the financial remuneration from the sale, were quite willing to let them go. In one of his books Kent remarked that "In Waldoboro beautiful [rugs] seem almost to have grown on bushes ready to be picked by some wise dealer."[17] That "wise dealer" turned out to be Creamer.

A copy of the auction catalog has a handwritten record of the prices realized and includes the notation of the phenomenal price of $1,550 for a pair of matching Waldoboro rugs. Putting this into perspective, in the same auction a rare Chippendale settee *and* armchair sold for a mere $425; a Hepplewhite inlaid mahogany card table realized only $80, and a Queen Ann walnut slant-top desk, $110.[18]

Why then, two months later, in July 1930, did Creamer not include the Waldoboro title in his ad in *The Magazine Antiques*? He stated, "As for hooked rugs, the finest ever made come from Maine and Warren Weston Creamer has the best of these."[19] There was still no indication of "Waldoboros," only "Maine" rugs. Possibly he didn't have any Waldoboros left after the sale just two months earlier. Finally, in April 1931, he included a photograph with his advertisement which now claimed "A fine assortment of the beautiful and rare Waldoboro rugs. We will be glad to send selections on approval to responsible parties."[20]

The Creamer sale was not necessarily all Waldoboro rugs. Since the individual descriptions do not identify which ones may be Waldoboros and not every rug is illustrated, one has to offer an educated guess. It seems strange that the known Waldoboros were not identified as such in the catalog. Possibly it was a sudden awakening brought on by the *Antiquarian* article, at which time the body of the catalog was already printed. There was still time, however, to redo the cover calling attention to the "Fine Specimens of Waldoboro, Maine Workmanship."

A study of the catalog shows similarities to at least two Frost patterns: "Animal Hooked Rug, features a seated mustard colored lion with cub in silhouette against an indigo background, with flowers and foliage in scarlet and green. Bound."[21] The disparity is the fact that the auction's lion was "seated" while all the Frost lions were lying down.

The second Frost-similar rug was described as "An elk head in soft brown framed by sprays of rosebud and leaves." One immediately suspects this is a Frost pattern. However, the dimensions of the Frost elk head pattern with its geometrical border do not coincide with the elk featured in the auction.[22] These two rugs may well endorse the theory of "borrowing" segments of designs to create a new "original" pattern. Other descriptions could definitely be categorized as from Waldoboro, including one

with "Leaf scrolls in mustard yellow and brown enclosing a posy of nicely colored flowers and leaves, partly in raised work, on an ivory field bordered in indigo."

Other questionable rugs include an "Antique Hooked Clipper Ship Rug showing a sailing vessel in a circular medallion, the corners of the field occupied by American flags and anchors. Lined. Rare." And there is one listed as "Made at the Shaker Colony, Maine. Showing bold leaf scrolls framing three single blossoms, with leaves in contrasted light colors on amethyst field bordered in green."

The attention given to this auction marks the point at which the majority of the greatest Waldoboro rugs left the State of Maine forever, dispersed to collectors, museums, and the marketplace in general. In all probability it was this single sale that catapulted the Waldoboro rug into the consciousness of the collecting public, causing prices to skyrocket. After the sales Creamer reduced his inventory and apparently retired. His advertisements disappeared from *The Magazine Antiques*. According to a local resident, Marjorie Freeman, Creamer's remaining inventory was purchased by James A. Duane of Waldoboro, who advertised it in the classified section of *The Magazine Antiques*, offering "Furniture, Prints, Glass, Waldoboro Hooked Rugs."[23]

Later reports of multiple rugs hanging on Waldoboro clotheslines to entice their purchase by passing tourists, support the probability that the phenomenal sum realized at the Creamer auction tempted many local women to suddenly become hookers. This would have resulted in a flood of inferior rugs on the market. Rugs were being hooked for money, not for the pure joy of creativity. It is fair to assume that this also tempted women from other areas to try to duplicate the Waldoboro experience. Many of the so-called Waldoboro rugs in today's market are from this era and fail to meet the quality standards established by the early Waldoboro hookers.

Fannie Brooks was the last of the Waldoboro hookers who would have been eligible to assume the title of being a Waldoboro rug-maker. Born in 1894, she would have been of an appropriate age (c. 1910) to have learned the craft from one of the original Waldoboro hookers. Her passing in 1984 signified the end of the true Waldoboro rug hookers. There would never be another. Any future attempts at making a Waldoboro rug would be a reproduction or copy of an original. It was the end of an era in rug-making.

Reminiscing several years later, Creamer noted:

This is one of the truly "great" Waldoboro rugs. It was pure whimsy on the part of the hooker to tip the flower basket, one of those artistic touches that collectors find so endearing in an early rug. It is nicely sculpted, with a central ground of the distinctive "Waldoboro green," and sheared wool with woolen yarn highlights on a linen foundation. Since black was a fugitive dye that changed color over time, the outer edge shows these spotty changes to a drab olive color. This helps to establish an early date for the rug. c.1880. Wool on linen, 29.75" x 60.50". *Courtesy Waldoborough Historical Society.*

A close-up of the basket details the careful and delicate shading that could be achieved with yarns.

Waldoboro has long been noted for its fine rugs. Between the years 1860 and 1885 there were a great many artistic rugs made in this section. The colorings were beautiful and during that period the work was splendidly done. I think the best were made between 1875 and 1885, reaching the highest point of perfection at approximately the latter date. Since that time the quality of the work has slowly retrograded and the quantity of rugs produced has diminished until at present there is practically no hooking done here and the few that are made are very poor as to quality and design. Beautiful rugs were made much earlier and I have had a great many that were probably produced as early as 1830 [contemporary to the Maine Charitable Mechanic Association Fair in 1838]. These were usually of yarn, very soft in texture and on a homespun linen foundation. There were also a good many of the needlework or reed stitch type of rugs made approximately one hundred years ago. They are becoming scarce.[24]

While the artistic excellence and the raised design have been major factors in identifying a Waldoboro rug, they do not necessarily determine the authenticity of a true Waldoboro.[25] Several other factors, including provenance, offer guidelines for such identification:

1. A foundation of linen (preferable tow linen) is a necessity. All early references to Waldoboro rugs definitely specify a homespun linen base despite the availability of other fabrics. "Factory warp," "factory cloth," and "factory shirting" were all available by 1817 at William Ryan's store in Belfast, also located in the mid-coast region of Maine. The traditional makers of Waldoboro rugs, however,

22

continued using homespun linen well into the twentieth century.[26]

2. The single most important trait of a Waldoboro rug as established in the marketplace is the sculpting or modeling of the design which resulted in a three-dimensional effect. While this tends to simplify the identification process, not all Waldoboro-made rugs were sculpted and not all sculpted rugs are from Waldoboro. Other characteristics must be considered.

3. According to early descriptions, the rugs must be clipped or sheared. This clipping process is essential in a Waldoboro rug, not only for those sewn with yarn but also those with fabric strips. This trait has resulted in confusion by some marketers and collectors whom, failing to recognize the distinction between *sheared* and *shirred,* suffer from the false hopes that their rug is a rare shirred rug, while in reality it is simply sheared. Shearing is common with all types of hooked and yarn rugs, not just ones from Waldoboro, and does not contribute appreciably to their value. Since the rugs were made of wool, it seems both appropriate and logical to use sheep-shearing tools for clipping or shearing process. At a later date, special scissors were developed for this procedure.

4. The delicate shading seen in Waldoboro rugs would have been impossible to achieve with the relatively heavy, hand cut fabric strips. This obstacle was overcome by hooking intricate details with yarns. Familiarity with the earlier yarn-sewn construction was an obvious advantage. Virtually all Waldoboro rugs have some portion of the design – usually a flower – hooked with yarn. This one significant aspect can frequently distinguish a true Waldoboro rug from a Waldoboro look-alike.

5. Basically, Waldoboro rugs are florals with central ovals of lush flowers, or baskets surrounded by floral vine borders or intricate scroll designs. Wreaths were common, including the so-called memorial wreath rugs, draped over the coffin to overcome the lack of wintertime flowers. There is considerable evidence of rug-makers using a simple design element in several rugs or even the copying of that motif by other rug-makers. In fact, the continued employment of certain design elements can contribute to the establishment of a Waldoboro rug's true authenticity.

6. Provenance, of course, is always desirable, but extremely difficult to come by. In the past, no attempt was made to record the rug's history and no mention was made of hand-made rugs in wills distributing the family assets; only the costly imported rugs were considered an asset in settling an estate. But provenance alone does not necessarily define a Waldoboro, for if it was made in Waldoboro on a burlap base, it is merely a "Waldoboro type" and not a true Waldoboro. The homespun linen foundation is a necessary component.

7. Colors have remained rather consistent through the years, with backgrounds of black, natural cream color, gray or a Waldoboro sage green, the latter not seen in other rugs. It is speculated that the green was specific to a woolen mill in neighboring Warren, and advertisements prove these Warren woolens were sold in Waldoboro in 1875. O. S. Head advertised a "large stock of Warren woolens" in his "stand over E. R. Benner's Drug Store."[27] Scarlet is frequently seen in the scrolls and flowers and it maintained its brilliance through the years, unlike black, a fugitive dye that changed from black to a mottled olive drab shade. Many early black rugs show striations of this color change and should not be interpreted as a whim of the rug maker. The reverse of the rug usually shows the original black shade more accurately since it was protected from fading.

8. No birds. While birds are frequently seen in rugs from the Pennsylvania area, they are rare in New England rugs and virtually impossible to find in a Waldoboro. They were a bad omen. According to a young woman raised in Waldoboro, she was warned that if birds were a part of the wallpaper design "they would peck the pennies right out of your pocket."[28] That superstition has not totally disappeared from New England, even today.

Geometric rugs are relatively rare although they may have been common in the early days. The difficulty of proving Waldoboro provenance accounts for their scarcity. No single factors in geometric rugs have been found to determine any unique traits for Waldoboro geometrics.

Animal designs are undoubtedly the rarest and might be eliminated from consideration entirely except that the late Elizabeth Coatsworth Beston, a noted children's author, wrote of just such a rug in *Down East* magazine in 1978:

> This is a miserable little book that I've been trying to fill. It's called *The Runaway Horse,* and it comes from a Waldoboro rug. The best hookers in this part of the country were in Waldoboro, and they did wonderful animal ones. The only rug I ever had that came from there was of a running horse – running hell-bent for leather, with red nostrils, feet out in front and feet out behind. The girth is still on, and the saddle blanket, but no bridle and no saddle. I used to have it in my study. I gave it to Kate [her daughter]. I've always thought I would write about it.[29]

23

No record has been found that she ever finished the book and all efforts to photograph the rug, which survives today, have failed. The possibility that such animal rugs might be found is intriguing.

Although each Waldoboro rug has its own individuality, certain elements often appear in more than one rug. Trading portions of designs was quite a common practice, as it is with today's hookers. As long as the design concept was original, elements could be "borrowed" without fear of condemnation for "copying." While the late nineteenth century saw a proliferation of commercially stamped patterns, the dedicated Waldoboro rug-makers continued in the old tradition of designing their own.

Each Waldoboro rug is unique in artistry and detail, but not all are unique in overall design. Pattern elements were frequently copied, but this is a duplicate of the overall design, not often seen. It could be by the same maker as the previous tipped basket maker or it could have been a copy – perhaps a mother and daughter combination. The dark indigo ground is a rarity in all rugs, but especially so in Waldoboros. It is interesting to study the different interpretations in the flowers. c.1870-75. Wool on linen with yarn highlights, 30.75" x 61.5". *Courtesy Sharon and Jeffrey Lipton.*

Duplication of design elements can be a significant factor in determining provenance. This rug has the exact scroll format as the rug with the tipped basket but the center design and the spandrels have been changed. While the rug is expertly hooked, the choice of background fabric rather "muddies" the rug's persona. c.1885. Wool on linen, 20.50" x 43". *Courtesy Waldoborough Historical Society.*

An unusual find was this copy of the tipped basket central design done in a square format. The odd shape is unknown in any other Waldoboro; perhaps it was made to top a table or chest. While the design is raised it lacks the sophistication of the original rug. The flowers are well defined but the fine detailing of both flowers and basket is missing. The intricate scrollwork has been replaced with a previously unseen plum-colored outer frame which contains three small inner frames. The Waldoboro green ground establishes its Waldoboro origin. c.1890-1900. Wool on linen. 23" x 23.50". *Courtesy Joseph Caputo.*

Another extraordinary Waldoboro rug depicts two sprays of roses encircling a nosegay of small flowers set against a background of natural fleece color. Two golden end scrolls anchor the design with its outstanding double frame, one of black and the other of scarlet. c.1870-80. Wool on linen with yarn highlights, 25" x 47.25". *Courtesy Waldoborough Historical Society.*

A close-up of the red corners reveals the true craftsmanship/art involved. The three-dimensional effect of interweaving the corners is enhanced with the variegated shading of the reds, and the outside edge hooked with a fine pink yarn, all emphasized by the sculpting. This is an outstanding example of the artistry found in the early Waldoboros.

A rug with a horseshoe as the central theme was a special "Good Luck" piece for a newly-married couple. Multiple borders of various colors frame the horseshoe festooned with a variety of flowers. The end scrolls, similar to the previous rug, support the Waldoboro attribution. c.1885-1900. Wool on linen with yarn highlights, 24.50" x 41.50". *Courtesy Beverly BaRoss.*

The marked similarities of the end-scroll designs of the two rugs above provides verification of this horseshoe design as a Waldoboro product.

Here, verification of authenticity is extended to the design itself. The floral garland for both horseshoes is almost identical. The first horseshoe now lends authenticity to a second horseshoe as a Waldoboro rug. Either they were made by the same person or the design was a freehand copy. While the first horseshoe rug is more subtle in coloring, this one stands out with its use of indigo in the frame, as well as extensive use of blue in the flowers. c.1890-1900. Wool on linen, 25.75" x 49.75". *Courtesy Beverly BaRoss.*

Despite the lack of any sculpting or raised work, the Waldoboro green ground marks this rug as an authentic Waldoboro. The arrangement of the dramatic rust-colored scroll work gives emphasis to a heart-shape in the simple but effective central floral wreath. It could well have been made as a wedding rug. The fading of the fugitive black dye in the frame is typical of most early rugs, c.1860-80. Wool on linen, 28" x 47.75". *Courtesy Waldoborough Historical Society.*

Once again, the Waldoboro green background stamps this rug as a Waldoboro. Not sculpted, it has an unusual red frame with gold and pink scrollwork. The simple central bouquet lacks the delicate intricacies usually seen in other Waldoboro rugs. It may have been an early attempt on the part of the maker. c.1890. Wool on linen, 29.25" x 61". *Courtesy Waldoborough Historical Society.*

Mrs. Sarah Eugley designed and made this rug as a wedding gift for her nephew, Alton Winchenbach of Waldoboro, and his bride, Nettie McLain, who were married on October 2, 1914. An unusual spray of oak leaves and acorns, both symbols of fertility, is seen at each side. The scroll has been substituted with a triple frame border of black, red and yellow. c.1910-14. Wool on linen; all vegetable dyes, 28" x 48". *Courtesy Maine State Museum.*

An unusual mauve background sets off a single central spray of sculpted flowers framed with more elaborate matching floral frames. The sculpted end scrolls are very similar to those seen in the horse-shoe rug. The number of similarities in this group of rugs indicates there was considerable interchange of pattern details. c.1900-10. Wool on linen, 29.50" x 56". *Courtesy Beverly BaRoss.*

Mrs. Fannie Brooks (1894-1984) of Waldo-boro was the last of the "Waldoboro hook-ers." During her childhood, she would have been exposed to the elite group of the best rug-makers and undoubtedly learned the craft from them. She created her own designs, dyed wool fabrics, many from clothing given to her by friends. The muted colors of the scroll work enhance the attention of the floral corners while a white ground sets off the central floral motif. This was a favorite design for Mrs. Brooks, who made several rugs of this pattern. c.1965. Wool on cotton, 34" x 56". *Maine Historical Society Collections. 2005.181.182.*

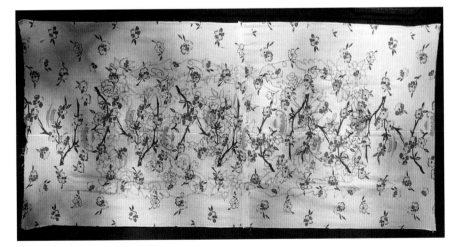

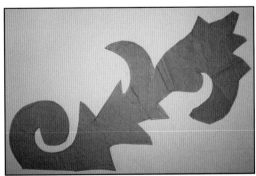

The original design for the rug above was sketched by Mrs. Brooks on a patterned grain bag popular in the second quarter of the twentieth century. Also pictured is the cardboard template used to trace the scroll design onto the fabric. A number of Mrs. Brooks's templates have been preserved. Pattern: 36" x 58"; template: 4.50" x 13.50". *Maine Historical Society Collections. 2005.181.001 and 2005.181.004 respectively.*

Mrs. Brooks was known to have hooked at least one rug with grapes. Here she used the fruit to compose a circular pattern for a chair pad, which would complement the grape hooked rug that once graced her dining room. Drawn with pencil on cotton, it was believed to have been done c.1940. 24" diameter. *Maine Historical Society Collections. 2005.181.002.*

Another Waldoboro rug is identified as such by the scroll of layered small leaves surrounding a central floral medallion. This design has been seen on at least two other rugs, one unfinished, from a Waldoboro closet. The undulating striations of the gold background provide interesting visual motion. The black frame shows evidence of the early period's fugitive black dye. The central motif is raised and is marked with unusual blue leaves. c.1900-1910. Wool on linen, 26.25" x 53.25". *Courtesy Jeff and Suzanne Good.*

A second rug with blue leaves raises the question of the likelihood that they may have been made by the same person. Blue leaves are a rarity in any rug, but it is seen in this Waldoboro as well as in the previous design. Both rugs show white highlights in the blue leaves. Also unusual is the blue-green ground in the previous rug and the blue-green scroll in this rug. Both have yarn highlights, but this rug is not raised. c.1880-1900. Wool on linen, 20.5" x 31.50". *Courtesy Joseph Caputo.*

30

Apparently not all Waldoboro rug-hookers designed their own patterns or even "borrowed" them. This example of a pattern on linen, found in Waldoboro, was made for sale. It bears the inscription "Welt. 60cts." (Welt was a fairly common German name in Waldoboro.) It has characteristics seen in Minnie Light rugs featured in Chapter IV and may be by her. Pencil on muslin. 56.25" x 34.50". *Courtesy Ann Seaver.*

There are some rugs that cannot be positively attributed to Waldoboro despite the fact they have all the attributes. This one is probably a mourning rug used to cover the casket during flowerless winter months. The ground – originally solid black – lends itself to grieving as does the circular broken wreath (a symbol that the life cycle had been interrupted) with "weeping" flowers visible at the top of the wreath. Its sculptured flowers are hooked with yarn. c.1880-1890. Wool on linen, 22" x 41". *Courtesy Sharon and Jeffrey Lipton.*

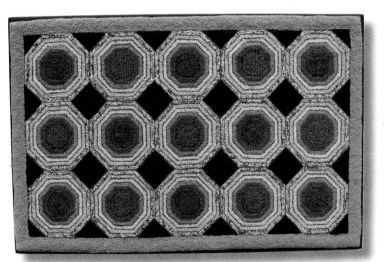

It is difficult to attribute geometric rugs to Waldoboro. This example has two important attributes: it is hooked on linen and it has always resided in the Waldoboro area. Although easier to design, the necessity of careful hooking remained a challenge even in the most basic geometrics. This one was expertly done with the series of octagonal lines precisely created straight and true. c.1900-1910. Wool on linen, 26" x 40". *Waldoborough Historical Society.*

Although sections of Pennsylvania, like the Waldoboro area, were settled by Germans from the Palatine, the typical "Pennsylvania Dutch" rug is set apart from Maine's German-derived designs. This charming rug shows features never seen in Waldoboro rugs, such as birds and the fringe. Waldoboro Germans believed that birds in a house were an evil omen and are rarely seen in any New England hooked rug. Here the birds are nicely sculpted and the flowers in the side borders emulate those observed on the decorated chests found in Pennsylvania. c.1900. Wool on burlap. 30" x 40.50". *Courtesy Sharon and Jeffrey Lipton.*

Chapter III
The Acadian Rug

Several early twentieth century authors writing about hooked rugs claimed that the Waldoboro rug faced stiff competition from the so-called "Acadian" rugs. *Collecting Hooked Rugs,* published in 1927, contains actual photographs of two such rugs. Co-authors Evelyn Waugh and Edith Foley described them as follows:

> They used hand-spun woolen materials exclusively and clipped the loops of their rugs, giving the surface a peculiar velvet-like quality. Extremely ornate floral wreaths formed their favorite designs; and they originated the idea, later copied by other makers of hooked rugs, of *raising* the design against the background so that it stood out in low-relief."[1]

Just two years later an article in *The Antiquarian* magazine described the Waldoboro rug as being "worked through closely woven homespun, so carefully and so evenly that the resulting texture is a marvel of velvety softness," adding that "the floral centers are notable for the delicate shading of leaf and blossom."[2] Waugh/Foley, addressing the Acadian rug, said that "A single pansy measuring one and a half inches in diameter shows seventeen different colors, no painter of flowers could have achieved finer nuances."[3]

It is interesting to note that there are seemingly two nearly identical styles of rugs, each defined by different points of origin and yet, prior to 1929, no mention can be found of any Waldoboro rugs, only Acadian ones. Yet, now nearly a century later, not a single "Acadian" rug can be found. They are not seen in museums, they never appear in auctions, at antiques markets, in exhibitions or advertisements. They have simply disappeared — *or maybe they never existed!*

Perhaps like Shakespeare's rose which by any other name would smell as sweet, the Waldoboro rugs had languished in obscurity for decades because they were being lauded under another guise. This would explain why two types of rugs, described as so similar, survive only under the Waldoboro title

today. It is important to note here that the Acadian rugs referred to in this chapter are the very early nineteenth century rugs and should not be confused with the later and present-day cottage industries that use the title "Acadian" rugs, such as those from the Chetticamp region of Cape Breton, Nova Scotia.[4]

An illustration in the Waugh/Foley book entitled, "Landscape rugs in the early American home of Frederick [Judd] Waugh, Kent, Conn.," contains a possible clue that could clarify why the confusion arose.[5] Certainly it is more than just coincidence that the book's author bears the same last name as this noted Connecticut artist, famous for his marine paintings created in that section of Maine long associated with the term "Acadia."

Evelyn Waugh was his daughter-in-law and the two obviously shared an appreciation of hooked rugs. Thus, it is logical to assume she would have accompanied her artist father-in-law on one or more of his numerous painting forays into mid-coast Maine.[6] These travels would have brought her into the very area where Waldoboro rugs proliferated. It is then logical to suspect that these so-called Acadian rugs that Waugh was discovering were, in fact, Waldoboro rugs that had yet to be ascribed by nomenclature to that region of Maine.

James M. Shoemaker of Manhasset, Long Island, New York, offered his choice collection of hooked rugs at auction in two sessions, both held at the American Art Association, Inc., in New York City.[7] The catalog sale was entitled, *Rare American Hooked Rugs.* The first session, held May 9-10, 1923, included 295 rugs. Of these, 14 were "modeled" or sculptured, but there is no indication they might have been hooked in the Waldoboro area.

During the second session on May 1, 1924, 180 rugs were sold and among them there were 16 with "raised work." This very large collection, therefore, contained 475 rugs of which 30 were sculpted or modeled. No mention was made of the term "Waldoboro," nor was it mentioned that they might be "Acadian." Notations on an extant Shoemaker catalog show the selling price of four of those sold in 1924 as $40, $70, $30 and $25, obviously giving no hint of the dramatic price increases to come in the late 1920s as typified by Creamer's 1930 auction noted in the previous chapter. The small number of sculpted rugs in the Shoemaker sale suggests this craft specialty was not widely known, had not yet been "discovered" by antique dealers and collectors, and likely was still closely circumscribed to the Waldoboro area.

A casual study of the catalog indicates that either Shoemaker had no interest in shirred rugs or they were extremely scarce since the collection included only one "chenille" rug, a term used at that time to designate shirred rugs. One other designation, a "hand-tufted" rug, suggests that it was a yarn-sewn made in the reed-stitch manner, indicating the rarity of this type of rug as well.[8]

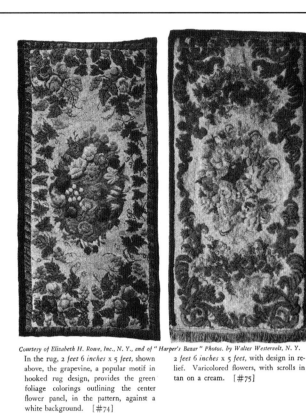

Courtesy of Elizabeth H. Rowe, Inc., N. Y., and of "Harper's Bazar" Photos. by Walter Westervelt, N. Y.
In the rug, 2 feet 6 inches x 5 feet, shown above, the grapevine, a popular motif in hooked rug design, provides the green foliage colorings outlining the center flower panel, in the pattern, against a white background. [#74]

2 feet 6 inches x 5 feet, with design in relief. Varicolored flowers, with scrolls in tan on a cream. [#75]

TWO RUGS IN ACADIAN MANNER

Hooked in New Hampshire and hardly used since the early part of the nineteenth century. Flowers modeled in pronounced relief.

Kent obviously compounded the error of misnaming Waldoboro rugs as being from "Acadia" in his book, *The Hooked Rug*. This volume, published just three years after the Waugh/Foley book, suddenly contains several "Acadian" rugs, including the pair seen here. The rug at the right has a remarkable similarity to the overall design layout seen in the Waldoboro rug with the tipped basket illustrated in Chapter II. Left: 30" x 74"; right: 30" x 60." Kent, *The Hooked Rug*, p. 89, plate 74-75.

What well may be the first of the so-called "Acadian" rugs ever photographed appears in the 1927 Waugh/Foley book. It is captioned "Antique French Acadian hooked rug showing elaborate floral motif in sophisticated design." The rug was "hooked of single strands of hand-spun wool." All the flowers and buds as well as the grapes were in raised relief. This is strong evidence that it was a yarn-sewn Waldoboro rug. Elizabeth Waugh & Edith Foley, *Collecting Hooked Rugs,* opp. p. 9.

Six "Good Luck" rugs featuring horseshoe designs were annotated in the catalog with the brief explanation that "Good Luck rugs were made chiefly for bridal gifts." Two such rugs with all of the Waldoboro characteristics are illustrated in the previous chapter. At this point in history, the Waugh book had yet to be published, providing an explanation as to why neither Shoemaker nor the auction gallery typed them as "Acadian." The name had not yet been coined. This collection also contained two "broken wreath" designs claimed by Kent to have been created as mourning rugs, the break in the wreath signifying a break in the family circle.[9]

However, just a year after the Waugh/Foley book was published, another auction was held. This one featured the hooked rugs collected by Mrs. Edward O. Shernikow of New York City, also held at the Anderson Galleries.[10] Occurring on March 14, 1928, the auction included three so-called "Acadian rugs": "#6 FLORAL HOOKED RUG. Velvety Acadian rug with large leaves in pale green and rose separating soft rose centre from black field. All wool, sheared;" and "#164, Two Acadian Hooked Rugs. Shaded rose scrolls and green leaves form symmetrical patterns on black background. All wool, sheared." Is this just mere coincidence that the descriptive term "Acadian rug" followed immediately upon the publication of the Waugh book?

Three years after the Waugh/Foley book, Kent reproduced for the first time a supposed "Acadian" rug in his 1930 publication, The Hooked Rug, and credited the photograph to The Magazine Antiques.[11] In a new edition published in 1937 he finally recognized two Waldoboro rugs, almost as an afterthought, while he still determinedly called eight rugs "Acadian" or of "Acadian Design." It seems logical that, in researching this revised edition of his book, Kent would have studied the Waugh/Foley volume, drawing the conclusion from Waugh that she had miraculously "discovered" some true "Acadian rugs" and was identifying them for the first time. Thus the lore that there was such a thing as an "Acadian" rug was confirmed without any historical substantiation.

In the later volume, Rare Hooked Rugs, published in 1941, Kent wrote: "It is fairly well known that very many of the best rugs were long ago made by the French or Acadians, but after these people were dispersed in Cape Cod and Louisiana the art gradually lost excellence and attraction."[12] However, in a second book, Hooked Rug Design, Kent admitted that he could find no historical trace of the Acadians carrying the craft of rug-hooking to Louisiana.[13] It would seem that Kent is saying that with their exile from Acadia in 1755 any interest in rug-making on the part of the deposed Acadians had simply vanished.

This implies that they were being made in Acadia prior to 1755 but not thereafter. Yet, there is no documentary evidence to indicate any non-woven rugs were made that early. Again, one sees the misinformation resulting from the historical inaccuracies prevalent in Kent's history of hooked and pegged rugs. The Acadians who settled in Louisiana were expelled from their Nova Scotia homeland approximately 75 years before there is any historical record that hooking existed anywhere as a craft form.

Dr. Marius Barbeau, the noted French-Canadian folklorist, seeking the origin of hooked rugs he discovered in the Province of Québec, reinforced the lack of any substantive evidence of "Acadian" rugs. He stated in a 1947 article in Antiques: "Hardly anything is known as to the source [of rug-hooking] and development among the Acadians."[14] It seems that, despite his lifetime of exhaustive research into Canada's folk lore and folk art extending over half a century, Dr. Barbeau found nothing of historical significance related to any early Acadian rugs.

Scott Robson, curator of the History Collection at the Nova Scotia Museum of Art in Halifax, oversees the historical collection of that museum's 20 different sites throughout the Province. This gives him a unique insight and knowledge of the artifacts of Nova Scotia. When asked about the so-called Acadian rugs he replied: "I cannot think of a single mat [in Canada the term "mat" is used as we use the word "rug"] with Acadian association that is yarn-sewn on linen. I can only recall perhaps three mats on linen, two with yarn-sewing and WITHOUT any Acadian or possible Acadian origin."[15]

Kent pictures another supposed "Acadian" rug, this one with the identical outer scroll frame seen at the right in the pictured pair on page 33. Although this rug bears all the hallmarks of a traditional Waldoboro, Kent defines it as an "Acadian French, Nova Scotia . . . probably not a stamped design, but well balanced and carefully executed." 28" x 48". Kent, The Hooked Rug, p. 91, plate 76.

Another similarity appears with this rug and the one at the left in the pictured pair seen pm [age 33. A frame of leaves and grapes surrounds a broken wreath, traditionally said to have been a memorial rug, signifying a break in the family circle. Grapes and grape leaves are a tradition in some Waldoboro rugs. Kent described this so-called "Acadian" rug as having "a soft tan field, on which appears a grapevine border in greens and tan, surrounding a broken wreath of old-time flowers of natural colors." 30" x 63". Kent, The Hooked Rug, p. 71, plate 64.

In using the term "Acadian" he continued:

There can be confusion that is inappropriate in a modern context. In addition to referring to people who are of Acadian descent, the term has been applied very generally to a large geographic area, which was (so long ago) called Acadia (or "Acadié" in French.) For instance, such terminology appears in vague and inaccurate terms in W. W. Kent's books, and in such works that derive from them. I think some of this came from the promotional literature of the early 1900s, in which the railroad promoted the Land of Evangeline, and Acadian associations due to the popularity of [Henry Wadsworth] Longfellow's epic poem, "Evangeline," as well as the establishment of the Evangeline memorial park at Grand Pré [Nova Scotia] in the early 1900s.[16]

In their book, Allan Forbes and Paul F. Cadman described the first French settlement in the New World by Samuel de Champlain and the Sieur De-Monts in 1604 at St. Croix Island in the St. John River which today delineates the international boundary with Canada. They stated that the French king named "DeMonts 'Lieutenant General' of all that part of North America called by the French 'Acadié,' lying between the fortieth and forty-sixth degrees of latitude, extending from Philadelphia to beyond Montreal . . ."[17]

Thus, "Acadié" was a huge area and it clearly included historically all of Maine, in fact all of New England. Acadia is the term still in use today to designate large parts of northern and coastal eastern Maine. There is today Acadia National Park and the Acadian Trail which extends along coastal U.S. Route 1 and leads to the Maritime provinces of New Brunswick and Nova Scotia.[18]

Certainly the term "Acadia" was, at the time Waugh/Foley were traveling up the Maine coast, in much more widespread use to designate the region surrounding Waldoboro. The uninformed or casual tourist would easily have considered it a part of the region known as Acadia. Thus, it would not have been absurd to consider rugs purchased in the Waldoboro area as Acadian rugs.

Grapes appear again, surrounding a floral center. Kent called this rug "a realistic floral of the Maine type," but he still failed to attribute it as a Waldoboro rug. A similar version, made by Fannie Brooks of Waldoboro, was seen in the 1999 Waldoboro rug exhibition in Lowell, Massachusetts. It is pictured in the exhibition's accompanying catalog, *Art Underfoot,* p. 21, fig.19. Kent, *Rare Hooked Rugs,* p. 43, plate 46.

The acanthus leaf scrolls and pineapple-like fruit at each end is strikingly similar to a rug at the Shelburne (Vermont) Museum which was included in the Waldoboro rug exhibition held in 1999 at the American Textile History Museum in Lowell, Massachusetts. (See: *Art Underfoot,* p. 14, fig. 10.) Kent calls this an "Acadian Type Antique Woolen Hooked Rug in Relief Design. Elaborate and finely worked piece with raised and molded flower designs in pastel colors on the white center. A border of tan acanthus scrolls; outer border in black." 32" x 62". Kent, *The Hooked Rug,* p. 97, plate 81.

Kent termed this an "Acadian modeled or raised pattern" He noted that the "field [was] unclipped, with clipped, raised flowers and scrolls. It was made, he said, "all of woolen yarn, except field of rags." Clearly the use of yarn for the highly sculpted design is very typical of Waldoboro work. Kent, *Hooked Rug,* p. 83, plate 71.

After becoming aware of Creamer's scholarship on Waldoboro rugs, in the third book of the Kent trilogy, *Hooked Rug Design,* the author's enthusiasm for Acadian rugs has diminished somewhat for he now singled out the Waldoboro rug, in particular, as having "excelled in color, blending, shading and detail" when compared with those of Acadia, New Hampshire, and other sections of Maine.[19] However, despite their obvious lack of documentary evidence, the Waugh/Foley and Kent books continue, even today, to sponsor among writers and collectors "proof" of the existence of such Acadian rugs.

Unlike these rugs, which were early-on known as "Acadian," but which lacked any documentation and are not found today in museum or private collections, the existence of the Waldoboro rug is now thoroughly documented by actual specimens and contemporary written evidence. They have taken their rightful place in the history of American rug-hooking.

Similarities of design are obvious when studying these rugs and comparing the so-called "Acadian" with known examples of Waldoboro rugs. This one, termed from "Acadia" by Kent, is similar in overall design with the one at the right of the pictured pair. Again, it is strikingly similar to the Waldoboro with the tipped basket in the previous chapter. The rugs seem to be a nearly homogeneous group bearing similarities that would indicate a tightly knit regional origin. 23.5" x 36". Kent, *The Hooked Rug,* p. 121, plate 100.

Chapter IV
Minnie Light

Documentary evidence relating to the output of any nineteenth century hooker-designer is exciting and rare. Even more unique is to locate that person's original rug patterns, which spanned two centuries from 1880 to 1940. The ultimate satisfaction comes in finally locating biographical details about the rug-maker, for the vast majority of early crafters has been and likely will remain forever anonymous.

Not so with Minnie Light, who was born in the Burkettville section of Appleton, Maine, a small town north of Waldoboro near the headwaters of the Medomak River. Although born and raised in Appleton, she had ample qualifications to be considered a Waldoboro rug hooker. Known affectionately to friends and relatives as "Aunt Minnie," she was a descendant of the German immigrants in Waldoboro and she spent several years doing housework and farm chores for a family at Orff's Corner in Waldoboro.[1] As a maiden lady this was one of the few employment options open to her. She should be lauded for overcoming that restrictive convention by developing her rug-hooking craft into what appears to have been a sustained and successful business — a true pioneer as a woman entrepreneur.

Born on June 22, 1864, Light made her first rug in 1880 at the age of 16. This is the period (1875-1885) when, according to

This is the only known photograph of Minnie Light, the noted rug designer from Burkettville. She is seen standing in the doorway of her modest rural home at the age of 76. The image was taken for a newspaper article in 1940. *Maine Sunday Telegram,* Jan. 31, 1940.

Creamer, the finest Waldoboro rugs were made, "reaching the highest point of perfection at approximately the latter date."[2] This time-line indicates that Light's early instruction had been through association with the best of the early Waldoboro rug-makers. From that meager beginning she would eventually become one of the best known hooker-designers,

sought out by collectors eager to purchase her rugs as well as her patterns.

Many years later she would sell her twenty-four remaining floral designs to Mrs. Hazel W. Bullard, a commercial instructor, designer, and pattern printer in Alfred, Maine.[3] In fact, one of her designs, still titled the "Minnie Light," remains in the current catalog of the Harry M. Fraser Company of Stoneville, North Carolina, a firm with the foresight to preserve the original designs that were made available to this author.[4]

In addition to Light's success as both a hooker and designer, tangible evidence suggests she created commercial designs for E. S. Frost & Company of Biddeford, well-known manufacturer of stamped rug patterns. (Frost will be discussed in detail in later chapters.)

Speculation comes into play in studying one of her recently found original designs of a modified version of Frost Elk No. 22. It was one of several such modified Frost designs featured in the late nineteenth century catalog of the Chicago-based Gibbs Manufacturing Company. Gibbs, as will be outlined in a later chapter, had definite ties, not only with the Northeast, but with Frost himself. Making up the third component of a triumvirate, Ebenezer Ross of Toledo, Ohio, carried still another version of No. 22.

The original elk pattern was recently discovered in the Waldoboro area.[5] The legitimate Frost pattern No. 22 presented the elk with a clump of flowers at the left side, while in the Gibbs pattern, also carrying the No. 22 designation, the elk is flanked by a squirrel-topped tree stump. It is otherwise identical to the Frost version including the Frost outer scroll-work. The Light design with the squirrel and tree stump is the same elk, now with a different scroll border and is designated as No. 23 in the Gibbs catalog and has the Minnie Light oval black frame and the identical scrollwork as seen in her original pattern. And finally, still another modified version was sold by Ebenezer Ross of Toledo, Ohio.

There is no evidence to indicate how Gibbs obtained the pattern, but obviously there was some association between Gibbs and Light. Since Light did not make her first rug until 1880, the earliest Gibbs catalog, undated, but assumed to be 1887, the Frost catalog (1885) and the Ross (1886), this establishes Light as a commercial designer early in her career.

A third original Light design, that of the cat on the "checkerboard" or tiled floor, while not an exact copy of a known Frost design, has all of the characteristics associated with Frost — the scrolled inner border, the animal, and the tiled checkerboard floor. Certainly, more than mere coincidence is involved!

Oral tradition in Waldoboro, claiming that Light sold some of her designs to Edward Sands Frost, is confirmed in a newspaper article published in 1940, three years before Light's death.[6] Mrs. Bullard, who knew Light personally, was quoted as saying that Light drew several original floral designs for Frost. However, Light would not have dealt with Edward Sands Frost himself since she did not hook her first rug until four years after Frost had sold his business and retired to California. Minnie would have been just twelve years old when Frost retired. It was the successor company, E. S. Frost & Company, owned by James Strout, who apparently sought out Light's talents.

She obviously had a penchant for creating "animal" designs as well as the lush florals for which she became noted. Pondering on how many designs she may have created for Frost & Company suggests the possibility that she could well have been a major designer. It seems unlikely that Strout would have "shopped around" for designers once he found one living in Maine that seemed more than suitable.

Chapter VI will discuss possible reasons for the many slightly modified versions of Frost designs among other rug pattern firms. The practice of incorporating a section of one design into another pattern, thus "designing" a new pattern, was not uncommon and was not frowned upon as unethical, but merely one of the offshoots of being in a competitive business. If Light was one of the principal designers for Frost, Ross, and Gibbs, it makes her a major figure in the history of hooking, not only in Maine but in the Midwest as well.

One of the hallmarks of Minnie's floral hooked rugs was a ticking fabric adhered to the reverse with what appears to be a paste made of flour and water. Although it was not unknown in other rugs, it was not a frequent consideration.[7] This raises another possible connection with Ebenezer Ross, the Toledo, Ohio, manufacturer who invented a punch needle machine and was selling Frost patterns as his own designs. (Ross will be discussed more thoroughly in later chapters.)

In 1891, Ross patented a second punch-needle machine. The patent papers for this invention contained the following suggestion:

> . . . After finishing the embroidery [these machines were consistently referred to as embroidery machines] and before removing the canvas from the frame the latter should be inverted and laid on the floor. The back is then covered with a thin coating of flour paste or some other suitable glue and a sheet of cheap material – such as calico or cambric – pressed tightly thereon and allowed to dry. This will cause the pattern to be flat on the face of the fabric and will prevent the loops from pulling out. . . .[8]

Although this procedure was occasionally seen in hooked rugs, it was a procedure consistently practiced by Light, hinting at another tie with Ross and Gibbs, the two Midwest pattern manufacturers.

As a youngster, Mrs. Muriel Kenoyer of Windsor, Maine, lived near Light and she has a vague awareness of Light's animal rugs. She emphasized that Minnie did a "lot of horses." Possibly the horse referred to by Mrs. Beston in the previous chapter was a Light design. Kenoyer also has recollections of entering the shed attached to the Light home in Burkettville and seeing Minnie, together with three or four other hookers, working on a large room-sized rug. She believes that it went to a New Hampshire buyer when it was finished.

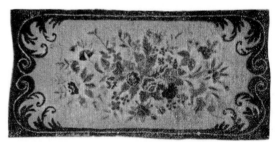

This is the first rug hooked by Minnie in 1881 as reproduced in Kent's *Rare Hooked Rugs.* The rug was originally photographed while it was in the possession of Mrs. Hazel Bullard of Alfred in 1941. It was described as: "Exquisite flower designs, field of neutral gray, scrolls a deep red, outer border a dull brown. Worked on old, heavy white cotton cloth." Unfortunately its present location – if it survives at all – is unknown. 27" x 54". Kent, *Rare Hooked Rugs,* p. 76, plate 90.

Kenoyer's mother, Mrs. Gladys Cunningham, had a number of Light patterns, but it is not known whether they were purchased or were gifts. A rug shown is a Minnie Light rug worked by Mrs. Cunningham. The pattern was not sturdy enough for hooking so Cunningham attached the cotton pattern to a piece of burlap and hooked through both fabrics. The original Light pattern can be seen through the woolen loops.[9] Although not hooked by Light, this rug provides a glimpse of the widely-acclaimed beauty of Light's many floral designs that she achieved in her maturity

Minnie's first rug coincides with the end of the "early pioneer days" in Appleton, at the peak of road-building in the town, resulting in an "evolution of the spirit of improvements in farm buildings, better implements, better roadways, travel and transportation by horsepower . . . making interaction between Appleton and Waldoboro more convenient."[10]

In 1940, just three years before Light's death on January 31, 1940, Mary Carpenter Kelley wrote an article about her in the *Maine Sunday Telegram* under the headline, "Never Took Lessons But Minnie Light of Burkettville Has Designed Beautiful Rugs."[11]

This is the story of a woman born in rural Maine who never took a drawing lesson in her life yet produced the remarkable collection of exquisite floral rug patterns that has recently been purchased by Harriet Wallace Bullard of Governor's Corner [Alfred, Maine]. These designs, 24 in number originated by Miss Minnie Light of Burkettville, will be known as "Minnie's Garden Series" and were bought with exclusive reproduction rights by Mrs. Bullard who at the same time purchased a very beautiful rug made by Miss Light 60 years ago, the first she ever hooked.

Through all her years of drawing rug patterns Miss Light's only teacher was Nature: in Summer the old fashioned posies growing in her own garden and the wild flowers in the fields about her home, in Winter those blossoming in her windows and in seed catalogs. These combined with the graceful scrolls in drawing which she was always adept, furnished her with all the motifs she needed. With naïve artistry she did not hesitate to place a pond-lily beside a carnation nor a modest bluet next to an opulent fuschia; her feeling for space and color compensating for any hint of incongruity. In fact it is these ingenious and unusual arrangements that give charm and individuality to the patterns which go to make up "Minnie's Garden Series."

Since she completed that first rug so many years ago, Miss Light has designed many patterns and hooked many rugs. Some she sold to Summer people for Burkettville is not far from the coastal town of Rockland with its large summer resort population. As time went on, they found her out and coaxed her into parting with some of her treasures, but in all probability she would never have sold her patterns had not Mrs. Bullard's husband, Harold A. Bullard, happened to call at her home one day six years ago and found her occupied with her favorite work — hooking a rug.

Mr. Bullard knows a great deal about hooked rugs, for Mrs. Bullard is not only a teacher of hooking, but gained considerable fame a few years ago when she reproduced in room-size that now famous old Alfred pattern known as "Aunt Harriet Emery's" rug. [This rug is now in the collection of the Shelburne Museum in Vermont.] So he saw at once that the rug on which Miss Light was hooking was quite out of the ordinary, that its soft coloring, its clear-cut design, its relation of figure to background were remarkable.

"Where did the pattern come from," he asked? "O, I drew it myself. I've made lots of patterns," said Miss Light unconcernedly. Whereupon she proceeded to show him how many different rugs she had designed and told him how simple it was, in her opinion, to draw a pattern.

Back at Governor's Corner, he reported the matter to Mrs. Bullard who immediately went down to Burkettville to see Miss Light and her rugs. They were far lovelier than she had imagined but Miss Light was not ready to sell any patterns and it was not until last Spring, when she came to the conclusion at the age of 76 that she would give up designing and hooking, that she consented to let Mrs. Bullard have the "Minnie's Garden Series."

The various designs were drawn on white cotton cloth, each as perfect in every detail as if some expert had stamped them instead of a woman who had only the simplest of tools with which to work. Her flowers were all true to nature. There was no confusion whatever, a rose depicted by Minnie Light could be mistaken for no other flower, a fuschia was certainly a fuschia and a pink, a pink. Medallions and corner figures, scrolls and borders were disposed upon the ground with a perfect sense of proportion. In fact all 24 patterns had been put together with such skill and taste that it was difficult to understand how a person with no training in drawing could have accomplished such results. And now Mrs. Bullard says that with the series as it is and such other patterns as she can make using motifs from one design combined with those from another, she has an inexhaustible supply of pattern material.

Miss Light was born in Burkettville near the house where she is now living, June 23, 1864. She is descended from the Hessians who first settled in that part of the country, the same area Ben Ames Williams has just made known to the rest of the world in "Come Spring,"[12] for Burkett-ville is a post office in the town of Appleton which adjoins Union. "Seven Tree Pond" is not far away and when Miss Light was a girl, Burkettville was as unsophisticated and quaint a little community as even Mr. Williams could have imagined. In fact it has not changed a great deal, for never having had a railroad or trolley line, accessible from the outside only by stage-coach, only the coming of the automobile has tended to modernize it.

"Minnie's Garden Series" designs are already very popular with Mrs. Bullard's classes and she is kept busy copying them on burlap for pupils. One of the loveliest, a medallion of roses, buds and leaves surrounded by a framework of delicate scrollery, on a very light colored background, has already been made by Mrs. Maude Clark of Alfred and was shown over at the Sanford Public Library during National Art Week. Another exceptionally beautiful number having a medallion with lily, roses, pinks and fuschias, and corner designs of the same flowers, no two of the four corners alike, on a white background, done by Mrs. Bullard herself, won a great deal of admiration when it was shown in the Spring and also when it was shown in Portland last week in the Chamber of Commerce.

Mrs. Bullard was a prominent Maine teacher and designer in her own right. Her original designs are identified by the inclusion of a characteristic butterfly, bee or ladybug.[13]

While Miss Kelley's newspaper article expresses surprise at the ease with which Minnie, an untrained artist, could be so adept at designing, her method was simple but not unique. The book, *Handcrafts of New England,* explains that Light would "select the flowers, lay them on paper, cut them out, and then place the paper designs on the burlap for tracing."[14] One of her original designs, photographed here, shows the pattern with some of the paper pieces still attached. A second pattern of the "Falmouth Flower Basket," is pictured in the Kent Book, *Hooked Rug Design,* and mistakenly claimed to have been the design of Hazel Bullard.[15] This design also is still carried in the current Fraser catalog of patterns.

These original patterns are historically significant in another way as well for they demonstrate the early methods of applying a design to a piece of fabric. Light always seemed to prefer old cotton sheets or muslin for her basic fabric, and her earliest designs were applied to this base with charcoal. She later used a tracing wheel perforating the paper, so it could be pounced with chalk. Finally, she employed the more modern blue transfer pencil. These methods allow the scholar to approximate the evolutionary dates of the patterns.

Although it is claimed that "Minnie's Garden Series" included the original floral designs sold to Edward Sands Frost, this is disputable. As noted above, she did not make her first rug until after Frost had sold his business to Strout, so the designs would have been sold to E. S. Frost & Company. Further study indicates that none of these "Minnie's Garden Series" designs ever appeared in any published form as a Frost design. Since she is known to have sold other designs to Frost & Company, it would be highly unlikely she would have sold Frost & Company the rights to the patterns and then, years later, sold those rights a second time to Bullard.

The late Robert Hall of Dover-Foxcroft, Maine, claimed he had purchased Miss Light's designs and sold them to Mr. Henry Francis DuPont for the collection at his Winterthur Museum, the world-famous institution in Delaware. Hall was a contemporary of Creamer and well known as a dealer in hooked rugs.[16] A check with staff at Winterthur found no record of such rugs. However, a number of years

In the same publication Kent showed another rug with the lush inward-curving scrolls that were to become Minnie's "trademark." Kent did not connect the similarity of the design in the previous rug to this one and failed to make a connection with Minnie. He simply called it an "Early American rug" and credited it to the collection of J. M. Shoemaker of New York. It had apparently been sold during one of Shoemaker's auctions. Dimensions not given. Kent, *Rare Hooked Rugs,* p. 39, plate 41.

previously Winterthur de-accessioned many of its hooked rugs as not falling within the parameters of the institution's collection policy. Hooked rugs, they felt, post-dated the historical period of their interest.

A study of Light's original patterns proves her mastery with magnificent and intricate scrolls. The inward curving scroll in the first rug she ever made was, with minor modifications, seen in several other rugs and helps to establish her as the originator of this particular design motif.

Light was a descendant of one of the earliest settlers in Burkettville. Her great grandfather was Henry Esancy, the object of some notoriety as a Hessian mercenary fighting on the wrong side in the Revolutionary War. He "came here as an enemy," according to the Burkettville history written by Light's brother, Elmer, but went on to redeem himself as an upstanding citizen of the town.[17]

Esancy was "a victim of the system and avarice prevailing in his time and native country in regard to the humbler class of people who were serfs or slaves to the land owned and controlled by Princes." Esancy was born in Braunschweig, Hanover, Germany, in 1754 and was impressed into the Hessian Cavalry for service in the British cause in the conflict with the American Colonies. He was later held as prisoner in Boston and either by parole or escape, found his way to Waldoboro where German colonists resided. He eventually made his way to Union and then to Burkettville, and was married to Susannah Rolfe, also of German descent through the Germans in Waldoboro.[18]

Their daughter, Sarah, married Daniel Briggs Grinnell, and their daughter, Sarah Grinnell, married Joseph M. Light, the father of Minnie and her three siblings. Minnie, the youngest of the four children, never married and following the death of her par-

Also in the 1940 newspaper article on Minnie was a photograph of her home in Burkettville, the ancestral residence of her mother, Sarah (Grinnell) Light. Since her siblings had married and moved away from home, as the one unmarried daughter, it is logical she inherited the family homestead. The U.S. Census shows her living alone and listed as "Head of Household." *Maine Sunday Telegram,* Jan. 31, 1940.

ents, resided on the maternal homestead in Burkettville near the home where she was born. She was fortunate (or perhaps unfortunate) to have received an education, for education was not necessarily deemed a desirable trait in a wife. She remained a spinster all her life. The Appleton census of 1880 shows her, at the age of 15, "at school," indicating that she was not living at home.[19] Possibly she followed in the footsteps of her brother, Elmer, who attended the State Normal School in Castine.

Elmer later taught at the Burkettville School and also served as a selectman. Although Minnie was employed doing housework and farm chores for a family in Waldoboro, it is likely she also earned additional money designing rugs for Frost & Company, Ebenezer Ross and Gibbs Manufacturing, certainly a rather unique employment opportunity at the time. Obviously she had enough interaction with relatives and friends in Waldoboro to become involved very early in the traditional craft of hooking.

Elmer's history describes the family's home life:

> Our garments were mainly home-produced. From wool we had our stockings, drawers, shirts, pants, jackets and capes. A cowhide tanned at the tannery for a fee was provided for the journeying cobbler to make up our winter footwear. Bright wheat or rye straw supplied the material for our summer hats. From a small patch of flax, after the required seasoning and manipulating, we had from Mother's loom our linen towels, bedspreads, tablecloths, and often Linsey-woolsey garments. No German or Diamond dyes were thought of then for coloring, but indigo, hemlock bark, elderberry, wild cherry and sumac were the ingredients that sent forth their odors from the dyepots.[20]

Minnie was exposed to the significance of color at an early age, and the lessons would stand her in good stead in future years. The 1920 census shows Minnie as head of household, owning her own home (the Grinnell homestead), free of mortgage, single, age 55, and able to read and write. It was also recorded that she, her mother and father "were natives" and her profession was listed as "farmer." Three years after selling her patterns to Hazel Bullard she died on January 31, 1943, after a significant lifetime contribution to the field of hooking.[21]

While she made her first rug during the height of the great Waldoboro period, hooking overall would decline in both artistry and technique from the period about 1885 until well into the twentieth century. Factory made goods had become less expensive so carpets and rugs were financially accessible to the average household. In addition, the Arts and Crafts Movement would bring in more sophisticated designers anxious to "improve" the craft. The temporary demise of hooking was further complicated by the effects of World War I. An article in *Good Housekeeping* in 1918 explained that "Of course, nowadays it would be immensely expensive as well as wastefully unpatriotic to draw in a rug of all yarn."[22] This certainly killed the yarn-sewn rug and to some extent inhibited the craft of rug-hooking in general.

It appears that, despite the periodic changes in the craft, Minnie maintained a steadfast inter-est in and production of both rugs and designs. In addition to the sale of her own rugs and designs, Bullard had an endless supply of "new" Light patterns by taking design elements from one pattern and combining them with elements from another. Thus, Light's designs continued to be a part of the craft long after her death in 1943. In some instances they survive even today and are sold through the Fraser Company, including one specifically named the "Minnie Light." It is more than likely that many rugs auctioned over the years in Maine have been Light rugs or, at least, Light patterns. Perhaps they still make their way to auction even today.

This is a very early example of the work Minnie would undertake and demonstrates her early skill in color and shading, as well as sculpting. The scroll is only slightly modified from that in the first rug she made. On her initial effort in 1881 she did not sculpt the design although it is documented that Waldoboro hookers were modeling or raising their rugs as early as 1877. The sculpting of the flowers and border scrolls is indicative of the best Waldoboro rugs. The sage green background is believed to have been obtained from the nearby Warren Woolen Company, which had a retail outlet in Waldoboro. c.1885-1895. Wool on cotton sheeting backed with ticking, 26.25" x 47.50". *MCP collection.*

Although this rug was not made by Minnie Light, it is her pattern, made available to the late Mrs. Gladys Cunningham of Appleton many years ago. The original design was outlined on a light cotton fabric. To make a sturdier foundation, Mrs. Cunningham attached the cotton sheeting to a piece of burlap and hooked through both fabrics. She also dyed her own colors. This rich and fulsome pattern demonstrates Minnie's continued development as a designer. c.1950s. Wool with vegetable dyes on cotton and burlap, 23.50" x 52". *Courtesy Muriel Kenoyer, Mrs. Cunningham's daughter.*

The cotton pattern is a documented original Minnie Light design which still remains in Waldoboro. It demonstrates her ability to draw animal figures, develop a pleasing composition and surround the design with an oval of lush scrolls. As seen below it became the basis for commercial patterns marketed by E.S. Frost, E. Ross, and A. Gibbs. It is not known how many other patterns Light may have designed for commercial use. Certainly her reputation was widely known and companies may have engaged her to design for them. Color suggestions are written in light pencil in each of the various areas which might lead one to believe Minnie was telling Frost, Ross or Gibbs how to apply different tints to the printed burlap. Cotton scrim, 28" x 54". *Courtesy Waldoborough Historical Society.*

This is the original E.S. Frost & Company elk No. 22. Frost's elk is flanked with a blossoming shrub and buds at both sides of the pattern instead of the squirrel on a stump. The mountain at the rear of the elk is somewhat modified but otherwise it is identical to Gibbs Nos. 22-23. Light definitely told Hazel Bullard she had sold designs to E. S. Frost & Company. Cotton scrim, 28" x 54". *Frost/Stratton catalog.*

In this instance Gibbs has left the basic inner portion of the Light design unchanged, but added a more Victorian-looking original Frost pattern for the outer border. The firm sold it as Pattern No 22. The possible connection between Frost, Ross and Gibbs is discussed more fully in a later chapter. *Gibbs Manufacturing Company catalog.*

The sequence of who first used Minnie's pattern is debatable but here Gibbs Manufacturing Company has published in its catalog Minnie's exact design with the squirrel on the dead tree stump and with her very identifiable scroll border around the oval central design. It is Gibbs's No. 23. *Gibbs Manufacturing Company catalog.*

The elk must have been a popular pattern and so it is no surprise to also find a version issued by Ebenezer Ross in his 1886 catalog, still again listed as No. 22. However, Ross "flipped" the zinc stencils so that the elk appears to be facing left, different from the other examples above. The dead tree re-appeared but the squirrel was not resurrected. This may be Ross's way, through a slight alteration, of legally copying the Gibbs or Frost patterns. *Ross 1886 catalog Maine State Museum.*

It is interesting to view Minnie's pattern for a cat on a multi-colored tile floor, and a Waldoboro rug (i.e., on linen) of the same subject. Rug-hookers will immediately see the close similarity of Minnie's design with the well known E. S. Frost & Company patterns of dogs and cats on the same type of flooring. Clearly Minnie had a wide influence on commercial rug pattern makers. The finished rug is identical to the cotton pattern except that the corner nosegays have been eliminated. Another identical rug, a mirror-image with different colorations, is known to have been completed by Mrs. Margaret Wellman of Waldoboro. Cotton pattern, 31.50" x 39." *Courtesy Muriel Kenoyer.* Rug: wool on cotton, 35.25" x 24.25" *Courtesy Jeff and Suzanne Good.*

Light preferred cotton fabric for her foundations. This original Light pattern, drawn on cotton sheeting, retains some of the original cut-out paper pieces she used in drawing the design. They are lightly pinned to the sheeting so she could trace around them. The flower petals show evidence of tiny holes made with a tracing wheel for pouncing. Cotton sheeting, 32.5" x 55.5". *All Light patterns are in the Maine Historical Society Collections.*

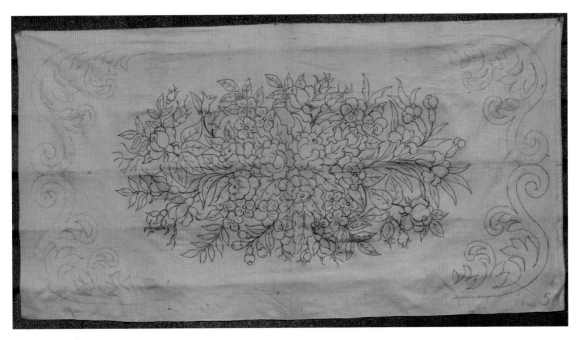

Like any good artist, Minnie's designs evolved over the years. Her floral medallions became richer and her scroll borders also underwent changes and modifications. However, at times she reverted to the past. Here is a pattern with a rich central medallion of flowers bordered by the distinctive inward-curving scrolls she had developed at the beginning of her career. Both interior and exterior elements were artfully combined into an attractive pattern. In the lower right corner is her "No. 5." This would certainly be an example of "Minnie's Garden Series" which Mrs. Bullard marketed after Light's death. It became Fraser pattern No. 248. Cotton sheeting, 29" x 56". *Maine Historical Society Collections.*

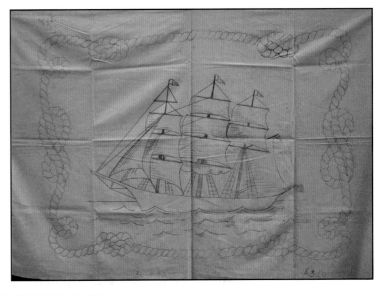

As she entered the twentieth century Minnie adapted to changing tastes in rug patterns. Summer folk especially wanted designs that reminded them of old-time Maine and so she produced this pattern of a three-masted vessel. Instead of her usual borders she used a rope motif to create a scrolling edge. Minnie's original price of $3.50 is seen in the lower right corner. Cotton sheeting, 35.5" x 53". *Maine Historical Society Collections.*

In the early part of the nineteenth century genre scenes began to creep into the rug pattern catalogs and Minnie joined the effort. This type of pattern did have a considerable following among rug-hookers in the 1920s and 1930s and retains its charm as a pattern for a child's room. Cotton sheeting, 24" x 34" oval. *Maine Historical Society collection.*

45

The distinctive scroll again allowed the attribution of this rug to Minnie Light when it came on the market in 1999. All of her early rugs show an adaptation of what became known as the "Waldoboro scroll," in which one edge of the scroll is straight while all the fronds are on the inner side curving toward the center. The rug also has ticking glued to the reverse with a flour-and-water paste, a feature often seen in Minnie's rugs. c.1885-1895. Wool yarn and fabric on cotton backed with ticking, 28.50" x 51." *Courtesy Sharon and Jeffrey Lipton.*

Just as the manuscript was being finalized, this Minnie Light rug came up for auction at the Constance S. Robie estate sale in Waldoboro. The collection of Minnie's cotton patterns provided the proof needed to attribute the rug to Light. Hooked on early hand-woven linen, it has the traditional Waldoboro green as the ground of the rug made of vegetable dyed wool yarns. Unfortunately, the leaves surrounding the central roses have faded to such a degree they have melted into the background. Nicely sculptured. c.1885-95. All wool yarn with wool fabric strips in the scrolls; on linen, 21.50" x 41.50". *Robert Foster Auction.*

This is Light's original cotton pattern for the preceding rug. In this version she eliminated the roses centered in the two end scrolls. Otherwise, the cotton pattern is exactly the same as the one found at the above auction. c.1885-1895. Pencil drawing on cotton. Dimensions of the squared design, 20.50" x 41.50". *Maine Historical Society Collections.*

Chapter V

Edward Sands Frost

Although the story has been told many times, any treatise on the history of rug-hooking in Maine would be remiss to exclude the peddler, Edward Sands Frost (1843-1894). Frost was praised by some and condemned by others, but his influence will be felt for all time. While there are indications that Frost was not, in reality, the first person to come up with stamped rug patterns, his actual achievements would leave a legacy of inventiveness that would far surpass that of any contemporary competitor.

The Wenham, Massachusetts, Historical Society collection includes rugs believed to be made from stamped patterns in the 1860s. The firm of Chambers & Lealand manufactured copper-inlaid blocks for stamping embroidery patterns, but they also made print blocks from wood of the size suitable for stamping rug patterns on burlap or linen. The blocks were eventually sold to Philena Moxley, an embroiderer, who also employed them to stamp rug patterns. There is no evidence that these patterns were commercially marketed to any significant degree.[1]

It was Frost, therefore, that history has acknowledged and glorified as the inventor of the first stenciled (and colored) rug patterns.[2] From his autobiographical memoirs, it is obvious that he was not aware of any earlier inventions. He would also come to be known as the man who destroyed the localization of design thus compromising the native creativity and naiveté so long associated with the craft of rug-making. And yet, he made a gigantic contribution to the industry

Frost was born at Lyman, Maine, on January 1, 1843. At the age of nineteen he enlisted in Company E of the 1st Maine Cavalry Regiment on August 7, 1862, and left Augusta with the rest of his unit to join the fight to preserve the Union. On his enlistment papers his occupation was given as "operative" (one who ran machines of one type or another). His health being delicate, Frost was separated from the service and "discharged for dis[ease]" on February 28, 1863.[3]

In frail health, he returned to the textile mill town of Biddeford and found employment as a machinist (a trade that ideally suited his later endeavors making rug stencils) at the Saco Water Power Company machine shop. He married Ellen Whitehouse and the couple took up residence at the corner of South and Green Streets. During the winter of 1864-65 ill health forced him to give up his position at the machine shop. His doctor thought an outdoor occupation would be best for him. This tends to enforce the tradition that he suffered from tuberculosis or "consumption," as it was known at that time.[4]

In terms of his health, becoming a tin peddler seemed to be an ideal trade to pursue. *Greenough's Directory of . . . Biddeford and Saco* for 1870 lists Edward S. Frost as a "pedler" [*sic*] living on the Buxton Road near its intersection with the Shadgee Road.[5] In a 1940 article in *The Magazine Antiques,* Kent quotes Mrs. Ella Jordan Marsh of Saco describing her childhood fascination with the peddler's cart Frost kept in his basement. "It had so many interesting things in it – tinware, rugs and patterns, calicos and everything."[6] In 1871 he is recorded for the first time as a maker of "Stamped Rug Patterns" in the *Maine State Year-Book*, an annual and, later, biennial compilation of facts and statistics relating to the State.[7] *The Maine Business Directory for the Year Commencing January 1, 1873,* lists Edward S. Frost at 180 Main Street, the same location of the business when it was later purchased and reformed as E. S. Frost & Company in 1876.

Peddlers were ubiquitous on the roads of mid-nineteenth century America, especially throughout New England. They were important economically, and popular socially, especially in rural areas. Not only did they bring merchandise to isolated peoples distant from urban regions, but they were a source of news, political gossip and tidbits of community happenings to those who rarely saw a newspaper. They could read letters to the illiterate, commiserate with the sick and infirm, and generally bring a ray of cheer to the wife and mother, often separated from any outside communication or social activities.[8]

To a child the peddler personified romance. He provided a tangible connection with that vague world of people and towns beyond the horizon. As one writer said, "Nineteenth-century boys dreamed of becoming a peddler as twentieth-century boy's dream of exploring the moon."[9] The traveling salesmen might have mastered a musical instrument, such as a mouth harp, fiddle, or ocarina, and folks would invite him in to spend the night and provide entertainment. Often neighbors would be urged to pay a visit and the peddler/fiddler could possibly make an extra 25¢ by impressing his audience with his talents as musician, story-teller, or magician.

As Mrs. Marsh remembered, the peddler's conveyance was an imposing sight. Starting out in the trade a young man might have only a "peddler's pony" (a walking stick), carrying his wares on his back. If he did well, he graduated to a two-wheel cart with goods packed ingeniously into baskets or tin trunks. Prosperity could lead to a single horse with 50-pound trunks swinging from each side of the saddle. Finally, as in Frost's case, the sign a peddler was well-known and well-patronized meant he could upgrade to a four-wheeled wagon drawn by one or two horses. It was such an outfit that came to be the trademark of the successful Yankee peddler.

One old-timer remembered that the cart seemed to him for all the world like a Trojan horse, full of an endless assortment of "goodies," and one elderly lady said her mother always wanted kitchen cupboards with compartments exactly like those inside a peddler's cart.[10] The wagons were always brightly painted and some even boasted of perfectly matched horses with silver-mounted harnesses. The peddler's cart was a store on wheels and to some appeared as colorful as circus wagons. Some peddlers, such as Frost, were their own bosses, buying all their merchandise, doing all the selling and reaping all the profits. Others worked for agents who provided the wagons and inventory. On the return from a selling trip, the peddler was paid in cash or in barter.

In fact, barter was a major element of peddling. If a housewife could not afford the peddler's new tin boiler, she would offer old rags, bristles, apples, butter and other commodities she made or grew herself. If her husband did not have cash to purchase the leather boots or new farm tools being offered, he would barter skins of raccoons, muskrats or deer, flax seed, or beeswax for them.

This is why, as Frost explains in the reminiscences below, he ended up with some old wash boilers in his stable. In fact, there survives an 1854 list of merchandise an agent peddler was allowed to trade for, with the prices he could pay for each object. For example, he could pay in trade 20¢ per pound for red deer skins but only 10¢ for gray ones. Likewise, he was given the authority to barter goose feathers for 50¢ a pound but could allow only 4¢ per pound for turkey feathers.[11] The peddler had to have a head for mathematics, a good concept of what he could or could not sell and resell, and, above all, a pleasing personality.

Several years after he had sold his highly successful business, Frost gave an autobiographical account of his career to a *Biddeford Times* reporter in 1888:[12]

By the advice of my physician [in the winter of 1864-65], who recommended outdoor work, I went into the tin peddling business which I followed until the spring of 1870. During this time, by close economy, I saved my first thousand dollars, and it was the proudest day of my life, when in January, '69, after taking count of stock, I found I had invested in household goods $200, in team $175, in sale goods and cash in bank $700. As profits do not average over two dollars per day, it had required strictest economy to support my family and save that amount. It was a hard struggle, but that is the only way a poor man can get capital to go into business with. It is easy enough to make money, if a man has money to work with.

It was during the winter of '68 that my wife, after saving quite a quantity of colored rags that I had collected in my business as a tin peddler, decided to work them into a rug. She went to her cousin, the late Mrs. George Twombley, and had her mark out a pattern, which she did with red chalk on a piece of burlap. After my wife had the pattern properly adjusted on her quilting frame she began to hook in the rags with the instrument then used in rug making, which was a hook made of a nail or an old gimlet. After watching her work a while I noticed that she was using a very poor hook, so, being a machinist, I went to work and made the crooked hook which was used so many years afterwards in the rug business and is still in vogue today.

While making the hook I would occasionally try it on the rug to see if it was all right as to size, and in this way I got interested in the rug. I had "caught the fever" as they used to say. So every evening I worked on the rug until it was finished. It was while thus engaged that I first conceived the idea of working up an article that is today about as staple as cotton cloth and sells the world over. Every lady that ever made a rug knows that it is very pleasant and bewitching work in a pretty design but tiresome and hard on plain figures; and so it proved to me. After working four evenings on the rug I told my wife

One of the first things Edward Sands Frost did upon entering the hooked rug pattern business was to design a rug hook with a bent shank which, he said, was easier to use than the old-fashioned home-made hook with a straight shank. This design is still used by many of today's hookers. *E. S. Frost & Company catalog*.

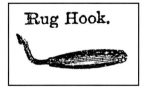

Rug Hook.

I thought I could make a better design myself than that we were at work on, so after we finished our rug I got a piece of burlap and taking a pencil, I wrote my first design on paper and then put it on cloth and worked the flower and scroll already for the groundwork.

We showed it to our neighbors and they were so well pleased with it that I got orders for some twenty or more patterns like it within three days. So you see I got myself into the business right away. I put in my time evenings and stormy days sketching designs, giving only the outlines in black. There was not money enough in it to devote my whole time to the business, and as orders came in faster than I could fill them I began, Yankee-like, to study some way to do them quicker. Then the first idea of stenciling presented itself to me.

Did I go to Boston to get my stencils made? Oh, no, I went out into my stable where I had some old iron and some old wash boilers I had bought for their copper bottoms, took the old tin off them and made my first stencil out of it. Where did I get the tools? Why I found them in the same place, in my stable among the old iron. I got there some old files, half flat and half round, took them to the tin shop of Cummings & West, and forged my tools to cut the stencil with. I made a cutting block out of old lead and zinc.

After fitting myself out with tools I began making small stencils of small flowers, scrolls, leaves, buds, etc., each one on a small plate; then I could with a stencil brush print in ink in plain figures much faster than I could sketch. Thus I had reduced ten hours' labor to two and a half hours. I then had the art down fine enough to allow me to fill all my orders, so I began to print patterns and put them in my peddler's cart and offer them for sale. The news of my invention of stamped rugs spread like magic, and many a time as I drove through the streets of Biddeford and Saco, a lady would appear at the door or window, swinging an apron or sun bonnet, and shouting at the top of her voice saying, "Are you the rug man? Do you carry rugs all marked out?" I at once became known as Frost, the rug man, and many Biddeford citizens still speak of me in that way.

My rug business increased and I soon found that I could not print fast enough; I also found it difficult to duplicate patterns, or make two exactly alike, as many of my customers would call for a pattern just like Mrs. So and So's. Then I began to make a whole design on one plate. At first it seemed impossible, but I was willing to try, so I obtained a sheet of zinc and printed on it and cut out a design. This process I continued to follow until I had some fourteen designs on hand, ranging from a yard long and a half yard wide to two yards long and a yard wide.

These plates gave only the outline in black and required only one impression to make a complete pattern, yet it was by far the hardest part of the whole affair to make stencils so as to take a good impression, and I think there is no stencil workman in this country that would consider it possible to cut so large a plate with such fine figures and take an impression from it. It required a great deal of patience, for I was just thirty days cutting the first one and when I laid it on the table, the center of the plate would not touch the table by two and a half inches. As the plate of zinc lay smooth before being cut out, I knew it must be cutting that caused the trouble; I studied the problem and learned that in cutting the metal expanded, so I expanded the uncut portion in proportion to that which was cut and the plate then lay smooth. This I did with a hammer and it took about two days' time.

When the plate was finished I could print it with a pattern in four minutes that had previously required ten hours to sketch by hand. I then thought I had my patterns about perfect, so I began to prepare them for market. I remember well the first trip I made through Maine and a part of New Hampshire, trying to sell my goods to the dry goods trade. I failed to find a man who dared to invest a dollar in them; in fact people did not know what they were for, and I had to give up trying [to sell them wholesale] and go house to house. There I found plenty of purchasers, for I found the ladies knew what the patterns were for.

Next I began coloring the patterns by hand, as there was some call for colored goods. The question of how to print them at a profit seemed to be the point on which the success of the whole business hung, and it took me over three months to settle it. I shall never forget the time and place it came to me, for it had become such a study that I could not sleep nights. It was in March, 1870, one morning about two o'clock. I had been thinking how I could print the bright colors in with the dark ones so as to make good clear prints. My mind was so fixed on the problem that I could not sleep, so I turned and twisted and all at once I seemed to hear a voice in my room say: "Print your bright colors first and then the dark ones." That settled it, and I was so excited that I could not close my eyes in sleep the rest of the night and I tell you I was glad when morning came so that I could get to town to buy stock for the plates with which to carry out my idea. [Basically Frost had recognized the necessity of making a separate stencil to apply each different color.]

At the end of a week I had one design made and printed in colors. It proved a success. Then I sold my tin peddling business and hired a room in the building on Main Street [in Biddeford] just above the savings bank, where I began in the month of April [1870] to print patterns in colors. I did my own work at first for four months and then I employed one man. In September I had two men in my employ, and in November I opened a [retail] salesroom in Boston through Gibbs & Warren.[13] Then it took four men in December and ten men during the rest of the winter.

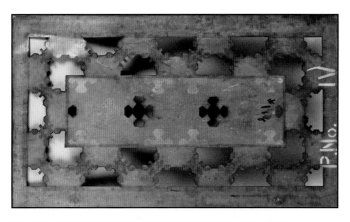

Frost was deservedly proud of inventing stencils to produce rug patterns. At top is one of the zinc stencils with wire reinforced border used to make Frost's Pattern No. 118. There was a different stencil for each color. When complete, the pattern measured 18" x 36." At bottom is how the rug appeared as a catalog line drawing. This is one of two Frost patterns which have been reissued by the Maine State Museum in a reduced scale. *Top: Courtesy Maine State Museum; bottom: Frost/Stratton catalog.*

Many of the business men here will remember what an excitement my business created, for there were very few men who had any faith in my bonanza. I remember having seen well known business men stand in the street near Shaw's block and point over at my goods that were hung out and laugh at the idea (as they afterwards told me) of my making a living out of such an undertaking. Well, I guess they will all admit that I did make a living out of it, as I continued to manufacture rug patterns there, all of my own designs, till the end of '76, when I was so reduced in health that I sold out my business and left Biddeford November 2nd, for Pasadena, California, where I have made my home since.

Looking at the chronology that Frost outlines in the above text several facts stand out:

1 – He started by improving the straight-shanked rug hook by bending it, making it more comfortable to use. Frost believed that by bending the straight shank then in use he was able to make an instrument that was more effective and easier on the hooker's wrist. He proved to be correct: his bent hook design remains in use to this day. In the E. S. Frost circular of 1885 it was available for 20¢ each or $2.40 a dozen, with the notation, "We have the sole right to sell Pat. Rug Hooks, the best in the world. . . ."

2 – While he and his wife were working on their first rug Frost came to the conclusion, after a mere four evenings of observation that he could design a better rug pattern. Obviously he possessed a sharp and inventive mind.

3 – After he had created his first design "within four days" Frost had orders for "twenty or more patterns" and he had completed fourteen different designs. These were only designs in outline, but showed that neighboring women immediately recognized the convenience these pre-drawn designs provided them.

4 – In March 1870, a little over a year after helping his wife with her rug, Frost came up with the concept of printing patterns in colors. It was an important step forward in relieving hookers of the need to make decisions they were happy to turn over to the pattern maker.

5 – From April 1870, when Frost first started printing in colors using multiple stencils, he went in a few short months from a single operator enterprise to adding ten workmen. In addition he opened an outlet in Boston. It was a rapid rise to fame. In about five years he had been able to give up the life of an itinerant and settle his business in a storefront on Biddeford's main thoroughfare.

6 – He was obviously proud of his achievements, and called the results of his creativity an "invention." He was also careful to retain all the dates and details of his enterprise enabling him to repeat them to the newspaper reporter years later. Frost felt he had developed something important and was justifiably proud of his achievement. The very first patterns Edward Sands Frost stamped in his own name are marked "Patent Applied For" but no design patent has been found in his name. It is very probable that he submitted a patent application but it was turned down.

While there are numerous surviving burlap patterns stamped "E. S. Frost & Company," very few are found today that were issued under the name "Edward Sands Frost" from the days when the peddler stenciled the patterns himself. Although not in the best of condition the present owner has had it professionally conserved. This pattern is an extremely rare document, not only being by Sands himself but also marked "No. 1," the first colored pattern he designed and manufactured.
The detail of the selvage shows the stamping, "E. S. Frost Man'fr 180-182 Main Biddeford ME." On another edge is marked: "No.1 Patent Applied For." There is no record, however, that the U.S. Patent Office granted Frost a patent on his method of printing patterns with zinc stencils. c.1870-76. Printed burlap, 36" x 70". *Courtesy Ann Seaver.*

For Frost the years between 1868 and 1876 were a true explosion of creative energy. The former Yankee peddler moved from a solitary tradesman to an enterprising manufacturer in less than two years. Frost was not only an inventive genius but a master at marketing his new product, quickly stepping into and dominating a field of endeavor ready to be exploited. The fact that he could design, manufacture, wholesale, and retail his rug patterns so rapidly indicates there was a considerable void to be filled. Such success could be achieved only by stimulating a widespread interest in the craft throughout New England.

Having made his mark on the trade and having achieved financial success, Frost remained concerned over his precarious health. In any case, he felt it was time to move on after a little over seven years. The sale of the business took place in November 1876 to James A. Strout and Jerre G. Shaw, two Biddeford businessmen doing business at 180 and 182 Main Street.[14] The following year (1877) the business was moved to 205 and 207 Main Street, Biddeford. However, the firm is not listed as E. S. Frost *& Company* until the appearance of the *Maine State Year-Book* in 1878. It was moved again in 1880 to 245 and 247 Main Street. Apparently the successful growth of the business required larger quarters.[15]

At the time of the take-over Strout and Shaw appeared fairly prosperous, both living in a good neighborhood, the former on Western Avenue at the corner of James Street, and the latter on the same avenue at the corner of Cutts Street.[16] In 1878 the Frost firm was honored with a Medal of Excellence at the American Institute Fair in New York, and a diploma from the Mechanics Fair in Boston for the "Best and Handsomest Patterns."[17] Frost died in California in May 1894.

Because the original burlap base does not stand up well over time, many of the Frost rugs in today's market were made from the original stencils, but do not date from the era of Frost or even Frost & Company. Rather, through the years the patterns have been continuously supplied to the marketplace by the various later owners of the stencils until Greenfield Village discontinued their reproductions in the early 1980s. The stencils are now back in Maine and at least two reproductions are again available at the Maine State Museum's retail shop.[18]

Top: While Frost may be accused of having stifled creativity in the field of hooking, some rug-hookers continued to personalize the pre-stamped patterns, either varying the colors or adding little personal touches. Here is an attempt at personalization of Frost No. 89. The lamb was hooked with raw wool, giving the animal a wonderful three-dimensional quality. The pattern also became Gibbs pattern No. 89 with very slight variation to the animal's head. Wool on burlap, 26" x 42". *Current whereabouts unknown.*

Bottom: In this instance the rug-hooker was impelled to personify the pattern by simply adding "candy cane" grass to the original pattern No. 54, making it unique when compared to other routine examples of this pattern. The low number probably makes this one of Edward Sands Frost's original designs. Wool on burlap, 23.25" x 38.75". *MCP collection*

Some of Frost's floral patterns have a repetitive sameness about them, but here the hooker has added her own touch to pattern No. 64. By hooking a striated background the rug takes on an individual personality. The border design is one of Frost's most attractive and most complicated. It is a border unique to this one pattern which is unusual for Frost. It does not appear in any other pattern. Wool on burlap, 34.50" x 60". *MCP collection.*

Pattern No. 80 of the elk's head is another low number and probably dates from the years Edward Sands Frost owned the business. The stencil for the intertwined border is found on several other Frost patterns. To show the close relationship between Frost and Alvin Gibbs, it should be pointed out that this pattern, with slight modification, is also Gibbs's No. 80. The antlers and bulkier head are more closely linked to the Minnie Light elk pattern than to Frost. Gibbs did not even change the pattern number! Wool on burlap, 23.25" x 34.50". *Cyr Auction.*

One of the largest and most desirable Frost patterns is the lion, No. 7. In the original E. S. Frost catalog it was the only design given a full-page illustration, as shown here. It was described as "a large lion with a baby lion in the background, with a fine scenery of flowers, brakes, etc." Unfortunately, during the latter part of the nineteenth century the large stencils became damaged and No. 7 was no longer printed by any of the successor firms to Frost. At times hookers refer to this as the "Ross lion" but the Ross lion has substituted palm trees for the foliage in the Frost pattern. Gibbs used the Ross adaptation, but altered it by eliminating the baby lion. *E. S. Frost & Company catalog.*

The bottom example is hooked in a bold and dramatic manner, with lush foliage and a visually strong border. Wool on burlap, 28.50" x 52". *Cyr Auction.*

Comparing the effort of two different rug-hookers working the same design illustrates how two completely different effects can be achieved. In the center example the lion becomes a stronger, darker mass of color, but the border, while following the pattern, is not as striking as in the other rug. Wool on burlap, 28.50" x 52". *Cyr Auction.*

Lions seem to have been among the most popular designs of Frost, Ross and Gibbs. American Rug Pattern Company also had a lion design with standing lion at the edge of a cliff. Two versions of Frost No. 144 show a stark contrast in coloration and corner shields unique to this design. They also are indicative of Frost's tendency to place his animals on some sort of foundation. Here the lions and foliage seem to be on a floating island of grass. Left: c. 1875-85. Wool on burlap, 34.75" x 61.25". *James Julia Auction.* Right: c.1875-85. Wool on burlap, 34.75" x 61.25". *Cyr Auction.*

Illustrated here are two rugs, made by the same person, with striped shield designs in each corner. A detail of the shield in the corner shows how closely it approximates the shield in the Frost lion rug. There is, therefore, an attribution dilemma as to whether this shield element was Frost-designed or Frost-copied. Frost was known to have frequently "borrowed" designs or design elements from various sources. While both rugs were found in Virginia they are most certainly of a Maine origin. The vast majority of early Maine rugs migrated out-of-state and still do. Basket of flowers rug, c.1875-1885. Wool on linen, 31.50" x 51.50"; floral medallion rug, c.1875-1885. Wool on linen, 30" x 52". *Both Courtesy Lionel N. and Gerry Sterling.*

Frost pattern No. 36 was a best-seller with a seemingly endless number of versions available to collectors today. The dog is well anchored on the tile floor, similar to the tiles seen in the Minnie Light cat pattern in Chapter IV. It raises the question, did Light copy Frost or was it the other way around. Having her own strong sense of design it is difficult to believe that Minnie had to copy another person's pattern. Wool on burlap, 27.25" x 44.50". *MCP collection.*

This large horse pattern, stamped "No. 101" on the lower edge is an aberration. It does not fit the design description of No. 101 in the original Frost catalog, nor is it the standard pattern bearing that number in later catalogs (Stratton, Greenfield Village, etc.). The size and Greek key border is correct but the standard No. 101 has a horse in a trotting position as well as an inner scroll and flower sprays, as seen in the pattern sketch. The burlap pattern illustrated here shows a standing horse and nothing surrounding it.

The selvage is clearly marked in green: "E.S. Frost & Co. Biddeford. Me." This is not a color usually used for the company legend. Also in green on the reverse is the price: "75 cts." Since the original Frost catalog price was $1.00 it is possible this oddity was either a special order or a reject sold at a reduced price. It was found in the same trunk from a Maine attic as the reed-stitch rug seen in Chapter I. Printed burlap, 33.25" x 68.50". *Courtesy Muriel Kenoyer; Frost/Stratton catalog.*

Frost floral patterns were extremely popular at the time they were issued. This example is especially attractive since the hooker has employed a cream colored background which allows the flowers to stand out sharply. In addition the individual flowers are crisply hooked. It is fairly common for a Frost design to be a half motif which is then flipped over to form the other identical half. This is Frost No.10. Wool on burlap, 32" x 50.5". *Waldoborough Historical Society.*

Chapter VI
E. S. Frost & Company

December 27, 1881 — a date of major significance in the field of rug-hooking. It deceptively implies that it only dates the specific catalog, but it has far greater significance for it celebrated the first patent for a punch-needle, a device for making rugs that would bring an entirely new dimension to the craft of rug-making.

It was Edward Sands Frost's successors who instigated this change and who set in motion a convoluted and twisted path leading from Biddeford, Maine, to Toledo, Ohio, and Chicago, Illinois. Several years following the 1876 purchase of the business from Edward Sands Frost, E. S. Frost & Company published a catalog of rug patterns, dated on the reverse "December 27, 1881," the exact date when a punch needle rug machine patent (Patent No. 251,381) was issued to Ebenezer Ross of Wauseon, Ohio.

Antique dealers, collectors, and hookers will immediately recognize this name as the rug pattern distributor who was selling Frost patterns stamped with his own name or that of his firm "E. Ross & Co." This establishes a definite business relationship between Ross and the Frost firm's new owners, James A. Strout, mayor of Biddeford, and Jerre G. Shaw, also a Biddeford businessman. Together, Strout and Shaw sought an inventor to develop a rug "machine" or punch-needle as it is more commonly called today.[1] This tool was an attempt to easily and inexpensively duplicate the era's increasingly popular commercially-made Turkish rugs. (Frost always referred to Oriental rugs as "Turkish.")

By 1878 the enterprise had become *E. S. Frost & Company*, still located at the original headquarters, 180-182 Main Street in Biddeford, and was listed in that year's *Maine Year-Book* as "Rug Pattern Manufacturers," obviously having made the leap from a small-market maker of patterns to the higher volume manufacturers of the same.[2]

The new company published a brochure entitled, *Descriptive Circular E. S. Frost & Co's Turkish Rug Patterns*."[3] Added at the lower edge of the cover was the phrase, "Colored Rug or Mat Patterns." In this *Circular* Strout recorded, in his own words, on

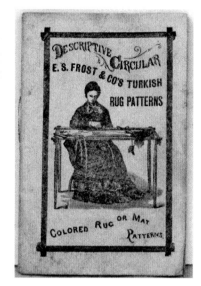

The front cover of the Frost catalog, with internal dates of 1882, 1883 and 1885, shows a woman seated at her hooking frame using the traditional hook. The original cover remained the same but the contents were updated over the years. *MCP collection.*

January 10, 1882, just two weeks following the issue of the patent:

Fully realizing the importance of, and believing in labor saving machines, we long came to the conclusion that a machine must be had specially adapted to "drawing in" rugs, that would not only save *time* and *labor,* but much of the *material* used by the use of ordinary Rug Hooks. We therefore sought the aid of the best inventive genius [Ebenezer Ross of Wauseon, Ohio.] within our reach, and at great cost to us, this machine, destined to speedily become the 'pet of the household,' sprang into being, illustrating with renewed force the old saying that 'necessity is the mother of invention.'

. . . This is an entirely new invention, having been patented December 27, 1881, and will undoubtedly prove to be one of the best selling articles ever offered to Agents affording large profits. We repeat, the Machine is new, the Turkish Rug Patterns comparatively so, and constantly increasing in popularity. The entire field is open, the goods are staple, easily handled, sell rapidly and pay an enormous profit, so that there is nothing to prevent any Agent, male or female, from making money. A few dollars and a little energy and perseverance is all that is required to secure a competency for yourself and family. Do not procrastinate.[4]

The back page of the brochure, equally as significant as the front cover, lists for sale this new and special rug machine that would minimize the amount of time required to make a rug. It shows a seated woman working with the new machine. It also prominently proclaims the date, "December 27, 1881" at the lower edge, the date the Ross patent was issued, obviously created with Strout's money.[5] In the five years since Strout and Shaw purchased the business, an inventor had been successfully solicited to come up with this special machine and Frost & Company had embarked on a new era in the rug pattern business.

Although Strout had found his inventor, time would show that he may have been overly optimistic about both the machine and his relationship with Ross. Since the new tool was developed "at great cost" to his company it is logical to assume that Strout received some consideration beyond the ability to purchase, along with everyone else, the machines from Ross, who maintained control of the patent rights. In return for funding the project, Strout received exclusive rights to this particular version of the machine since he seems to have been the only firm ever to sell it.

Interestingly, a short time later Ross was selling Frost & Company patterns in Ohio, now marked "E. Ross & Company." Obviously, he had been granted rights to sell the patterns, indicating a Frost/Strout partnership that attempted to monopolize the market. While Ross gives every indication the patterns are his, Strout certainly gives the impression that the rug machine is a total Frost & Company accomplishment. The Frost & Company catalog never mentions Ross nor does Ross ever mention Frost despite an obvious business relationship.

At the same time Strout introduced the new machine in early 1882, a fresh competitor opened in Biddeford known as "The American Rug Pattern Company." It offered, in addition to stamped patterns, a product called the "Novelty Rug Machine," which Ross interestingly had chosen as the name for a modified version of his original patent that he would soon sell under his own name, independently from Frost. The result was that Ross was now offering a simplified version of his machine to a Frost competitor, located just a few doors down the street from Strout's headquarters.

This emerging Biddeford enterprise seems to have reaped the greater benefits from the now slightly altered, but considerably improved invention. The Frost & Company machine was originally designed with a cumbersome attached reel to hold the yarn being "punched" into the rug. This reel was intrusive, awkward and had to be constantly replenished with filler material. The illustrations show an enlargement of the design seen on the Frost *Circular* compared with the Ross patent design copied from the patent papers, both having the obvious reel.

The redesigned Novelty Rug Machine eliminated the awkward reel and substituted a simple "screw-eye" through which the filler material could be fed into the rug from a basket placed on the floor beneath the rug frame.[6] This new tool was far more comfortable to work with and had a constant supply of filler without any rewinding.

According to testimonials received by The American Rug Pattern Company, the Novelty Rug Machine was highly successful for them. (The American Rug Pattern Company will be treated in greater depth in Chapter VII.) It appears that Ross, as the sole distributor of the new Novelty Rug Machine, denied Strout access to this improved version, forcing E. S. Frost & Company to be stuck with the already outdated reeled machine. It seems highly unlikely that Strout would not have taken advantage of the new version had he been given the opportunity.

In his original patent application Ross had made three "patentable" claims, one of them being the reel.[7] Even by dropping the reel, his other two claims were still in force, and while he may have given Frost exclusive rights to the original version, he apparently could legally offer the new, improved Novelty Rug Machine to The American Rug Pattern Company. In making the newer machine merely a simplification of the original design, Ross, through his 1881 patent rights, had complete control of both versions of the machines. Thus he had the option of denying Strout access to the improved implement, which meant Strout maintained exclusive rights to a machine that did not work very well. It also meant that Ross continued to have access to the Frost patterns.

Although Ross claims to have "invented certain new and useful Improvements in Machines for Embroidering and Ornamenting Rugs,"[8] his accomplishment seems somewhat diminished by the fact that embroidery machines had already been invented and patented years previous. The accompanying illustration shows how closely such "embroidery work" is allied with the "tufting" or "turfing" technique of a hooked rug.

Strout took anticipatory advantage of the new tool by totally revamping the business, even adding new machinery to facilitate the marking of the patterns. In a section entitled, "An Entirely New Business," the *Circular* explains: "To meet this requirement we comenced about five years ago to manufacture our improved Turkish Rug Patterns, or 'bodies,' printed or stamped with a great variety of beautiful artistic designs, and all ready for 'working' or 'drawing in'. These patterns, by perseverance and *large outlay* for the necessary machinery and apparatus, we have finally brought to absolute perfection and are now furnishing to our agents about one hundred and twenty-five different styles [of patterns] ranging in size all the way from 7/8 to 3 yards."[9] It was clear he also depended on "agents" – self-employed canvassers – to spread the fame of his patterns and his new machine.

The older method of using zinc stencils that had been inherited from Edward Sands Frost did not require machinery, but merely hand labor with an inking applicator that applied the ink through the stencils onto the burlap underneath.

The answer to the new "machinery and apparatus" apparently comes to light in a catalog of Frost patterns published in 1972 by The American Life Foundation in Watkins Glen, New York. The cover of this catalog boasts that their burlap rug patterns were being printed [*not stenciled*] "from the original hand cut printing plates made by the E. S. Frost Co. in the . . . nineteenth century. . . . These patterns are beyond all doubt [the] rarest and finest collection in the world and should not be compared with the cheap stencil outlined patterns."[10] This is a direct disparagement of Stratton and Greenfield Village who were using the old Frost stencils.

Thus, it appears that the expensive machinery was a *printing press* that employed engraved metal printing blocks to produce the burlap patterns. Such a press would have been large in size to accommodate the printing blocks (up to 33.75" x 68.50" for the large Frost No. 101 lap robe) and would have entailed the outlay of considerable funds. The use of a printing press was clearly more efficient and allowed burlap patterns to be printed much more expeditiously and less expensively once the cost of the press and printing blocks was amortized.

It explains why the old stencils, no longer being used, survived in such relatively good condition and were passed on to Whiting, Stratton, and Greenfield Village for their small-scale operations. It would have been cost-prohibitive for these producers to purchase and install the expensive presses and hire the skilled printers needed to use the printing blocks.

Using the stencils was not only a low cost but a low skilled process.

Unfortunately The American Life Foundation no longer survives and attempts to contact descendants of the firm's owner have proven fruitless. What happened to the printing blocks is unknown at this time. Apparently, the Foundation never sold any patterns, but the catalog offers directions on how to "grid" their images to enlarge the designs to an appropriate size for making a rug.

To return to the story's chronology: a year later, in 1883, Ross, now with a partner, Joseph L. Parks, also of Wauseon, decided to form a company selling Frost rug patterns under his own name along with the newer version of the punch needle tool (the Novelty Rug Machine).[11] The new tool was advertised in a brochure of original "Turkish Rug Patterns" published under the Ross name. He continued to provide the new device to American Rug, and apparently still fully enforced his original agreement with Frost & Company to sell the Frost patterns under the Ross name.

One can logically assume that Strout was providing the patterns for Ross, so it was a mutual endeavor. Looking at the parrot design, No. 127, stenciled with the legend "E. Ross & Co. MFR," it obviously is identical to the Frost & Company design No. 127. This indicates that the company name was applied with a stencil. However, evidence indicates the pattern was printed, not stenciled. In printing patterns for Ross, it would have been a simple matter to omit the name on the pattern edge, ship the patterns off to Ross who could then stencil his own name on the piece. In any event, Strout undoubtedly did benefit from the sale of patterns to Ross, although probably at a wholesale or discounted price.

It seems likely that the original agreement gave Frost exclusive rights to the first rug machine. In return Frost paid an unknown amount of money to Ross and also gave him the rights to sell the Frost patterns under the Ross name. It is likely the agreement was in force for five years. This theory is given credence by the fact that Ross published a new catalog in 1886, (five years from the patent date of the machine) which now carried a few new, original Ross designs as well as a number of Frost look-alikes.

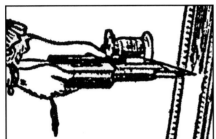

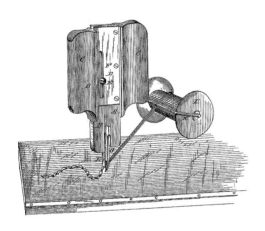

The back cover of the Frost catalog illustrates a woman at an upright easel hooking frame using the newly patented Ebenezer Ross punch needle or "turfing" machine. The patent date is proudly proclaimed at the bottom.

An enlargement of this cover clearly shows the cumbersome reel that fed the yarn or rag strips to the needle. Also illustrated is the original drawing submitted by Ross to the U.S. Patent Office. The patent protection was granted December 27, 1881. *U. S. Patent Office.*

It seems as though Ross attempted to modify the patent privileges granted to Strout by slightly altering the machine and offering it to the American Rug Pattern Company. The illustration of an altered machine shows it still bears the original patent date: "E. Ross & Co./Patented Dec. 27, 1881." The original patent was granted to Ebenezer Ross, and he transferred the patent rights to his new "E. Ross & Co." still utilizing the original patent date. However,

it no longer is the original machine since it lacks the reel.[12]

Perhaps a more likely scenario would be that American Rug Pattern Company, new in the market, sought to use the machine being touted by Frost & Company and was turned down by Ross because Frost had been granted exclusive rights. The next logical step would be to contact the inventor to come up with a variant machine for The American Rug Pattern Company. This would have spurred Ross to devise the newer, simplified design. It also is interesting to learn that Ross and American Rug Pattern used identical images to illustrate and promote the use of the newer version. There was clearly some business collaboration between these two companies.

In any event, Ross now had total control of both the original machine he made available to Frost and the simplified "Novelty Rug Machine" version sold by himself and American Rug Pattern. He, alone, determined who was allowed to use his invention and obviously he eliminated Frost & Company as a major competitor in the sale of punch needles by withholding the revised tool.

There is no indication that Frost & Company ever used anything but the more awkward version, and evidence in The American Rug Pattern Company's own *Circular* suggests that American Rug Pattern was highly successful in selling the new instrument. The Frost & Company brochure contains testimonials related to their patterns, but not a single endorsement for their machine with the reel. The firm's *Circular*, updated to 1885, indicates that, despite having their rug machine on the market for four years, they had no testimonials to offer and

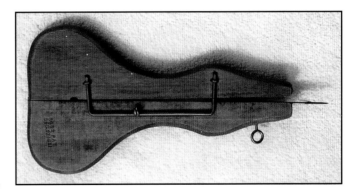

This is the altered "improved" version of Ross's punch needle, showing the reel replaced by a simple screw-eye through which the filler material was passed. This eliminated the need for the ungainly reel. The detail shows the impressed patent information on the handle. This was the version supplied to the American Rug Pattern Company, as explained in Chapter VII. *MCP collection.*

63

the older version was still being offered. Had their machine been an instant success, it seems likely the updated *Circular* would have reflected this success. On the other hand, American Rug Pattern Company published several pieces of mail lauding their machine. All appearances seem to indicate that Frost was stuck with a dud!

The 1886 directory entitled *Leading Manufacturers and Merchants of Ohio* contains an "Historical and Descriptive Review of the Industrial Enterprises" of several Ohio communities, including Toledo. The volume lists E. Ross & Co. as "sole manufacturers of the Novelty Rug Machine at Nos. 254 and 256 Summit Street"[13] and describes the firm as follows:

> One of the most interesting and successful businesses in Toledo is that of Messrs. E. Ross & Co. . . . It was established three years ago [1883] by Messrs. E. Ross & J. L. Parks, and has grown with such rapidity that a large trade is now prosecuted in all parts of the Union. This has been accomplished on account of the superior excellence of specialties offered to the public – this applying with particular force to the novelty embroidering machines, of which Messrs. Ross & Co. are the patentees and exclusive manufacturers . . .

> We have invented a machine known as the novelty rug machine, with which a beautiful rug can be filled, either with rags or with yarn, in a day, that would require weeks to do with the hand hook. By the use of this machine the rug does not need to be clipped, as the loops are all the same length, which will wear much better and many think them prettier than clipped . . . Messrs. Ross & Co. manufacture rug patterns extensively, carry a full and complete stock and exhibit many beautiful and elaborate designs that cannot fail to interest and instruct all who appreciate art in one of its most pleasant and attractive forms. A handsome catalog is published, which will be mailed to any address on application.

At the time of this Ohio publication, Ross had issued a new catalog of colored designs, many of them take-offs on the Frost patterns. The catalog contains some new designs intermixed with original Frost patterns. This indicates that Frost was no longer supplying Ross with printed patterns and the Ohio firm had now started printing or stenciling their own burlaps.

Thanks to Ms. Nancy Curtis, reference librarian in the Science and Engineering Department of the Fogler Library at the University of Maine, patent papers were "de-coded" and accessed for this period of time. Another patent of special note was issued on November 10, 1885, to Josiah J. Deal of Wilmot, Ohio, who, for some reason, assigned all rights to his fabric turfing implement to Ebenezer Ross and Joseph L. Parks, both of whom were now living in Toledo.[14] It was totally different from the Ross machine, made with a round wooden handle "having a hole bored through the axis."

Pulling a metal ring at the top of the handle maneuvered the needle back and forth. The patent papers explain that "The operation of this implement is precisely like that of the others now in use; but in consequence of the bend in the shank of the needle and the square groove on the underside in contact with the loop-holder, the loops are made with greater regularity."[15] There is no indication, however, that the machine was ever manufactured under the Ross name. Conceivably Ross and Parks purchased the rights to Deal's machine to keep it off the market for fear that it would compete with their own successful invention.

A study of the patent papers indicates that on August 10, 1886, just 13 months later, Deal had patented another version of his original design.[16] No record was found as to whether this new version was assigned to Ross, nor is there any indication that Deal ever promoted the machine under his own name. Meanwhile the immense success of the rug pattern business led to many other patents for turfing or tufting implements, as the U.S. Patent Office records demonstrate.

However, Melville C. Ayer, co-owner of American Rug Pattern Company, decided, some years later, to enter the invention competition, and on August 27, 1889, Ayer was granted a patent. Thus, after a period of seven years he eliminated the need for doing business with Ross and his Novelty Rug Machine. Probably the most significant aspect of this new patent was "They have no wearing parts that need oiling and any part can be duplicated." This indicates that the machine parts were interchangeable.[17] (See Chapter VII.)

Guess who then came up with a patent for a machine "with moveable parts?" Two years after the Ayer invention, on November 17, 1891, Ross was issued still another patent for an improvement on his original design of December 27, 1881, this time without his partner, J. L. Parks. Among other things it featured interchangeable parts! The patent specifications state that "The parts of this device are of any desired sizes, shapes, and materials, and several sizes of needles are usually furnished with each pair of members, a spring being also provided which corresponds with each needle."[18]

Still another curiosity appears in the saga of the Frost patterns. Offering some original and some slightly altered versions of the Frost patterns late in the nineteenth century was the Gibbs Manufacturing Company in Chicago. A clue was seen in Chapter V where Edward Sands Frost, in his autobiographical report, claimed that in November 1870, he opened a salesroom in Boston through a firm known as Gibbs & Warren. The *Boston Directory for the year . . . commencing July 1, 1871* shows "Alvin Gibbs and Samuel Warren, rug patterns" at 22 Tremont Row. Both men lived on Winter Hill and billed themselves as sellers of "rug patterns."[19]

A year later, Samuel Warren is still in business now featuring *colored* rug patterns, but Gibbs is no longer listed in Boston. He moved to Chicago, taking copies of the E. S. Frost & Company patterns with him. Gibbs altered the patterns slightly and published an undated catalog which claims the business was "Established in 1875."[20] This was a year before Frost sold the business. There are no dates in the catalog to confirm this. In fact, the years have been obviously omitted from testimonial letters which give only the month and day.

Thanks to helpful research assistance from the Maine State Library, an extremely rare copy of the initial Gibbs catalog was located in the Winterthur Museum and Library. Undated, it does carry one testimonial letter of April 9, 1887, from Scatterwood, Dakota Territory, eliminating the possibility of a publication date prior to that year. The format of this catalog differs from Frost and American Rug Pattern inasmuch as it provides illustrations of each rug design. The look-alikes carry the same pattern numbers assigned to the original Frost patterns

While there are no Chicago directories available prior to 1881, *The Lakeside Annual Directory of the City of Chicago* for 1881 shows an Alvin Gibbs, "rug patterns," at 158 State Street, but he is not listed in the business section under either "Fancy Goods" or "Rug Patterns."[21] The firm was not noted as a "company" so apparently it was a small operation. While many of the Gibbs's patterns are of Frost origin, they have been slightly altered, obviously intended to circumvent originality issues. The fact that Gibbs's unworked patterns are occasionally seen in Maine auctions indicates that he had some widespread success in distributing his wares.

The listing remains the same through 1886, the year Gibbs moved to 88 State Street. There are no listings in 1887 and 1888 for the business and Gibbs is no longer listed as alive in 1887.[22]

The 1889 Chicago directory, shows the rebirth of the enterprise as the Gibbs Manufacturing Company at 88-90 State Street with Louis Karcher as president, and E. W. Shoesmith as secretary. Obviously they had purchased the business from Gibbs or his widow, mistakenly convinced the business was a golden

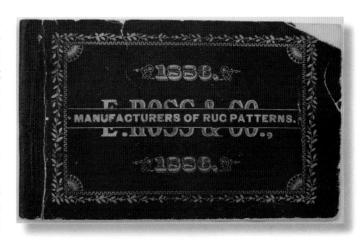

In 1886 Ebenezer Ross published an attractive color catalog of his rug patterns, the great majority of them being altered copies of those issued earlier by E. S. Frost & Company. Pictured here is a page with three patterns. The one with the two ducks, originally by Frost, is reversed and there are changes in the foliage at the right. Ross even kept the same number as the Frost No. 17. The dog pattern is very similar to a Frost pattern which has the dog on a tiled floor and a different frame. *Maine State Museum.*

opportunity to corner the Midwestern market in the field of rug machines and patterns. The firm was now renamed The Gibbs Manufacturing Company which published a new "Descriptive Catalogue" offering Turkish Rug Patterns, Rug Machines and Rug Yarn, Hooks and Clamps "manufactured and for sale" by them.[23] Their optimism was misplaced for they would cease to exist after a brief lifespan of approximately four years.

After serving as Edward Sands Frost's Boston agent, Alvin Gibbs moved to Chicago, apparently taking with him a set of Frost's original burlap patterns. He established himself in business in a small way, never incorporating as a company. Illustrated here is the Chicago directory listing for Gibbs in 1886. It was only after Gibbs sold the business that it became Gibbs Manufacturing Company. *Chicago Public Library.*

This was a much more elaborate catalog with colored illustrations of fifty patterns. Of these, thirteen were adapted Frost patterns. The alteration, in some cases, is so slight as to be hardly detectable. For example, in the Frost pattern of the spaniel dog lying on the tiled floor, only the size of the diamond shaped tiles had changed, becoming somewhat smaller. Otherwise, it is the Frost pattern and even carries the same pattern number as seen in the Frost catalog.

The copies of the Frost florals, in fact all of the Gibbs florals, have simplified arrangements. The leaves and flowers are rather widely separated as opposed to Frost who featured densely structured floral arrangements including the floral borders.

The cover of this second and final Gibbs catalog claimed they were "Manufacturers and sole owners of the Celebrated Jewel Fabric Tufting Machine, 88 and 90 State Street, Chicago."[24] No patent record was found for any such machine, which looked very similar to the forthcoming Ross patent of November 17, 1891.

Referring to the Gibbs machine, the catalog states:

> It is so simple that any ten year old child can operate it successfully, and make any desired fabric, as Turkish Rugs, Ottomans, Curtains, Stair Carpets, Hoods, Mittens, Slippers, Lap Robes, Quilts, Piano Spreads or Table covers, which have all the gorgeous appearance of the genuine Turkish or Persian designs, and are much more durable, though costing but a small fraction of what is paid for Smyrna or Constantinople goods. . . .
>
> Our invention solves the whole problem. It is strong and durable, all its working parts being made of the finest steel, exactly on the principle of the sewing machine.
>
> With presser foot and automatic feed, it measures its own stitches and makes the loops perfectly regular in length and as closely together as desired. . . . What has been struggled for and suggested by others, has been attained by us and reduced to practice, and we are able to furnish our patrons with the perfect machine, which is so adjustable in its parts that it is capable of embroidering with the finest silk or working the coarsest rags on heavy canvas, making the "pile" an inch and a half high. None of these important qualities have ever before been possible in any machine.
>
> At an enormous outlay, we have perfected this invention, and built special machinery for its manufacture on a large scale, so that we are now able to furnish it at a very low price. We desire to introduce it into every home in this country, well knowing that when once seen and understood, it has a certain road to success and universal use.

Without the success they had anticipated, Karcher and Shoesmith sold Gibbs Manufacturing in 1890 to John E. Bratt and Alfred J. Pruden. The former was president and the latter, secretary/treasurer. Both men had been previously listed as "clerks" in the Chicago directories since 1888. In an attempt to resurrect a failing business, they immediately changed the focus, dropping all mention of rug patterns and calling themselves "dealers in fancy goods." The firm continued until 1894 when Gibbs Manufacturing Company disappeared and was reformed as Bratt & Pruden, fancy goods, moving to 189 Fifth Avenue.[25] Since it no longer dealt in rug patterns, its further history is not continued here.

However, still another interesting twist occurred. While Gibbs Manufacturing went out of the business of selling patterns in 1890, just a year later, Ross shows up again, having been issued a new rug machine patent and simultaneously publishing a new catalog of 56 colored patterns, many of which were Gibbs copies. He now was offering a metal machine in addition to the traditional wooden product. It is noteworthy that Gibbs had previously made its "Jewel Fabric Tufting Machine" in both wood and steel. These clues lead one to conclude Ross had purchased the defunct Gibbs Manufacturing Company, including the rights to sell the Gibbs Jewel Fabric rug machine.

Ross continued this firm until 1899, when Ross & Company gave up the rug business and became The Automatic Hatching Company. Major national retailers were now providing rug patterns, such as Montgomery Ward's, which first offered patterns in their 1887 catalog. Since E. S. Frost & Co. was still functioning at this date, it might indicate they were printing the patterns for major retailers. The competition from the merchandising giants was too great for the smaller, regional companies to survive. The Toledo city directories show "E. Ross & Company, (Ebenezer Ross and Joseph L. Parks), Rugs," between 1885 and 1899. Ross died on January 12, 1904. Parks, then in the furniture business as Stolberg & Parks, lived until March 7, 1916.[26]

The original machine offered by Frost & Company in 1881 was an obvious failure, but Strout must be credited as the progenitor or instigator of a whole new approach to the craft of rug-making. Not only was it his vision to develop such a machine, but he provided the necessary funds to see it fulfilled.

In copycat fashion a whole new field of inventions was developed around the original concept. While some saw this as a positive accomplishment, others rued the possibility that the naiveté and charm of the earlier hand-hooked rug would be lost forever.

The fashionable new look for rugs was of machine-made perfection, each loop perfectly aligned and each one the exact same height. There was no longer any feeling of spontaneity that only comes to the rug-maker with that sense of humor or almost child-like innocence so admired in original creations. True, the punch-needle rug could be quite wonderful, but, still, something important had been lost. The whimsy is lacking. Rugs were now machine-made, a fact often disputed by punch-needle workers on the basis that the machine is hand-held, therefore the rug is "hand made."

While Frost & Company offered no testimonials in reference to their rug machine, they do offer a couple of endorsement letters for their rug patterns. In November, 1876, Jacob Childs of Worcester, Massachusetts, wrote: "I have been selling your Turkish Rug Patterns long enough to satisfy myself what I can do with them. I want to know the very least I can have them for in lots of not less than one hundred dozen. I think I want to increase it two hundred dozen per month after I get all my agents started."[27] That would be 2,400 patterns per month, certainly a sizeable order for just one agent. It provides some insight into just how significant Frost was in the rug pattern market. The Biddeford company had permeated the national fabric of rug patterns and they continue to be widely known today.

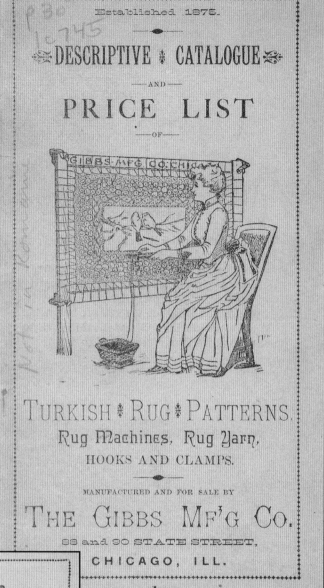

These illustration are from the only known copy of Gibbs's earliest catalog. Internal evidence dates it from c.1887. To give a sense of its contents, the cover, a pattern page and an advertisement for the firm's Jewell rug machine are pictured. No. 36 is the same as Frost No. 36 except for the number of the tiles in the floor, and No. 76 is identical to Frost's same number. On the other hand, No.150 is not the same as any Frost Turkish pattern and No. 95 is an original Gibbs design. *Courtesy Winterthur Library. Printed Book and Periodical Collection.*

In 1885 E. S. Frost & Company added still another new marketing tool — the publication of color card illustrations of a few select designs. Under the heading *"ILLUSTRATED PATTERNS,"* the January 1, 1885, circular explains:

> We beg leave to call attention of our Agents and all others interested in our fabrics to a few of our Illustrated Patterns which we send with this circular.
>
> These Illustrated Patterns are exact representations of the originals, reduced in size, of course, but showing not only the design, but every flower, leaf, vine, or figure, in colors, printed on manila colored ground, and in all respects precisely like the original patterns.
>
> The few *Illustrated Patterns* herewith presented will give everyone a correct idea of the whole list, and will greatly assist Agents in canvassing for the sale of our goods.[28]

Four of these pattern cards are illustrated here. Each bears a legend at the bottom containing the name of the company, E. S. Frost & Company, the price and size of the rug, and the inventory number of the particular pattern.

Urging people to become agents for the Frost patterns, the circular makes it sound very lucrative:

> There is no business in which agents make money so fast or so easy as by selling our Turkish rug patterns. It doesn't make any difference whether they sell and deliver the goods on the spot, or take orders for samples, or sell at retail or wholesale, there is money in it in any way. The business is new, the entire field is open, the goods sell rapidly and pay a large profit. From one to a dozen rugs can be sold in nearly every house, and large quantities can be disposed of to storekeepers, traders, dry goods peddlers and others to sell again. Many ladies are earning wages by making up the rugs and selling the finished article instead of the pattern. Some make up one or two rugs and take orders from them as samples. When they are well made from fine stock it is almost impossible to tell them from the best imported Turkish rug. . . . [29]

Many of the early rug pattern catalogs depended on written descriptions. To make it easier to visualize a specific design, E.S. Frost & Company published a series of colorful lithographed "cards," which the company and its traveling agents could mail or hand out to stimulate sales. Since they were printed on cheap pulp paper and because they were larger than the catalog and therefore did not slip easily into it, these brittle "cards" had a short life. They are rarely found today. Notice that along the bottom edge is given the price, dimensions of the pattern and its catalog number. *MCP collection.*

Another enticement tactic stressed the significance of having a good product:

There is no question at all that an agency business of the right kind is now about the only source of money making, and the great secret of the agency business seems to be in getting hold of some specialty and pushing it. This applies not only to the regular trade but to all kinds of peddling and soliciting. Of course, you can make a living at common day wages, even by sawing wood, but the chances of making anything more than a living at such an employment are very small. And so with nearly every other ordinary vocation at the present time — there is no money in them. The fact is something new is required, and not only something new, but something meritorious, or it is no use at all for an agent to give it the least attention. And then again, you must not only have a good article, but it must be an article which has not been hawked all over the country until the very name is sickening to everybody. Look at the chromo business, which has been so completely "run into the ground," to use a vulgar phrase, that no good agent in his senses would think of engaging in it; and so with the lightening rod business, life insurance, subscription books and many other things. [30]

Countering all of these pitfalls, the company claimed to have an article "which fully meets all of the necessary requirements for a pleasant, permanent and profitable agency business."[31]

E. S. Frost & Company would survive Ross for a brief period, but the entry into the market of national firms, especially large retail catalog companies such as Montgomery Ward and Sears, Roebuck, spelled doom for the smaller manufacturers. Added to this was the rapid approach of the Arts & Crafts Movement's involvement in the rug hooking craft with its "designer rugs." (This phenomena as related to Maine rugs will be examined in later chapters.)

Strout continued the E. S. Frost & Company in Biddeford until 1900. The stencils, no longer being used, were purchased around the turn of the century by Henry F. Whiting of Lowell, Massachusetts, a belt manufacturer. Market conditions for stamped patterns in that period were depressed and the scarcity of Whiting patterns leads to the supposition that the business was not highly successful. It is not uncommon, however, to find in the Lowell area examples of Frost rug designs still bearing the E.S. Frost name, but with a Lowell identification.

From there, in 1936, the stencils went to Charlotte K. Stratton of Montpelier, Vermont, and later

A hooked example of the cat pattern No. 39 shows the faithful reproduction of colors as suggested in the original pattern. Competitors obviously used Frost as a source for their own designs. This one seems very similar to American Rug Pattern Company No. 106: "Group of kittens playing ball. Old cat looking on enjoying the sport." Wool on burlap. 28" x 51". *Cyr Auction, ex-Curtin Collection.*

Deerfield, Massachusetts. She sold them to John Dritz & Sons, a New York firm in 1946 and repurchased them in 1950. Mrs. Stratton continued to stencil and sell the patterns until 1958 when she sold them to the Henry Ford Museum and Greenfield Village in Dearborn, Michigan. They were used in the crafts department during the 1960s and 70s. In the early 1980s, the craft program was discontinued and the stencils were retired to the Henry Ford Museum. In June 2003 the Ford Museum gave a majority of the 742 stencil plates to the Maine State Museum, Augusta.[32]

Several catalogs of Frost patterns have been published through the years since the original firm went out of business, but none has come up with a complete survey of all the patterns listed in the original E. S Frost & Company circular. Stratton published two catalogs, one in 1939 and the second in 1952. The Edison Institute, parent company of the Henry Ford Museum and Greenfield Village, published their catalog in 1970, the one most often used to identify Frost patterns.

The American Life Foundation's catalog, *Choice Hooked Rugs and the Original Frost's Hooked Rugs Patterns,* claimed the illustrated patterns "are the original E .S. Frost & Co.'s hooked rug patterns and are made from the original hand cut printing plates made by the E. S. Frost & Co., in the early nineteenth century. Even the cuts or plates used in this catalogue are the original used by them in their first illustrated catalogue printed in the 1800's."[33] Provenance doesn't get much vaguer than this.

While Frost & Company did enclose a very few chromolithographed examples of various patterns, as illustrated above, they were not known to have published a complete catalog illustrating all of their designs. The American Life Foundation statement that the catalog was created from the original hand cut printing plates made by Frost & Company in the *early* nineteenth century is incorrect. Frost wasn't born until 1843 and Frost & Company did not exist until 1876.

The American Life Foundation produced the black-and-white catalog of designs (interestingly some not recorded by Stratton and Greenfield Village), but they did not offer any patterns for sale.

Despite its sale of the manufacturing portion of the business in 1900, E. S. Frost & Company maintained an address at 245-47 Main Street in Biddeford until 1904-05.[34] It seems logical that this retail outlet was kept open to dispose of surplus inventory of patterns stamped with the firm's name and address, since they would have been of no use to Whiting who was stenciling his Lowell address on the patterns.

At this point, a puzzling successor appears on the scene. John A. Borrows is recorded as a "junk dealer" in Portland, Maine in 1903 and the following year he elevated his profession to one dealing in "antiques." He is also listed as a traveling salesman.[35] He would eventually bring Frost patterns back to the market for a brief period.

The pieces of the story begin to fall into place when a firm, John A. Borrows, Inc. is formed and opens at 67 Union Street, Portland, dealing in "hooked rugs." It can be assumed that as E. S. Frost & Company was disposing of surplus stock in the 1900-1905 period, that a junk dealer who morphed into an antiques dealer, could have purchased the now out-dated inventory, as well as the machinery, and tried to sell it himself. This is given further credibility since Borrows was a traveling salesman, much like the original pattern maker, Edward Sands Frost.[36]

These suppositions are validated by examining the accompanying illustration which shows one of the E.S. Frost & Company publicity "cards" with the bottom legend carrying the Frost name cut off and the reverse printed with Borrows's business address.

In the 1903 *Portland City Directory*, Borrows is listed as in the junk business at 133 Sheridan Street; a year later morphing into an antiques dealer at 46 Portland Street, residing at 34 Hancock; listed the same in 1906 only now residing at 43 Huntress; in 1912, he was a traveling salesman, living at 931 Forest Ave. In 1924, the listing appears as "John A. Borrows, Inc., hooked rugs, 67 Union. H[ouse]. Saco." The listing remains the same for 1925, adding that Borrows was president of the firm and was living at 64 Montreal Street. In 1927, he had moved to Manchester, New Hampshire, and had no further connections with Maine.[37]

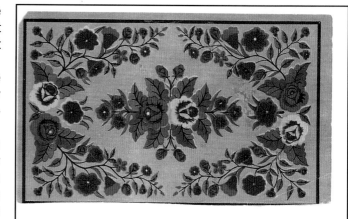

Proof that Borrows purchased the liquidated stock of E. S. Frost & Company comes in the form of one of the Frost sample "cards" with the Frost information cut off from the bottom edge and overprinted on the reverse with information about Borrow's business. The stamped "10" on the reverse is the number of the original Frost pattern. An example of a completed No. 10 is illustrated at the end of Chapter V. *MCP collection.*

His Portland advertisements had offered to "Buy Your Old Hooked Rugs." Possibly he repaired them for resale or simply resold them for a profit or copied the designs. Taking advantage of any other possible source of income, he capitalized on the curiosity of his customers offering to send any other information for 10 cents. He obviously had hopes of resurrecting the rug pattern business, deciding to become a manufacturer at some point. Borrows is known to have issued at least one original pattern under his own name. The creation of even one original pattern would qualify him to be listed as a pattern *manufacturer.* One can only guess that Borrows also bought the printing press from Frost & Company, the press that eventually showed up in the catalog of The American Life Foundation.

Outside of city directory listings the author has found very little that documents John A. Borrows as a manufacturer of hooked rug patterns in Portland. It was a great surprise, therefore, to find this pattern with his name and address. As can be observed, it is an original design and does not duplicate anything done by E. S. Frost & Company. The detail shows Borrows's name, address and the prominent number "1." Printing at least one pattern would have qualified him to be listed in directories as a "Manufacturer of Rug Patterns," as an aid in selling the left-over Frost inventory. Current whereabouts unknown.

However, there is still another minor puzzle. Another of the Frost "cards" exists with an advertisement on the reverse for Borrows selling his hooked rug patterns out of something called "Studio Farm, Saco, Maine."[38] The Portland directory shows Borrows living in Saco in 1924, apparently selling patterns from his home while still commuting to his business on Union Street in Portland. With his obvious lack of success, another short-lived rug pattern dealer passed from the scene, leaving behind two printed cards and one extremely rare stamped pattern issued under his own name.

It appears that Borrows could not financially justify having his small operation in Portland so towards the end he was selling his patterns out of his home in Saco. Again the Frost caption has been cut from the bottom. This was No. 60, one of Frost's more attractive floral designs. *MCP collection.*

HOOKED RUG PATTERNS

Sizes 36x60 . . . . . . $1.00
" 30x50 . . . . . 1.00
Door Sizes ~~24x36~~ *half round* .75¢
Larger Sizes to Order
We Buy Your Old Hooked Rugs
Send 10 cents for Any Other Information to
JOHN A. BORROWS, Inc.
STUDIO FARM
Saco, . Maine

Alvin Gibbs's pattern No. 49, is listed as a "cat lying on a cushion: handsome scroll border. Size 1/2 by 1 yard; price, 40 cents." It is the Frost cat No. 49, but with an entirely different border and inner frame. Every now and then a rug-hooker indulged in a little bit of whimsy to individualize her rug. Here she has attached bone buttons to accentuate the cat's eyes. Wool on burlap, 23.50" x 41". *Courtesy Joseph Caputo.*

In an attempt to compete with expensive rugs being imported from the Middle East, Frost, Ross, and Gibbs all carried patterns for what they termed "Turkish" rugs. These allowed the middle class to cover their floors with rugs that approximated the real "Persian" carpets being acquired by the wealthy. Frost was relatively successful with these designs and had more available than Ross and Gibbs. Here is a well-worked example of Frost No. 109. The original stenciled burlap had dimensions of 29" x 50," but it is not unusual for the finished rug to vary from the original measurements. In the completed rug, both ends show some reduction of the outer border. Wool on burlap, 30" x 44". *Courtesy Lionel N. and Gerry Sterling; pattern from Frost/Stratton catalog.*

Frost's original No. 127 was copied and bears the Ross legend. It is such a crisp, pristine example that it strongly suggests it was done during the five-year period when it is assumed Frost was providing patterns to Ross. Comparing it with the catalog drawing one sees slight variations that occurred when creating the sketch for the printing plate. For instance, the parrot's eye is more detailed when hand-drawn and the tail in the catalog version falls over the lower leaf while the Ross pattern's tail is partially hidden. It is obvious from a study of this pattern that the stencil was traced for the catalog and finer details were filled in by hand. *Pattern and Frost/Stratton drawing, both MCP collection.*

At first glance the rug with the white background appears to have the identical parrot in the center. A close examination reveals differences, however, leading to the belief that someone liked a completed Frost/Ross rug so well at a neighbor's home that they made a freehand copy of the parrot and added a border of their own design. Wool on burlap, 25.5" x 42". *Courtesy Jeff and Suzanne Good.*

This embroidered bench cover (now framed) shows why Ross chose to adapt an embroidery machine for "tufting" rugs. It involves virtually the same process as the punch needle machine for hooked rugs. In the rug-making process, however, the ability to create extremely intricate details was lost due to the use of a much larger needle to accommodate the bulkier filler material. All the design elements are very highly sculptured, making the bench cover three-dimensional. A worm can be seen crawling out of the bottom of the white flower at lower right. The textile was found in southern Maine. Wool on wool, 29.50" x 56". *Courtesy Beverly BaRoss.*

Chapter VII

The American Rug Pattern Company

Stamped rug patterns were an overwhelming success, so it is no surprise that they spawned a number of imitators. The Biddeford section of the *Maine State Year-Book,* the *Maine Business Directory* and the Biddeford city directory all listed several competitors to E. S. Frost & Company in the third quarter of the nineteenth century.

Henry B. Bennett, like Borrows, was located in Portland. He advertised that he was a "manufacturer of colored rug patterns."[1] Starting in 1873, even before Frost sold the business, Bennett seems to have been the first challenger. Located at 111 Federal and 29 Temple streets, the firm changed addresses slightly in 1876, staying at 29 Temple and moving from 111 Federal to 213 Federal. The following year the firm had become "Henry B. Bennett & Company" and was now at a better address, 381 Congress Street. Incorporating as a company apparently did not improve business for by 1879 there are no further listings for the firm. It had lasted only six years, proving that the market for printed rug patterns was a competitive and cut-throat business not leading to sudden fame and wealth.

Daniel Pond, initially noted in 1870 as a retailer of piano fortes and other musical instruments in *Greenough's Directory of . . . Biddeford and Saco* and the *Maine State Year-Book,* remained in the music business until 1878 when he decided to challenge the Frost firm's monopoly in the manufacturing of rug patterns. D. Pond & Company appears for the first time as a "Rug Pattern Manufacturer" at 164 Main Street, Biddeford.[2] Three rare patterns, the only designs known today to have been Pond originals, are pictured in this chapter.

Apparently he was not a serious threat to Frost, but an example of a worked Pond pattern proves that he had at least one customer. From 1878 both D. Pond & Company and E. S. Frost & Company are noted as dealers in "stamped rug patterns." They compete against each other until 1880, when the *Year-Book* fails to list Pond.[3]

In 1873, a stencil cutter in Portland by the name of Henry B. Bennett decided there was money to be made by going head-to-head with Edward Sands Frost in Biddeford. Possibly Bennett felt that being in Maine's largest city would give him an edge. To announce his entry into the field he took an advertisement in that year in the *Maine Business Directory.* By 1879 he was out of the rug pattern business, but still making stencils. No rug pattern with his name on it is presently known. *From The Maine Business Directory.*

In 1881, the year the Ebenezer Ross rug machine was patented. Frost & Company, with this new patented rug machine, moved to 105-107 Main Street and in 1882 the firm shifted location again to 245-247 Main Street. At this point Pond reappears as a competitor at 24 South Street, and a new entry, the American Rug Pattern Company, appears for the first time. In this year (1882) the *Biddeford and Saco Directory* shows that Pond, ever restless, had now relocated his business to Wells Court and was residing at 22-1/2 South Street.[4] In the 1884 and 1888 city directories there are no changes except that Pond has down-sized and is now doing business out of his home at 245 South Street. Pond disappears again for good in the 1890 *Maine Register.*[5]

However, the American Rug Pattern Company seemed to have been a serious challenger to E. S. Frost & Company. It is first listed in the *Maine State Year-Book* in 1882 at 227 Main Street, Biddeford, just a few doors down from Frost. This firm was a partnership of John S. Grant and Melville C. Ayer. The *Maine Register* makes it clear that Grant was the principal owner. He resided at 3 Union Street and Ayer lived at 10 Center Street.[6]

This is one of only three known patterns produced by Daniel Pond. Along the top edge is the notation "D. Pond Biddeford Me No. 40." A pleasant pattern but hardly competitive with the more sophisticated floral designs marketed by E.S. Frost & Company. Anything related to Pond's career is extremely rare. Printed burlap. *Courtesy Jane Nylander.*

This burlap is clearly marked with Pond's name, address, the number 51, and the price of 50 cents. The name and address of someone in Portland is written on the reverse.

The extreme rarity of Pond patterns calls into question the high numbering system. If there were fifty other burlap designs they apparently were not big sellers. It seems unlikely that there were many other patterns issued by this enterprise. Printed burlap, 21" x 48". *Maine State Museum.*

The final Pond pattern is marked "No.12" with a price of 35 cents. It is an interesting design, seeming to presage the Art Nouveau spirit of a quarter-century later. Certainly Pond was not slavishly imitating Frost. His deigns are quite different than his competitor and it appears he was trying to establish his own identity in the rug pattern field. Unfortunately, he was not successful. Printed burlap, 28.50" x 41.50". *Present location unknown.*

This rug proves that Pond had at least one serious client. The completed rug shows how carefully some hookers relied upon the pattern for guidance, not only for the design but the colors as well. Even the color of the burlap was duplicated as a background in this example. The rug-hooker, however, did alter the border shades. Wool on burlap, 24.50" x 37". *Courtesy Lionel N. and Gerry Sterling.*

Although the city directories show the enterprise to have been in business as early as 1882, it was not until about 1888 that what is now an exceptionally rare catalog was published by the American Rug Pattern Company.[7] The catalog contains testimonials dated 1883 praising the firm's "Novelty Rug Machine." This machine is the simplified version of the one originally patented by Ross in 1881 for Frost & Company. It was the "Cadillac" version as opposed to the "Model T" implement Strout was forced to use. Under the date of Nov. 3, 1883, the circular claims "We have hundreds of recommendations like the following" from Garrett, Indiana:

I want an agency for your Novelty Rug Machine, please send terms &c. I bought one of your Rug Machines from a couple of ladies who were selling them at a fair, made an ottoman, 16 x 16, in three hours, and it was beautiful. A number took it for Kensington painting a little piece off. I would not take ten dollars for my machine if I could not get another

From Union City, Tennessee, May 13, 1884:

I received the Rug Machine a few days ago. I made a rug with rags, and went out one-half day and took orders for 24 machines. Enclosed find the money order to pay for the same — please send immediately. My next order will be a large one.

And from Puyallup, Pierce County, Washington Territory, December 28, 1883:

I received your Rug Machine over two weeks ago. I worked the pattern you sent me, and am so well pleased with it that I now send for some machines to sell, as they will sell well here. All my friends who have seen the work want one. I send $7.00; send me all the machines you can for that amount. I will soon send for 100 machines.

It is surprising that within the period of only a year between the founding of the firm and the first dated testimonial letter, the machines had achieved such widespread geographic distribution. The catalog claims that "We have hundreds of [such] recommendations." The firm's success towered far above Frost's, at least in this aspect of the business. The Frost firm mentioned not one single testimonial in support of its machine.

Late nineteenth century city directories indicate the American Rug Pattern Company was located at 227 Main St., Biddeford. This rare photograph shows the appearance of the building shortly after the defunct firm vacated the premises. The two men standing near the power pole are directly in front of the former American Rug Pattern store. (The sign, placed by a later occupant, reads: "W. Schneider & Co./ 227/ [Men's] wear Manufacturers." When E.S. Frost & Company was at 180-82 Main it was diagonally across the street to the east of American Rug Pattern Company, and at the time this photograph was taken it was located at 245-47 Main, just a few doors down the street to the right, probably hidden by the trolley car. *McArthur Public Library.*

The high level of success with the newly adapted machine they were supplying to American Rug Pattern Company seems to have motivated the Ross/Parks partners to establish their own rug manufacturing business, independently from any initial agreement made with Frost. They apparently promoted the newer implement while still making use of the original pact with Frost which allowed them to sell the Frost patterns. Instead of cooperating with Frost, they were now in competition using Frost patterns to promote the new machine, while obviously refusing to provide Frost with the improved machine. Adding "insult to injury," they were providing American Rug Pattern, Frost's major competitor, with unlimited access to the refined implement.

This is the cover of the only known copy of an American Rug Pattern Company catalog. Printed on cheap pulp paper, it was issued in 1888. It totals 22 pages and is in the author's collection. *MCP Collection.*

It seems highly unlikely that the consumer would purchase the machine from Ross and then contact Frost to purchase a pattern when they could buy that same pattern directly from Ross or another set of designs from America Rug Pattern Company.

The cover of a Ross pamphlet carries an illustration of a woman seated at the rug frame using the Novelty Rug Machine. It is the identical illustration carried by American Rug Pattern in its 1888 catalog.[8] Who originated the design cannot be determined, but there obviously was some cooperation or collusion between the two firms. It leaves open the possibility that some of the non-Frost designs "created" by Ross may have been copies of patterns created in Biddeford by the American Rug Pattern Company.

Things changed dramatically for American Rug in 1888 with the proud announcement that "We Have Made The Best Rug Machine In The Market: 'The American'."

> We say this because we believe it. We believe it because it does perfect work and is not liable to get out of order; two merits that we have failed to find in other machines.

THESE
RUG PATTERNS
Are printed on heavy Burlaps (cloth), in various colors. They are to be finished by the purchaser with Rags, Worsted, Yarn or Carpet Filling, cut into narrow strips and drawn through from the under side with a hook.

They should then be sheared off to imitate Turkish Rugs. They will outwear several Imported Velvet Rugs. Remember, all our Patterns are

NEW DESIGNS,

offered now for the first time.

Address all letters to

American Rug Pattern Co.,
BIDDEFORD, ME.

The fourth page of the catalog contains a few interesting points, two of which are that the patterns are printed on "heavy" burlap (possibly a dig at competitors) and that "carpet filling" could be used to hook the patterns. The most important point, however, is that American Rug Pattern Company boasted that they used only "new designs" and not knockoffs of E.S. Frost & Company patterns, as did Ross and Gibbs.

We have been engaged in the manufacture of colored rug patterns for several years, and have handled nearly all if not quite all the machines in the market. In every one we have discovered some serious fault — some indeed proving entirely worthless.

To make a first-class, reliable machine, we have spared neither time nor expense, and in placing the "AMERICAN" on the market we do so with the utmost confidence of its merits.

In our tests of different machines we have become convinced that a perfect working machine cannot be made to operate by a crank; [a remark obviously aimed at the eggbeater-like design of John F. Blake's Patent No. 342,569] and we are as fully convinced that a machine using a tubular, half round, hollow, oval, or three cornered needle, cannot do good work.

Our machine carries the best form of needle that will not tear or cut the canvas.

The feed is automatic and *positive.*

It is made of the best material and finely finished throughout.

It is made and adjusted especially for drawing in rugs, lap robes, crumb cloths, mittens, etc.

Our machines are new in principle and patent applied for. They have no wearing parts that need oiling and any part can be duplicated.

Remember, we shall manufacture and sell the "AMERICAN" only, in the future.

Remember, our machines are not of that clap trap class that are good for nothing and sold cheap. . . .

This machine which American Rug Pattern was touting so positively, was invented and patented by Melville C. Ayer, partner in the American Rug Pattern Company. U.S. Patent No. 409,900 was issued to Ayer on August 27, 1889. The specifications state that "The invention relates to embroidery-machines such as shown and described in Letters Patent No. 251,381, granted to E. Ross, December 27, 1881."[9] (Virtually all of the patents for turfing or tufting implements seem to be based on Ross's original patent, which, in turn, was linked back to an earlier patented embroidery machine.) The new "American" rug machine sold for $1.25 in the 1888 catalog,

The Ayer "American" "turfing implement" was designed "to provide a new and improved device specially intended for turfing [machines] or rug machines, and serving for automatically feeding the machine forward, being very simple and durable in construction and very effective in operation."[10] Another positive recommendation for this machine was that it had no wearing parts requiring oiling and any part could be duplicated.

This machine was made especially for working with rugs and was not recommended for fancy work, as some other machines were. American Rug Pattern Company claimed that "A machine cannot be made to do both light and heavy work without disarranging the adjustment, when poor work results. . . We shall soon place on the market a machine designed especially for very fine work such as tidies, pillow shams, table scarfs, etc." No record was found that Ayer patented this lighter version machine.[11]

Despite their fond dreams, the new invention of a rug machine and the publication of a catalog, the Company lasted only until 1892, a little more than a decade, but it was a major competitor when compared with Pond's more modest efforts. The *Maine Register* volume for 1893 leaves only E. S. Frost & Company in the rug pattern business in Biddeford. The final entry for the American Rug Pattern Company is in the *Year-Book* for 1892-93. By the turn-of-the century, Ayer was listed as an electrician and Grant as a grocer.[12]

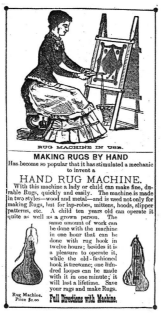

It is interesting that the design used to illustrate a lady hooking at an easel in the American Rug Pattern Company catalog (at right) is identical to the one used by Ebenezer Ross in his rug pattern pamphlet dated 1882 (at left). It proves a close relationship between the two firms, as noted elsewhere. Notice that the lady is working on a "Turkish" pattern. American Rug Pattern Company listed only one such design: No. 105, "very handsome indeed. Cannot be described." Its price was 60 cents and the size was 30" x 45". *Right: MCP collection. Left: Maine State Museum.*

To draw even more attention to its newly patented rug machine, American Rug Pattern issued an insert for its catalog featuring a bold and striking eagle as a masthead. Clearly the firm was proud that its owner, Melville C. Ayer, had been able to develop a better substitute for the machine they had been buying from Ross. The flier makes certain that not a single claim touting the machine is left unsaid.

Mrs. Pearl McGown lists five establishments manufacturing designs in 1888, three of which had established businesses in Biddeford: James A. Strout operating as E. S. Frost & Co.; Daniel Pond was another; and the third she believed to be someone named "Ayers" [*sic*]. Unknowingly she obviously was referring to Melville C. Ayer, partner in the American Rug Pattern Company. The non-Maine competitors were listed as E. Ross & Co. of Toledo, Ohio, and John E. Garrett of Burlington, Vermont. Mrs. McGown found two patterns identifiable as "Ponds," but she never found any by "Ayers."[13]

The discovery of an original catalog published by the American Rug Pattern Company was a rare pleasure for this researcher. As far as known it has never been republished in any form, so some space will be devoted to it here. The firm was listed as a legitimate competitor to Frost and Pond in Biddeford only between 1882 and 1892, but during that relatively brief ten-year lifespan it manufactured at least 106 burlap rug patterns, advertising that "We manufacture Colored Rug Patterns and supply Rug Machines, Hooks, Dyes, Yarns, &c." These were the exact same type of items being offered by Frost and the American Rug Pattern catalog was nearly identical in format to the one produced by Frost.

The unique copy of the American Rug Pattern 1888 *Descriptive Catalog of Colored American Rug Patterns* boldly claims on its front cover that these are "The only New Patterns in the U.S.," obviously trying to capitalize on the fact that the Frost pattern selection had remained relatively stable for some time and that the Ross and Gibbs patterns were merely Frost knockoffs. The American Rug catalog, being extremely rare, offers a unique insight, not only defining the company, but in describing its patterns.

Lack of access to the catalog has made it impossible for collectors and dealers to identify any of American Rug Pattern Company's designs. Few collectors are even aware there was such a competitor. In an effort to compensate for this lack, the animal and genre patterns are being listed here.

Due to the extreme difficulty of identifying patterns with similar central floral designs by printed descriptions only, these are not included here. Below are the exact listings as they appear in the original catalog. Some will definitely be recognizable by interested persons. As far as can be determined, this is the only list currently available for this company.

Since so little has been written on American Rug Pattern many rugs hooked from their patterns have entered the market without proper attribution. Shown here is American Rug Pattern No. 74, similar to No. 45 but of a different size and with another border. It was sold as No. 267 at the James Shoemaker auction in 1924 with no attribution to American Rug Pattern Company. The description in the Shoemaker catalog, however, is very close to the one in the firm's catalog: "bird perched on a branch in oval medallion flanked by clusters of leaves in mulberry, green and soft brown on a buff field." The same rug is also pictured in Reis, fig. 17, p. 39. *Shoemaker catalog and Reis book both MCP collection.*
    Rug c. 1895-1920. Cotton and wool on burlap. 30" x 40". *Milne Historical Society Collections.*

A casual scan of several early publications on hooked rugs includes some definitely designed and manufactured by this company without being identified as such. One such rug is figure 17, page 39, in Estelle H. Ries's book, *American Rugs,* published in 1950. It is clearly American Rug Pattern Company No. 74 and not the E. S. Frost No. 160 with a similar motif.

On the other hand, some of the American Rug Pattern Company's designs sound a great deal like they were cribbed from those circulated by E.S. Frost & Company, such as No. 62, with two ducks, which could be a take-off on Frost's No. 17.

A listing of the animal and genre designs includes:

No. 30 — Tigers and their Cubs, their mother lying amid a green foliage, one cub standing upon its hind legs playing with its mother's ear, the second cub upon its back between its mother's fore paws, she in the act of washing it, while the third cub sits watching the proceedings; all surrounded by an appropriate border. One of the finest patterns ever offered. Size 40 x 62; price 85 cts.

No. 34 — Lion in a defiant attitude with head and tail erect, standing upon a projecting rock, surrounded by a set border, the ends of which are filled with beautiful flowers. Size 40 x 60; price 85 cts.

No. 35 — American Eagle standing with spread wings upon a shield and coat of arms surrounded in red, white and blue, with a handsome flower border and corners, consisting of rose buds, morning glories, etc., the whole handsomely colored. Size 40 x 54; price 80 cts.

No. 37 — A pair of parrots sitting upon a branch, (so life-like you could almost see them move), a grape vine loaded with grapes, inside border, with a handsome flower and bud outside border. Size 40 x 54; price 80 cts.

No. 41 — Horse in the act of jumping a bar. Position active and lively. Horse shoe corners, plain border in two colors. Size 32 x 52; price 70 cts.

No. 43 — Rooster, hen and pair of chickens standing upon the edge of a pan drinking. Life-like and original, surrounded by a handsome scroll and flower corner border. Size 32 x 52; price 70 cts.

No. 44 — Dog in the act of bringing a duck from the water, showing only the head and shoulders of the dog. The foliage etc., enclosed in a circle, with an extensive scroll border. A very life-like pattern. Will please. Size 32 x 52; price 70 cts.

No. 45 — A pair of birds standing upon the edge of their nest which is built in a cluster of roses and sprigs of purple flowers, all surrounded by a half scroll and half flower border. Very, very handsome. Size 31 x 52; price 70 cts. [Similar to No. 74 below

but of a different size and border.]

No. 47 — Cat, black and white, lying upon a red and orange sofa pillow, (looks as natural as life), surrounded by a vine and star cornered border. Very taking [*sic*]. Size 32 x 52; price 70 cts.

No. 50 — Cat lying upon a sofa pillow, with ornamental border, leaf corners. Nicely colored. Size 32 x 46; price 60 cts.

No. 51 — Boy and girl skating with outstretched arms, inclined to fall, girl easy and graceful with head slightly turned towards the boy; ice centre, land and trees rear and ends. Something entirely new and bound to sell. Size 32 x 46; price 60 cts.

No. 57 — Something new. Boy sitting at table, knife and fork in hand, plates, cups, saucers and pitchers on table, lady in act of hanging a tea kettle upon a crane suspended in an old-fashioned fireplace; printed in taking [*sic*] colors and not difficult to work. A fine pattern. Size 30 x 40; price 50 cts.

No. 58 — Large butterfly centre, printed in orange, red, brown, green and black, surrounded by flowers and vines with double colored border. A brilliant pattern. Size 30 x 40; price 50 cts.

No. 59 — A fine shaped horse, handsomely colored in easy working colors; grass ground work; red and black plain border with ornamental corners. Showy. Size 30 x 40; price 50 cts.

Warren Weston Creamer owned this rug without realizing it was American Rug Pattern Company No. 61, described in the firm's catalog as "A bird in the act of flying but upon a branch of a tree, enclosed in a circle with four corners of autumn colored leaves branching from a circle . . . Size 30 x 40; price 50 cts." When Creamer auctioned his collection in 1930 this rug was item No. 171. Kent, *The Hooked Rug,* p. 207.

No. 61 — Bird in the act of flying but upon a branch of a tree, enclosed in a circle with four corners of autumn colored leaves branching from the circle, enclosed by a double colored plain border. Size 30 x 40; price 50 cts.

No. 62 — A pair of beautiful colored ducks, printed in six colors, appropriate ground work, plain border in three colors. Size 30 x 40; price 50 cts.

No. 64 — Stag's head centre with heavy scroll border. A very pretty pattern. Size 30 x 40; price 50 cts.

No. 68 — Cluster of roses, buds and ferns tied with a blue ribbon, a beautiful butterfly in each corner, with small set figures between, all surrounded by a plain border in two colors. Size 30 x 40; price 50 cts.

No. 71 — Stork standing in pond of water surrounded by lilies, grasses, etc., ornamental scroll corners with plain border. A very pretty, neat pattern, and cannot fail to please. Size 30 x 40; price 50 cts.

No. 72 — Dog's head enclosed in circle, with same border as No. 69. (highly ornamented inside border with roseate corners, with plain outside border). Size 30 x 49; price 50 cts.

No. 73 — American Eagle, shield, spears, flags etc., enclosed in pointed border with ornamental corners. One of the handsomest style eagles ever designed. Size 30 x 40; price 50 cts.

No. 74 — Bird's nest, roses, buds and foliage centre, same as No. 45, with plain border, ornamental corners. Size 30 x 40; price 50 cts.

No. 75 — Parrots upon tree branches, surrounded by grapes and foliage. Very handsome and attractive. Size 30 x 40; price 50 cts.

No. 78 — Dog's head centre, double striped border, circle corners; for door or carriage mat. Size 22 x 36; price 40 cts.

No. 80 — Dog, Russian blood hound. This is taken from the dog "Hero," a hound at "Libby Prison." [in Richmond, Virginia, during the American Civil War.] His weight was 198 pounds, length 7 feet 10 inches, height 3 feet 2 inches. It makes a noble looking pattern either for rug or carriage robe. Size 36 x 54; price 75 cts.

No. 81 – Jersey cow. A fine pattern. Perfect. Will work up neat and easy. Appropriate border. Size 36 x 54; price 75 cts.

No. 87 — Good luck. Horse shoe, with words "Good Luck" in shaded colors in centre of shoe, scroll leaf corners with outside border of three colors. Size 20 x 36; price 40 cts. In ordering this pattern state if you wish to work with *hook* or *rug machine* as the *letters* must be printed different. [This is a very interesting comment made nowhere else in any rug pattern catalog. It does hint, however, at how the introduction of the rug machine changed the technical aspects of rug-hooking.]

No. 23 [*sic*] — Kitten lying down for centre. Pointed border in three colors. Size 14 x 20; price 20 cts.

No. 90 — A very pretty spaniel dog, with ornamental inside border, roseate corners and plain outside border. Size 30 x 40; price 50 cts.

No. 91 — A very pretty cat centre with handsome scroll border inside and plain cut border outside. A very pretty pattern and easy to work. Size 20 x 36; price; 40 cts.

No. 92 — A large sized lion lying down, with paws extended, surrounded by an appropriate border of red, black and purple. Size 40 x 62; price 85 cts.

No. 97 — The owl folk's concert. Four owls sitting on the branch of a dead tree with singing books in their claws. You can almost hear them sing. The whole surrounded by handsome Turkish border with scroll corners. Size 36 x 54; price 75cts.

No. 98 — A magnificent design of a horse in an attitude of mingled fear and defiance. Heavy scroll border. This is pronounced by judges to be the finest design ever executed. Size 36 x 52; price 70 cts.

No. 101 — Design of dog. Handsome black and white English setter lying down. Appropriate surroundings and heavy Turkish border. Size 36 x 52; price 70 cts.

No. 102 — Design of lamb lying down among the grass and flowers. Very pretty. Size 36 x 52; price 70 cts.

No. 106 — Cat and kittens. Group kittens playing ball; old cat looking on enjoying the sport. Size 30 x 40; price 50 cts.

The American Rug Pattern Company has the distinction of being the first to produce stamped genre patterns, described in the catalog as the skating boy and girl, as well as the kitchen scene. While many genre designs continued to be made over the years by various companies, they have never been highly popular. The firm also went outside accepted designs by including some with a bit of comic humor, such as No. 97, the owl folk's concert.

In making Rugs with a common rug hook the yarn or rags are drawn up through the pattern, the frame resting on legs, backs of chairs, or any convenient thing

The American Rug Pattern Company catalog also demonstrated how to make a rug hooking frame that allowed a woman to work her burlap pattern horizontally instead of on an easel, as illustrated earlier. The clear impression is that the "American" rug machine was best adapted to use at an easel and the old fashioned hook was preferred on a horizontal frame. Notice that the bent-shank rug hook is slightly different from the earlier Frost version pictured in Chapter V.

The catalog includes illustrations of only two designs, both reproduced here.[14] No. 98 was said to have been "pronounced by excellent judges to be the finest design ever executed." These judges obviously were not rug-hookers, for the design is much too detailed and intricate for ease of hooking whether with a traditional hook or punch needle.

The American Rug Pattern Company machine remains very similar to the prevailing machine in use today. A "Parisian Hooked Rug Shuttle Needle" made by Sears, Roebuck & Company was very similar in its basic mechanical concept to the earlier American Rug Pattern device.[15] Sears was seeking a patent (date unspecified) at about the time (1906) Grenfell mats were being made at the Labrador Mission. Since Grenfell mats were noted for using silk or rayon stockings as filler material, it is noteworthy that directions on the original Sears box suggested the use of silk stockings or rayon strips in lieu of yarn.

The user is advised: "After you have cut them [the stockings] into strips, be sure to take hold of both ends and stretch as far as possible to take the stretch out of the material, as they will then work better with the needle." The implication is that the buyer, with this machine, could produce mats of a quality equal to or surpassing the Grenfell mats, highly lauded for their delicate and perfect manner of hooking.[16]

This admiration for the workmanship in the Grenfell products continues today as reflected in the prices collectors are willing to pay for the mats. While the American Rug Pattern Company machine seems to have been the superior one, it failed to significantly enhance the overall business of the Company which would continue in business only briefly, giving way to the rapid advancement of changes brought about in the Arts and Crafts Movement.

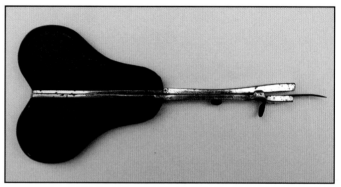

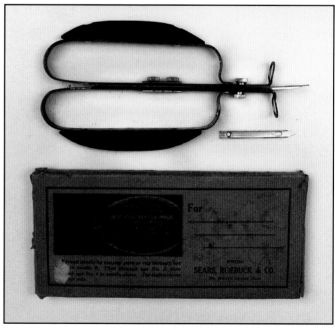

There are only two illustrations in the American Rug Pattern Company catalog, the remainder of the rug descriptions are given by text only. The caption for the horse claimed it was "pronounced by excellent judges to be the best design ever executed." The burlap pattern cost 75 cents.

The only other illustration is pattern No. 95, featuring a wreath of roses, buds and other flowers in a "handsome set border of red, purple and black." It is an original design and unlike any Frost, Gibbs, or Ross pattern.

The end of the nineteenth century saw the small rug pattern companies going out of business as large, national catalog retailers entered the field. Ross tried to fight back by patenting and manufacturing a solid, well-made machine in 1891. Within a few years, however, Sears, Roebuck & Company was on the market with their inexpensively made version. The tide had turned. *Both MCP Collection.*

Chapter VIII

The Sabatos Industry

An early 1900s article described New England hooked rugs as being "much despised," with an "absence of attractiveness." It urged "women of taste and experience in art methods" to seek improvements in the industry.[1] During this period a philosophical and design movement emerged to counteract the rather "primitive" image of the rug hooking craft as it was practiced primarily in rural areas. It was part of what became known as the "Arts and Crafts Movement," the age of Gustav Stickley and Mission furniture. Urban designers in New York and elsewhere were eager to professionally design rugs they felt would improve the quality of the "primitive art" practiced heretofore. America's love affair with "folk art" would not come into full bloom until after World War I.[2]

The same period saw the growth of the Ethical Culture Movement founded in 1876 by Felix Adler. It stressed, among other things, the responsibility to improve the quality of life, not only for one's self, but for others as well.[3] The two movements, one aesthetic and the other social, meshed into a perfect vehicle to transform the country's rural poor, both culturally and financially, or so it seemed.

The involvement of "outsiders" from urban areas into what had been a rural craft led to many changes in the field. In the nineteenth century rug-making had been practiced not only to provide inexpensive floor covering, but to bring a treasured adornment and note of color to an otherwise drab home. At the same time, it provided an outlet for the creative urge and required little outlay for materials. It could be done in one's own time following other rural chores and obligations. No financial profit was gained nor expected.

Once the wealthy visitors from the big cities discovered that the Adirondacks, the Blue Ridge Mountains of western North Carolina, coastal and pastoral inland Maine, and the verdant hills and valleys of Vermont and New Hampshire offered a peaceful respite from their crowded urban existence, a change was about to ensue. In a thoughtful missionary manner the well-to-do tried to ameliorate and uplift those they looked upon as uneducated, unsophisticated and/or culturally deprived, resulting in a profound effect on rug hooking and other crafts. This crusading effort, combined with the Ethical Culture philosophy, encouraged the growth of "cottage industries." Established by outsiders to benefit the native populace, they also introduced the concept of sale for profit.[4]

The Arts and Crafts Movement was born in England in the last quarter of the nineteenth century, a reformist undertaking greatly influenced by the English author and critic John Ruskin and William Morris, the artist, writer and socialist. It was a revolt against the increasing "soulless" mechanization spawned by the Industrial Revolution. Considering the machine as the root cause of society's evils, those involved in the Movement sought a return to hand craftsmanship.

As a result, this new philosophy influenced British decorative arts, furniture, all the crafts (including textiles), and even garden design. The speaking tour of Oscar Wilde to 120 towns and cities throughout North America during 1882 helped spread the Movement's influence. Soon locally made Arts and Crafts products were specified by trend-setting American architects and designers and selected by wealthy homeowners for their stylish suburban homes, town houses, and summer "cottages."

It is easy to see, therefore, what happened when affluent urban families saw the "old fashioned" handicraft products of rural folk around Asheville, North Carolina, or Cranberry Island, Maine. Their pottery, weaving, woodcarving and rug-hooking were judged primitive, crude, untutored and unsophisticated, all those terms that today define "folk art." Just as the process of "mechanization" had changed the overall characteristics of hooked rug "art" through the process of pre-printed patterns, a new movement would take over the craft's next evolution.

It became a mission for those "from away," who believed their wealth, social status, and education made them better able to determine what was considered good design, good color sense, and good craftsmanship (or so they believed), to uplift the disadvantaged. From this missionary zeal came the growth of several cottage industries that had a strong influence on rug-hooking at the start of the twentieth century. And, if by paying rural folk for their work, and then selling their products in retail outlets in New York, Boston, or Philadelphia, monies could come back to the producers, so much the better, it was felt by the founders of these home/community industries.

At the time these cottage industries were being developed, events in America's far Southwest greatly influenced their outlook, meshing well with the aims of the Arts and Crafts Movement. It commenced when a modest caterer, Fred Harvey, was commissioned by the Atchison, Topeka, and Santa Fe Railroad to open a series of restaurants in railway depots along the Santa Fe's transcontinental lines through the southwestern part of the country. Staffed by the genteel "Harvey Girls," and combined with an extensive publicity campaign to encourage easterners to visit the southwest by rail, it was highly successful.

Soon the railroad depots/restaurants featured gift shops selling Navaho weavings, Hopi pottery, and Zuni jewelry. Eastern designers were quick to incorporate these Native American designs into house interiors by way of fabrics, wallpapers, and other decorative arts. They fitted in beautifully with the new Art Nouveau and subsequent Art Deco furniture and decorative arts then in vogue [5]

A November 1906 governmental report, "*The Revival of Handicrafts in America*," published by the U.S. Bureau of Labor, within the Department of Commerce and Labor, clearly shows that the government had assimilated the Arts and Crafts philosophy. It was seen as "in part a protest against the conditions of modern factory production, with its minute division of labor and mechanical processes, and the expression of a desire for conditions of production so that the producers may take pleasure in their work and such as are more favorable to the development of the facilities."[6]

The report added:

Craftsmanship implies not only thoroughly good workmanship, but a positive interest and satisfaction in the work on the part of the worker. Advocates of handicraft consider it desirable that workers should, as far as possible, exercise the faculty of design in connection with manual labor, and so impress their individuality upon their products. [This, of course, contradicts the wish to stamp out the "primitive" designs heretofore seen in rug-hooking in favor of the newly preferred "designer" rugs.]

Aside from the efforts of individual craftsmen in their homes or in private studios or workshops, the arts and crafts movement in America has manifested itself in several kinds of organized efforts, which are more properly the subject-matter of this paper. There has been, in the first place, a rapid organization of arts and crafts societies in the cities, bringing together at meetings and exhibitions the craftsmen in various lines and specimens of their work. From the long list of these organizations which hold annual arts and crafts exhibitions, a number of societies have been organized even in small villages, and the products of domestic industry are exhibited and sold both at local exhibitions and in the larger exhibitions held in the cities. Finally, little groups of craftsmen from the cities have formed themselves into corporations or otherwise associated themselves together for the purpose of living and working in the country, thus avoiding in part the high pressure of city life and combining congenial association with the other advantages of country life.

While Maine was a leader in many aspects of rug hooking, the idea of turning the craft into a rural cottage industry did not originate in Maine, although a Maine-connected artist, Douglas Volk, would be the inspiration for its inception across the New Hampshire border. The Abnákee rug industry under the tutelage of Mrs. Helen R. Albee was the country's first such industry, founded in the mountains around Pequaket, Carroll County, New Hampshire.

An article in the *New York Tribune* in February 1900, tells of Albee's meeting with Volk during a demonstration at the Ethical Culture School in New York:

We had been talking, she said, about handicrafts and William Morris and Ruskin in an artist's studio one afternoon, and George De Forest Brush and Douglas Volk were there. Suddenly Mr. Volk turned to me and asked: "What are you doing for those women in New Hampshire?" I was not doing anything; that although our relations were pleasant, I found it hard for us to meet on the same plane. Mr. Volk said "But what right have you to do nothing?" His question stayed by me, but when I put my services at their command they did not want my help.

Mrs. Albee showed a rug which she said was a fair example of the ones that have been made by people in rural districts for many years and said as she held it up: "There are forty years wear in that rug, and in it lie all the opportunities that I am trying to develop." It was made of old rags of all sorts drawn through burlap and across the centre was represented a house. Mrs. Albee said she forgot when she began to introduce her ideas that the New Englander had traditions and she was constantly confronted with remonstrations when she showed her designs. 'My son's wife works houses and cats and flowers that you can almost smell, upon hers,' a woman would say to her rebelliously when asked to make a rug with a conventional [i.e., "modern"] design. The people, she said, were actually needing money and work, yet only dubious looks and smiles met her when she suggested to them her project.

She was unable to understand the situation until she discovered a spy in the camp — a young country girl — who explained that the trouble was that she did not employ bright colors and animals and flowers. Then she understood that the people she was trying to help did not endorse her ideas of art. She then went to work and made twelve or fifteen rugs from her own designs and, in the materials that she had proved to her own satisfaction to be most suitable, and had an exhibition in the little village hall. People came from far and near until horses were tied to every available place.

Women brought their babies and tiptoed about and talked in whispers as they looked upon the novel creations. It was a great day, more eventful even than Sunday. Summer guests came too and to her great surprise she found when the day closed that she had taken a number of orders and was involved in an industry. After that there was a change in attitude and those who had been most antagonistic changed most readily.[7]

Albee eventually wrote a small booklet, *Abnákee Rugs: A Manual Describing the Abnákee Industry, the Methods Used, with Instructions for Dyeing,* long since out of print. In it she outlined her personal reasons for developing the industry:

How shall educated and trained men and women, who go into the country, use their influence to keep the country-bred youth at home? It is obvious the most important thing is to give them congenial and remunerative employment, as it is to seek employment that they have left their homes. . . . That this employment should be of an artistic nature was to my mind the first requisite; for, if there is any one thing which the average American mind needs, it is an awakening of the artistic sense. Beauty of form and color are not a daily necessity with us. As a people we are ingenious, fertile in resources and imitative; we are rapid in execution and quick-witted to devise new conveniences and to meet new conditions; but for some mysterious reason, the artistic feeling which is so evident in Oriental, in some European and in nearly all savage races is a thing to us unknown as a nation. . . . in short, every sort of commodity produced by the common, average mind and bought by the common, average public are tawdry to the last degree. They are overloaded with meaningless ornament, they are for the most part crude in color, and utterly commonplace in conception.[8]

Albee set about creating simple, conventional designs adapted chiefly from Native American sources. The immediate and obvious result was the further destruction of hooking as a "pure" folk art. It had crossed the boundary where now designers would attempt to control the direction of the craft and define what they considered was a "good" hooked rug. Not long thereafter, those in the fine arts would lend their influence in an attempt to turn the "craft" into "art" in the traditional definition. (e.g., see Chapter XII)

Although Albee had anticipated that the workers would eventually assume total control of the industry, this never happened and she was forced to continue management of the project. But, according to the Labor Department *Bulletin* published more than six years into the project, "Even under these conditions she has found it difficult to obtain work of a uniform quality . . . Mrs. Albee has trained about thirty people, but only half of these attained proficiency, and some of the skilled ones have moved away. A few of the workers can be relied upon to carry out the most elaborate patterns."[9]

This early attempt of the Abnákee industry strongly influenced the development of a similar project across the border in Center Lovell, Maine, where Mr. and Mrs. Douglas Volk of New York City had a summer home, "Hewn Oaks," located some 14 miles by stagecoach from the nearest railroad station in Fryeburg. The house was entirely handmade, with "tons of oak in the heavy beams. The plates and sills and posts are all hand hewn with the axe, dovetailed and pegged with wood."[10]

A 1906 magazine article in *Country Life in America* described the village:

Center Lovell is a more than commonly prosperous village. Many of its inhabitants are of old blue-blood Maine stock, who have refrained from growing excited over the rush city-ward. Sheep are on their hills, and among the people a weaving tradition to the third and fourth generation. The village homes and outlying farmhouses welcome the feet of guests with native "drawn" rugs. Beyond the memory of man they have been making these.[11]

The *New York Press,* on the other hand offered an earlier version of the village on January 13, 1901:

> The Volks have a country place in that remote country far beyond the disturbing influence of railroad traffic, commercial hubbub and confusing marts . . . Primitive simplicity prevails throughout the locality, and the artist and his family bring in no new ways from the larger world. Unfortunately, with the simplicity there exists a lack of prosperity among the natives.[12] Mrs. Volk took exception to such a description in a letter to the *New York Herald*: "The people of this locality, descendants, many of them of good old New England stock, are, in general, contented prosperous farmers with attractive homes and one would travel far in the country to find a more kindly and well informed community.[13]

While the Ethical Culture philosophy was considered patronizing to some of the recipients, those involved in furthering its aims took strong issue with that intent. In a letter critical of an article that appeared in the *New York Herald* on November 25, 1900, Mrs. Volk cited the interest in the development of the "little village industry" as being "genuine and friendly, not altogether founded on pecuniary motives. The tone of the article in question rather suggests the patronizing attitude, which is decidedly unfortunate; patronage being something they [the people of Center Lovell] do not need or ask for."[14]

Mrs. Volk also wrote in defense of the homemade rugs which were described in the *Herald* article as "distressingly crude things with awful combinations of color." She responded:

> Please let me state, that this no more applies to the average household rug of home make than it would to all Oriental rugs, because some happen to be crude and bad in effort. It is only just to state that very many of these quaint home made floor coverings possess a charm and interest which give an attractive aspect to the rooms they help to adorn. For one thing, they are hand-woven, and not all of them by any means are made crude through the use of aniline dyes. The assertion, to which exception is taken, would possibly apply more aptly to the vast quantity of inharmonious pretentious carpeting manufactured for profit alone, which is seen on every hand in our big cities.[15]

Contradicting the *New York* Press statement that the Volks brought in no "new ways" from the larger world, they went ahead and founded the Sabatos Industry, obviously attempting to practice what Mr. Volk had preached to Albee a short time earlier. He was an artist of some repute and the son of another noted artist and sculptor, Leonard Volk. The elder Volk was most famous as one of only two artists ever to make a life mask of President Abraham Lincoln. Executed in 1860, the Volk mask was praised as "the most reliable document of the Lincoln face, and far more valuable than photographs, for it is the actual form."[16]

Douglas was known for his portraits and romanticized historical views of Colonial America, the latter interest obviously contributing to his decision to reproduce the early methods of making hooked rugs. In 1881 he married Marion B. Larrabee of Chicago, the first instructor at the Minneapolis School of Fine Arts. She would be the one to take charge of and develop the rug-hooking division and, as time permitted, her husband would assist with other crafts that might be pursued by interested Lovell residents, as well as maintaining his own painting career.[17]

Despite having ceded its status of "first" in the field of cottage rug hooking industries to the Abnákee enterprise, the group at Center Lovell was the most complicated, the most demanding, and the most unique. Started in 1899, (there are conflicting dates of origin: either 1899, 1900, and 1901) a neighboring mountain "Mount Sabatos," lent its Indian name to the industry.[18] A decision was made early on that the craft would be developed exactly as it had been carried on in its early nineteenth century infancy, but opting to combine the yarn-sewn and hooking attributes in an attempt to achieve both the durability and beauty they sought. Forget the self-indulgence of the more current aniline dyes, the fabric strips, and the burlap foundation! While the results may have been worthwhile aesthetically, it was arduous, time-consuming, and expensive and may well have been overdone to the point of forced extinction.

Upon the death of Mrs. Wendell (Jessie) Volk in 2005, the last of the Volk family to reside at Hewn Oaks, the Smithsonian Institution was given the opportunity to retrieve items of interest to them. Among the items selected was a scrapbook of clippings and copies of photographs made available to the author through the Maine Historical Society. Although many of the clippings lack attribution, they have been invaluable in providing unique insights and descriptions of the industry. The remainder of the Volk estate was auctioned in Gray, Maine, July 19, 2006, a treasure trove of Arts and Crafts memorabilia so extensive and so well-documented that it may never be equaled again in this country.[19]

One of the unidentified clippings titled "The Centre Lovell Art Colony," emphasized as impractical the tremendous effort required to become a long-lasting industry:

While this revival of the handicraft of other days is interesting, it is not apt to become far-reaching, as the quantity of articles produced is necessarily small, and the price is rather out of proportion; but through his art connections in New York, Mr. Volk is able to dispose of practically all the furniture and fabrics made at Centre Lovell at prices which really place them in the museum price category. Stressing the thorough craftsmanship demanded by the industry, it claims "one of the boasts of the colony is, that not a pound of glue nor a single screw is used in any of their furniture. The curtains are woven in wool and linen, and follow the styles made in Maine many years ago.[20]

Marsden Hartley, a Lewiston, Maine, native who would one day become internationally known as a great Modernist painter, traveled to Center Lovell in 1903 to paint and write poetry. Despite the arduous travel, he rented the old cobbler shop at the entrance to the Volk estate, but decried the transportation facilities. "To get to North Lovell one rode up from Fryeburg on a 'real Buffalo Bill coach and four' that made a single trip each day which meant that a person had to perch wherever there was a place, usually

Variations of this popular Indian motif are seen on several Sabatos rugs and also at the lower edge of the hand printed history illustrated at left. This was an early sample rug hooked on burlap. While the design obviously was acceptable, the burlap was not. It shows signs of considerable wear at the edges. It also lacks the knots found to be essential in the later, improved hand-made webbing foundation. It was part of the estate auction held in July, 2006 in Gray, Maine. c.1900. Handspun wool, vegetable dyes on burlap, 35" x 57". *Cyr Auction.*

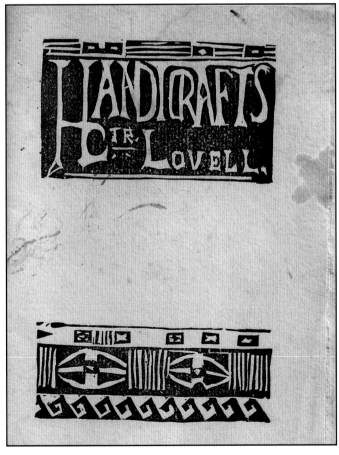

The dedication of the Sabatos Industry to the philosophy of hand crafting is obvious in this publication of the industry's history written by Wendell Volk, son of the founders. It is hand printed on hand-made paper and published by the Sabatos Press, Center Lovell, Maine, in February, 1902. *Lovell Historical Society.*

The reverse of the rug bears an attached label. True to the group's principle that everything must be handmade, the label is hand embroidered on linen. No label has been seen on any of the other known rugs in the Volk collection.

atop some supplies, rarely on the seat," he said.[21] Hartley tried unsuccessfully to sell his paintings through the industry's local exhibitions, perhaps in direct competition with Volk. Obviously friendly with Mrs. Volk, he provided a brief description of her:

> I didn't get close to Douglas Volk but it was Mrs. Volk who impressed me — a large woman of maternal energies flowing out of her and every now and then singing quietly in magnificent mezzo-soprano tones . . . The Volks were all for the restoration of New England folk arts then and were having wool combed and spun into pillow cover lengths with applied design on them. Nothing much came of this however.[22]

An article in the *Lewiston* [Maine] *Journal* also described Mrs. Volk as "a woman of unusual charm."[23]

Mrs. Volk's "maternal energies" probably explains, in part, how she was able to motivate the local women to help with the hooking of rugs, but it is interesting that Hartley, although not familiar with textiles, sensed the project was going to be neither profitable nor long-lasting. Or perhaps he was judging the industry on its failure to sell any of his paintings.

At some point during the summer of 1902 or 1903, Hartley camped out in a tent in the backyard of the home of Percival Chubb, a summer resident prominent in the Ethical Culture movement. His family liked Hartley, who in turn enjoyed their company and would perch for hours on the porch steps of their house, talking eagerly about ethical culture, light and color, and many other things. Chubb's daughter [Mavis Chubb Gallie, memorialized in the Sabatos rug recently gifted to the Maine Historical Society] remembered Hartley as something of an aesthete, lean, gangling, a bit "Greenwich Villagey," and clearly anxious to be part of their group.[24]

Although several other crafts became affiliated with the Sabatos Industry, the hooked rugs were the signature product and the most widely acclaimed. Two of the rugs were accepted for exhibition at the Louisiana Purchase Exposition of 1904, more commonly known as the St. Louis World's Fair. Exhibition competitions featured 807 categories and involved more than 40 countries, 43 states, and several U.S. territories. Mrs. Volk was awarded a silver medal for her entry of two Sabatos rugs.[25]

The official catalogue of exhibitors listed her in Group 14 – "Original objects of art workmanship – Volk, Mrs. Douglas, New York, #867: 'Sebatos' [*sic*] rug, pine tree design, and #868 'Sebatos' rug, Indian border design. Lillian Lord, collaborator. The rugs are made on a foundation of hand-spun hand-woven wool, into which the pile of hand-spun yarn is drawn and knotted. The colors are from fast vegetable dyes."

Interestingly, the next entry was for "Volk, Wendell D., New York: #869: 'Sebatos curtain.' White field with blue figures and stripes (Linen and wool. Vegetable dye. Wool hand-spun)."[26] In his book on the Fair, *The Universal Exposition of 1904,* David R.

The entwined letters M and V identify this as a Marion Volk signature on a miniature version of a Sabatos rug. A green fringe leaves elongated hooked loops uncut along all edges. The loops in the body of the mat are all cut or sheared, resulting in a soft, velvety texture. c.1900-1905. Hand-spun wool, vegetable dyes on burlap base, 8.75" x 14.50". *Maine Historical Society Collections.*

Francis, president of the Louisiana Purchase Exposition Company, explained that award winners were given a graded series of medals (grand prize, gold, silver, and bronze medals) accompanied by a diploma or certificate "representing the formal decree of the award and bearing the name of the recipient exhibitor, a description of the exhibit upon which the award was made and the signatures of the proper officers of the Exposition Company. The awards were distributed a little more than a year after the close of the Exposition. There were 33,158 medals made and issued while 41,052 diplomas were issued. Mrs. Volk's certificate was sold at the Gray auction, but the whereabouts of her silver medal is unknown.[27]

An excerpt from the *Lewiston Evening Journal* of February 16, 1905, gave recognition to the Volk award:

> It ought to be a source of pride to Maine people interested in the arts and craft movement in this State that the international jury of the St. Louis fair have awarded a silver medal to Mrs. Marion L. Volk, wife of the artist, Douglas Volk, for the Sabatos rugs made at Center Lovell, Maine.
>
> What is more, these hand-made rugs were the only American ones accepted by the jury for admission. It will be remembered that the *Lewiston Journal* told the story of these rugs at length last summer and presented its readers some pictures of the Volk home, "Hewn Oakes," where the Sabatos rug was first made. What is Mrs. Volk's honor is also that of her many co-workers in Lovell and of the State at large.[28]

While experimenting with ways in which to create the Sabatos rug, Mrs. Volk used machine-made burlap as the first foundation. The recent Volk Estate auction sale contained one of the early burlap-backed rugs as well as a small mat, also on burlap, both bearing the Marion Volk monogram. [It is assumed they were made by Mrs. Douglas Volk, but both mother and daughter were named Marion, and so had identical monograms.]

True to Mrs. Volk's intuition, the burlap did not come up to her standards for durability. There is considerable damage to the edges of the large rug, and somewhat less damage to the mat. There is no knotting of the loops in either rug. The large rug has an attached label which maintains the integrity of the industry's founding principle by being a totally handmade and hand signed linen product.

A second attempt was made, using cotton warp woven on an old-fashioned loom "which one of the farmers resurrected from his garret after diligent search throughout the neighborhood."[29] This was better, but other options also were considered until she finally settled on the hand-woven wool webbing as the most desirable. This special foundation devised by Mrs. Volk is unique to the Sabatos rug. It was a hand-woven webbing made totally from hand-spun wool from locally-raised sheep, carded at an old mill in South Waterford, then spun and woven by local women. The yarn spun for this undyed webbing was "a double and twisted string . . . as this needs must be strong for both woof and warp."[30]

Because the weave created was not tight enough to firmly hold the home-spun woolen yarn loops, Mrs. Volk developed a special knot for attaching the loops to the backing. The resultant rug was by far, the most original in the entire craft of rug-hooking. A handwritten letter of February 8, 1901, from Allen Whiting, secretary of The Society of Arts and Crafts in Boston, clearly showed his "intrigue" with the rug project: "Your description of the work is extremely interesting and I feel that among all the rug makers I know of in this Country, you are the only one whose work at all approaches the ideal or standard as established by the Orientals."[31]

With their reputation in the art world behind them, the prestige of a silver medal at the Fair, the zeal and fervor to improve the lot of Maine folk around Center Lovell, and the funds to indulge their dreams, it would seem that all the elements were aligned for the Volks to make a success of their new Sabatos Industry. Unfortunately, despite good intentions not everything was simple and straightforward.

The quaint patterns of some of the rugs are delightful. No photograph however, can give any idea of the beauty of coloring

A 1906 article in *Country Life* featured, among other things, a group display of the Sabatos rugs. The popular Indian motif band is seen once again at the center left. While the photographs are not in color, most of the rugs featured indigo as the major shade. *Country Life Magazine.*

Chapter IX
The Sabatos Industry—Continued

A history of the Sabatos Industry was written by Wendell Volk, son of the founders (illustrated in Chapter VIII). His pamphlet, *Handicrafts Ctr. Lovell,* was printed in February 1902, by the Sabatos Press, another undertaking of the enterprise, to encourage the craft of authorship and hand-printing. The name of the industry had various spellings in different publications, but the name used here is that seen in the original history which is excerpted and reproduced here slightly reformatted for readability.[1]

The development of the Press may have been influenced by the huge success of the Roycroft Press in East Aurora, New York. As a resident of New York City, Volk would have been well aware of the handicraft community founded about 1895 by Elbert Hubbard. While the rug division in Center Lovell was totally within the realm of Mrs. Volk, the remaining portion of the industry was designed and developed by Douglas and followed very closely the concepts of the Roycrofters.

Volk wrote in his history:

A rug, although it occupies a very lowly position in our home, has nevertheless something about it which has always made it one of the dignified objects of our household possessions. Probably this is traceable to the fact, that so many of the human activities are involved in its production

All the steps are interesting from the time the sheep is captured on the hill side, is given his unwilling bath and shorn of his winter fleece until the completed rug is placed upon the floor.

The wool, which is put through the various processes of carding, spinning, and weaving, passes through stages which have been dignified by usage from time immemorial. In our country hand weaving of various kinds of cloth and textiles formed one of the important industries of the past. Unfortunately these old and valuable products are being displaced by commercial wares, which, it is to be feared, are made more for the love of profit than well doing.

It is especially to be regretted that in country districts, where the home industries have been

fostered the longest, this outside demand for factory made articles has drawn the young people to large towns and villages, where an opportunity is offered for work, no longer afforded at home. In the village of Center Lovell, Maine, an effort is now being made by Mr. and Mrs. Douglas Volk in conjunction with some of their village friends, to revive a few of the old industries that were carried on in the farm houses fifty years or more ago. Mr. Volk has given such time as he could spare from his regular occupation to the furthering of this phase of the crafts movement, while Mrs. Volk has taken under her charge a special feature of the work in shape of the "Sabatos" rug.

A close-up detail of the rug's reverse shows the finely woven wool webbing that made up its foundation. When removed from the loom the ends were tied off and fringed.

An exceptionally rare example of the Sabatos rug demonstrates the Native American designs so prevalent in the Arts and Crafts period. The rare use of indigo in a rug made it highly coveted and was a hallmark of Sabatos rugs. c.1901-1906. Handspun wool, vegetable dyes on handwoven webbing with knotted loops, 35" x 57.50" including fringe. *Maine Historical Society Collections; family gift in memory of Mavis Chubb Gallie. 2006.095.001.*

This was the first thing undertaken by her and is the result of many months of experimental effort. Though this rug may fairly be said to be the offspring of the New England rag rug, it is also a development of and a departure from its progenitor in many ways. The rag rug is made from strips of cloth or rags drawn or hooked through a foundation of burlap. From the first, however, a wool yarn pile instead of cloth strips, was employed by its originator in making the Sabatos rug. The first one was drawn through burlap, but this foundation was at once given as not being of the same durability as the pile; and experiments were made with other [cotton] foundations woven on a hand loom, but of material that was in turn discarded in favor of an all wool home spun, hand woven webbing so that the rug as it stands today is a product in every particular of Lovell industry.

Briefly described the chief processes employed in creating a Sabatos rug are as follows: Sheep are raised by many of the farmers in and about Lovell. After the Spring shearing, the wool is carded into rolls ready for spinning The wool used for this rug is spun by hand, an occupation that is fortunately still carried on by a number of the inhabitants who are experts in the art. In many a cosy [*sic*] farmhouse one can find the house wife standing before the huge wheel, mysteriously converting the delicate rolls into the stout thread of yarn. When the spindle is quite full, its contents are reeled off upon a clock reel, with loud ticks occurring at even intervals to mark off the forty threads, seven knots being requisite to make a skein.

The large skeins are now ready for washing, a task that

becomes a pleasure when undertaken by lake shore or brook side. When ready, the skeins, if not dyed indoors are carried perhaps to the pine woods nearby, where the dying is often done in huge kettles suspended from stout green poles over the bon fires. Here the fleecy white skeins are plunged into their baths of color and thence taken out to dry.

The wool, having been carded, spun and dyed, is ready for the webbing, the old time hand loom now continues the work and there are happily quite a number of people about the country who are adept in its use. The process of making a web is intricate and difficult to describe. Briefly it may be stated that the skeins of warp are wound upon a set of thirty or forty spools, with the aid of a swift, clock reel, and spinning wheel. The spools are placed in the scarn or creel, and the ends of warp from the different spools are deftly gathered together and tied, the whole being banded on the huge upright warping bars.

In doing this, one takes a "lease" requiring an accurate and delicate handling of the separate threads to insure an even webbing on the loom. This long band of warp is carefully removed from the warping bars, in the form of a chain, and has to be most carefully adjusted to the huge yarn beam of the loom. Each separate thread is passed through the filmy harness or heddle, and then through the sley or reed.

Now commences the actual process of weaving, through the drawing back and forth of the "weft" by means of the shuttle. When sufficient has been woven to form a rug of the desired length, the completed webbing is taken from the loom and stands ready for the rug frame. Thus is made possible the fringe of warp at either end so characteristic of Oriental rugs. If the worker is not practiced enough to work from a drawing, the design is drawn, but not stenciled upon the webbing, which is then secured to the frame, after which the laborious work of drawing a rug begins, the yarn being drawn through the webbing and regularly knotted. The employment of a knot is observed in all Oriental pile rugs, and the use of one devised by Mrs. Volk, in the "Sabatos rug" is one of the points of departure from the rag rug or strip rug. Recognizing that a knot is an important feature of a rug, Mrs. Volk invented one to meet the requirements.

A careful examination of the rug illustrated herein displays the knot that Mrs. Volk had "invented." *Making Rugs Again,* an unattributed scrapbook clipping, describes the process: "She has recently invented a clever knot which securely ties each strand after it is pulled through and puts the New England rug on a par with the Oriental for durability. The ends pulled through the web are the 'pile' which is sheared from time to time as the rug is filled in. It takes about six weeks to make, from start to finish, a 3 x 5 foot rug."[2]

Mrs. Volk had inadvertently invented what is known today as the latch-hook rug knot. Mrs. Volk's rug hook lacked the modern latch, making it awkward to pick up and hold the several threads of yarn, an extremely time-consuming project. Today, craftsmen use only a single strand of a fairly heavy yarn and the attached latch on the hook holds the yarn within the hook while it is being worked.

Weaving the rug foundation, of course, required a loom, which Mrs. Volk did not possess. From the scrapbook clipping *Making Rugs Again:* "A spinning wheel she possessed, but a loom she did not, and great was her delight when one of the natives dug out from his woodshed and presented to her a fine old loom of beautiful red oak, all made by hand, put together with pegs. There was not a suspicion of a nail in it and it was over 100 years old."[3]

This manuscript page shows how either Douglas Volk or Marion assisted the local designers with sketches of different rug designs and indicating the colors to be used. Two different interpretations of ocean waves are seen at the ends hooked in blue and white with a green band at the top and a white band at the lower edge. The central band design was green with white figures. *Maine Historical Society Collections.*

Another good example of the use of Native American designs by the Sabatos Industry is seen here in shades of gold. Many of the rugs dispersed by auction in 2006 were apparently "rejects" withheld from the market for one reason or another and eventually worn out as scatter rugs in the rented summer cottages at "Hewn Oaks." As a result these rugs showed great use and wear. Gold seems to have been used infrequently while indigo was the major color of choice. The introduction of the dark shade at one end of this rug seems out of character with the overall color and may be the reason for the rejection. The rug has all the essential features: knotted handspun yarn, hand-woven webbing and vegetable dyes, 40" x 72". *Cyr Auction.*

Continuing Wendell Volk's history:

The designs used in the Sabatos rugs have from the first been mainly adaptations from native Indian motifs. These not only furnish opportunities for broad color effects, but have a character and interest which appeal to most of us. Great stress is laid on the quality of the dyes used in obtaining the color effects. Vegetable dyes are employed as being harmonious and agreeable to handle, and only such dyes are accepted as have stood all reasonable tests as to "milling" and fastness to light. Mr. Volk at the beginning of this enterprise was interested in seeing some of the old time fast dyes adopted in the work.

A few of the Lovell people still use steeping of the bark of different trees and plants, coloring wool and cloth, and from them he received many valuable hints, which, together with some experiments of his own furnished a basis for a working system. Some of the names of these dye barks and flowers alone are interesting: such as the yellow oak; golden rod; maple and apple bark; St. John's wort; [and] barberry, fustic, and madder root. Many of the colors obtained from these sources are practically fast, though it is a fact that almost all dyes will fade more or less in the course of time.

Making Rugs Again suggests that it was not all drudgery:

She [Mrs. Volk] gives "Barking Bees," when they all go out a-picnicking to gather bark and other vegetable matter for dyes. From the bark of different trees they get excellent browns and tans, from acorns a good gray, and from sumac the beautiful yellows. These "Barking Bees" are popular social events in Center Lovell. No less fascinating but limited to her pupils, for it is an important business, are the "Dyeing Bees" on the border of the lake near the Volk homestead. Here

This rug, found at "Hewn Oaks" at the time of its dispersal, is also assumed to be a reject. It has an indigo and sage green design derived from Southwest Native American motifs on a cream-colored ground. It is difficult to explain the reasoning for its rejection. In this case it could well be the distortion of the central indigo line or the mismatched designs in the lower left and upper right corners. Homespun, knotted yarn on hand-woven webbing and vegetable dyes, 31" x 66". *Cyr Auction*

teacher and pupils build bonfires, over which they put huge brass kettles containing the dye. While it is heating they wash the wool [to eliminate air and all traces of lanolin, a natural fat that would interfere with the absorption of the dye] then throw it into the kettles, and later spread it out on the rocks to sun and dry.[4]

One great advantage, however, of the vegetable dyes is that, if they change color at all, it is to harmonious tones. They preserve their original character and grow old beautifully. Thus it is held advisable to avoid the "quick and easy" commercial dyes which though readily manipulated disappear in most cases or change into shades absolutely foreign to the original intent of the dyer. Even in Persia the superb blues and other colors once obtained in the native rugs are becoming a thing of the past, owing to the introduction of commercial coloring matter. Mr. Mumford in his book on Oriental rugs cites the law lately promulgated by the Shah of Persia, prohibiting the importation of aniline dyes. He says during his stay in the Empire, over four thousand pounds of aniline dyes were publicly burned. This action indicates that the Persians are alive to the danger of having a once famous industry disappear.[5]

One of the most beautiful, enduring and difficult dyes to obtain is the old vat indigo blue, which is one of the predominant colors of the Sabatos rugs[;] it being used by a few people in the vicinity who still preserve a knowledge of how to obtain this practically imperishable dye. Thus in the various processes employed, technical difficulties are not avoided where their mastery affords pleasure or results in any advantage to the work. No pretence is made of making the rug more than a result of local possibilities, but within these limits care and sincerity are the key notes of the whole thing; therefore short cut methods are not adopted for the sake of expediency.

Interest in the best way, not in the quickest, is the motive that has kept the workers steadily going ahead in the enterprise. This circumstance accounts for the fact that but a small number of rugs is turned out in Lovell at present, during a year, for it is impossible to make a rug, say three by five feet including all the steps necessary in less than six or eight weeks.

Mrs. Volk is quoted in the *Lewiston Journal* article:

I am sorry that the impression has been spread abroad through some periodicals and papers in the past that we have a big rug-making industry here at Lovell. It is not so. We only began the work in the summer of 1900 and this season we have done practically nothing; so that in four years, I have made but seven rugs entirely by myself and the whole output is less than forty. [6]

This is better put into perspective when compared with the Maine Seacoast Mission group (discussed in Chapter XI) which was said to have created as many as 100 rugs in a single winter and as many as 300 rugs were made by the Albee enterprise in a single year. It also explains and emphasizes the extreme rarity of any Sabatos rugs today.

The magnitude of the effort that went into the creation of a Sabatos rug would today seem overwhelming. Just the one facet of using only vegetable dyes imposed unusual demands on the workers, including the decision to use vat-dyed indigo, a color used extensively at Center Lovell. It was a tedious and intricate procedure, but, fortunately, some women in the area were still capable of carrying out the process.

Interestingly, the only true blue obtainable in vegetable dyes is acquired through the use of indigo, a dark blue pigment obtained from the decomposition of indicant found in the sap of various herbaceous shrubs. It is not generally seen to any degree in country hooked rugs, not only because of the difficult dyeing process, but because it was also the only color that had to be purchased. Due to that expense, the priority use of the indigo was for the bed coverlets commonly referred to as "linsey-woolsies."

Unlike other dyes, indigo needs no mordant, but relies on a fermentation process that requires several days' advance preparation. Once the ingredients (indigo, madder root, wheat bran and soda ash) are combined with warm water, the mixture must be kept at a relatively constant tepid temperature and allowed to steep for about a week. If the temperature is not stabilized the fermentation will not proceed properly. This, of course, was done in the days when there were no temperature-controlled appliances. However, once the dye was made, it could be kept for a considerable period of time, even a century or more, being "renewed" or re-fermented periodically with the addition of more indigo. In another unattributed clipping it was noted that "The dye vat of one of the oldest residents of Center Lovell has been in constant operation for over half a century, and on this neighbor Mrs. Volk relies for her blue wools." [7]

Gentle stirring every day insured that any sediment was reincorporated into the solution. The operative word here is "gentle" for the intrusion of any

air into the mixture changed the color. Surprisingly, indigo first turns yellow, eventually changing into green and immediately changing to blue upon exposure to air. The dye is ready when a test piece of fiber dipped into the liquid is covered with a coppery yellow color, and emerges a bright green, rapidly turning blue when the air hits it.

Now, the yarn or wool can be dyed, another tricky process. Since protection from oxidation is vital, all air must first be removed from the yarn. This is accomplished by thoroughly wetting and then squeezing the wool or other fabric, forcing out all water and air. Finally ready for the dye pot, it must be inserted very gently to avoid the introduction of air, carefully and gently working the yarn while it is submerged. After several minutes the yarn can be carefully lifted out of the vat, squeezing out the excess dye while only slightly above the surface to prevent the introduction of any air from drops of liquid splashing back into the pot. The bright green yarn immediately turns blue. Depending upon the desired depth of color, it can be redyed several times, becoming darker blue with each bath.

This was just one of the dyes being used. The Sabatos Industry opted to use all vegetable dyes, gathering barks and other organic materials and turning them into dyes. Mrs. Rosalind Tufts, whose family summered in the area for a number of years, recalls her grandmother talking about the myriad of blueberries that would be picked by the young boys for use in the dye pots. [8]

Explained in her own words to the *Lewiston Journal* Mrs. Volk told of the difficulties encountered:

When it came to the dyeing of the pile yarn, we met our greatest obstacle. We knew we must have permanent colors and the right shades and that to secure these we must use vegetable dyes. To use the chemical, aniline dyes would mean certain fading of the colors in time. Only recently such dyes have been ordered confiscated by the Shah of Persia, a sure proof that the Persian rugmakers were in danger of using this non-permanent chemical. But there was nothing in print on vegetable dyeing to help us. Even William Morris's book on this subject proved of no practical value. Mr. Mumford's book on rugs, which is considered authentic, we found stated that the Orientals have lost the art of permanent dyeing.

All this so discouraged me that I would have given up the work at this point, in utter despair. But Mr. Volk was interested and persistent. We found the native women used the butternut and sweet apple bark with good effect, but we wanted the beautiful fast colors of indigo blue, the madder reds and gray greens, colors from vegetable dyes that would be sure only to mellow and soften with age. So we kept experimenting with the different barks until at last we produced just what we were after: and it is this feature of permanent dyeing, in difficult but desirable shades, that was the hardest and is the most commendable, feature of our work.

Then we taught the natives how to shave the bark from the branches and put it into condition for the yarn. The task of matching the colors is very, very hard, and we have done most all of the dyeing for the rugs made here during these four years. Sometimes the wool has to be put in at the beginning and slowly steeped. Again, it has to be put in when the dye is at a certain temperature and soaked slowly and for a long time. But the results were satisfactory. Our indigo blue, so hard to get with vegetable dyes, is our greatest achievement.[9]

Concluding Volk's history:

No effort as yet has been made to put this little village enterprise upon a formal commercial basis. Mrs. Volk and her fellow workers execute such orders as the exacting nature of the work enables them to fill; thus far they have been unable to keep up with the orders received. Many inquiries are sent regarding the number of rugs made and the question is often asked why are not more rugs seen for sale? As stated, but few can be made by one person in a year, and the fact that every step in the creation of the result is painstaking also prevents the rug from being produced at a very low figure; some cost as much as certain kinds of Oriental fabrics others less. It is pleasant to note that all who have cooperated in this "infant industry" in Lovell have worked with a commendable interest and sincerity; and though the number of workers is comparatively small, it

A page from a dye book prepared by Mrs. Volk records different strengths of madder dye with alum sulfate as a mordant. Examples of the dyes are seen in attached yarn samples. The Sabatos Industry prided itself on using only vegetable dyes. *Maine Historical Society Collections.*

constantly increases as the work becomes better known.

Other branches of home industry have also been started at Lovell. An exhibition of handicrafts, held here last summer, demonstrated the fact that not a few craftsmen in wood, iron and other material, are still to be found here. Among other products a hand woven fabric of linen and wool is being made that is very effective for portieres, window hangings, table covers, etc. This material is not expensive and comes into play admirably in summer houses. The wool used in this weaving, as in the case of the rugs, is hand spun and of native growth, and efforts are being made to have flax also raised for hand spinning. Attention is likewise being given by some of the people to the making of hand woven cloth, blankets, flannels, home spun knit goods, etc. A small hand press is also doing some service in the cause, and certain literary work participated in by some of the urban contingent may be developed in connection with the movement in general.

The undertaking, which has been called a village industry, is not as yet an extended enterprise. Mr. and Mrs. Volk live in Lovell a good part of the year, and being deeply interested in the crafts movement, have simply given the time consistent with other work to practical development of home industries in their locality. Whether or not the industry will grow depends largely upon the interest which the village people themselves continue to take in the work, as well as on the patronage of the outside public. It may be stated, however, that active steps are being taken by some of the influential people of Lovell to organize this local handicrafts movement; thus it is not unlikely that the growing interest in the work will take more tangible shape in the near future.

Inquiries are often received from different parts of the United States as to how the rug or weavings could be produced in other localities. Answer may be made that it would be possible for a person to carry on the work only in places where, besides the wool etc., there exist spinners, and weavers, unless he procured from Lovell or some other favorable place the necessary hand made material. He would of course have to know how to color in the proper way and would naturally have to learn how to execute the rug, whether he was furnished with the "webbing" or not; but no half-way methods can be encouraged or furthered in any way, as when, for instance, it is proposed to use manufactured yarn, foundations etc., the effect and result in such case, would be quite different from the standard required. Examples of the Sabatos rugs and weavings may be seen from time to time at the various Crafts exhibitions and orders given will be received and filled as soon as possible. Correspondence regarding prices and other matters may be addressed to Mrs. Douglas Volk, Center Lovell, Oxford Co.; Maine.

The *Oxford County Advertiser* reported an organizational meeting held on Friday, February 14, 1902:[10]

The Sebatos [sic] Handicraft Society was organized at Lovell Center at the home of Douglass [sic] Volk. Mr. Volk returned from New York, Tuesday night, and Wednesday evening a number met by invitation at his house and spent a very enjoyable evening. A fine lunch was served of scalloped oysters, cake and coffee. Marion Volk gave a recitation. [This likely would have been the Volk daughter who was named after her mother.]

The charter members of the new society are: Mr. and Mrs. George Eastman, Mr. and Mrs. Mell Eastman, Mr. and Mrs. Joseph Farnham, Mr. and Mrs. Mell Charles, Mr. and Mrs. J. Z. McAllister, Georgia Putnam, Mrs. C. Smith, Deacon Cyrus Andrews, Mr. and Mrs. Cushman Sawyer, Mr. and Mrs. C. Lord, Mr. and Mrs. Albra Lord [Albra Lord would become noted as a Maine basket-maker], Mrs. Warren McKeen, Ella Charles, Miss G. Abbott, Mr. and Mrs. Weston Palmer, J. Kendall, Ernest Hatch, Mr. and Mrs. J. Hatch, Mr. and Mrs. Owen Eastman, Mr. and Mrs. Will Stanford, Mr. and Mrs. Fredric Coburn.

The Sabatos rug industry at Lovell was started in the winter of 1899 [This is a conflict of date since it was also reported that the organizational meeting was held in 1902] by Mr. and Mrs. Volk, who had long been convinced that there would be a market for the old-fashioned New England drawn rugs, if proper pains were taken to secure beautiful designs, harmonious colorings, and technically excellent dyeing and weaving. As a tentative venture several people worked in conjunction upon three or four rugs which were shown in New York [at the Gustav Stickley rug exhibit] and which created something of a furore among artists and others who saw them. Orders for a number of other rugs were promptly placed and for the past two years a great deal of weaving and spinning, dyeing and drawing has been going on. Heretofore there has been no organization, no guild of the workers.

A catalog "printed on hand made paper at the 'Hewnbeam Press' [obviously named as an adaptation of the Volk summer home, Hewn Oaks], Center Lovell, by Wendell Volk and A. E. Hanson," lists the participants in the first Handicrafts Exhibition of the Society held on Aug. 24, 1901, from 10 a.m. to 9:30 p.m. at the Center Lovell town hall.[11] Among those exhibiting "textiles directly related to the Sabatos Industry were Mrs. Benjamin Andrews, Strip Portieres — indigo dye; Emily Colt, home spun cushion cover; Mrs. George Eastman, Home spun knitted goods; Mrs. Joseph Farnham, Sabatos rug, hand woven webbing, wool Indigo and vegetable dyed, strands knotted, made to order; Althea Farnham, Home spun cushion cover; Lillian Lord, Sabatos Rug (unfinished); Georgia Putnam, Rug — vegetable dyed; Mrs. Cushman Sawyer, Hand woven linen and wool portiere (Made to order); Mrs. Lottie Seiferd, Hand woven table cover; Marion Volk, Sabatos rug and hand woven cushion; Mrs. Douglas Volk, Sabatos rugs."

Douglas Volk also exhibited a Pewter belt cup. Local basket-maker Albra Lord displayed an "Oak and basket work settle, and baskets."

A manuscript page from the Smithsonian scrapbook lists "Center Lovell residents who were associated with Mrs. Volk in making Sabatos' rugs. Weaving, spinning, drawing, carding, indigo dyeing etc. Mrs. Joseph Farnham, Mrs. Albra Lord, Mrs. Mell Charles, Mrs. Sam Beardsley, Mrs. Jane Hatch, Mrs. Nelly [?], Mrs. Warren McKeen, Mrs. Benj. Gray, Mrs. Cyrus Andrews, Mrs. Aubrey Kimball, and one or two more not recalled."[12]

Information published in 1906 claims the Society had thirty members and had held two exhibitions in Lovell, the more recent attended by 300 people. "Every sort of handicraft industry was represented. There were prizes for the best spinning, weaving, woodcarving, basket-making, iron and wrought-iron work." The Industry also participated in the 1903 exhibit in New York City sponsored by Gustav Stickley.[13]

Although her interest always centered on the rugs, Mrs. Volk encouraged all types of weaving. It was this endeavor which became a significant aspect of the life of her son, Wendell, also noted for his woodcarvings. Wendell was a weaving instructor in the Domestic Art Department of Teachers' College, Columbia University, New York. He also gave classes in weaving in Center Lovell, while wood carving classes were provided by Karl von Rydingsvärd. According to his stationary Wendell also created "Sabatos handwoven college cushion covers made of linen and silk with the initial letter of your college embroidered in the college colors."[14]

The letterhead under Wendell's name further advertised Sabatos looms as being "used by Teachers' College, Ethical Culture School, New York; Boys Branch, West Side Settlement Schools, New York; Dr. Grenfell's Mission in Labrador, and others."[15]

The Sabatos rugs sold for approximately $50 and measured on average 3 x 5 feet. "The weaver proceeds at a pace of little more than half of a square foot each day. She is paid from $1.50 to $2 a day. [In 1902, the national average salary was .22 cents an hour with an average annual salary of $200 to $400 a year. Putting that into perspective, a person today making $40,000 per year, would have to pay $5,000 for one of the rugs. The price is even more staggering when considering that it is not a carpet, but a scatter rug.] And before the prospective rug was ready for weaving it had been through various processes that consumed about seven days of one person's labor."[16]

A study of this rich green rug reveals a possible reason for its rejection. The design is worked with tightly spun yarn while the body is of a loosely spun fiber which resulted in the tendency for the loop to slip out of the knot. This caused loss of the filler material. The design, however, is intricate and most attractive. Homespun, knotted yarn on hand-woven webbing with vegetable dyes, 40" x 72". *Cyr Auction.*

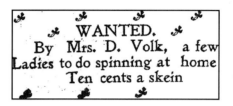

WANTED.
By Mrs. D. Volk, a few Ladies to do spinning at home Ten cents a skein

If Mrs. Volk did not have enough volunteers for her rug industry she did not hesitate to advertise. Her husband, Douglas, printed "The Fire Fly," a small weekly local newsletter, on his Hewn Beam Press. It carried "Editorials, Local News, Essay[s], Poem[s], and Miscellaneous." This advertisement is from the first issue of August 4, 1900. *Lovell Historical Society.*

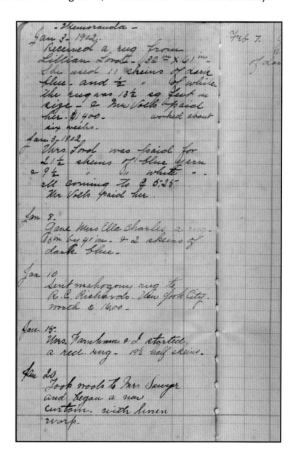

Mrs. Volk kept an account book recording the financial status of her rug industry. On January 3, 1902 she "Received rug from Lillian Lord – 32 in. x 61 in – She used 11 skeins of dark blue – and 1/2 [skein] of white. The rug was 13 1/2 sq. feet in size – and Mrs. Volk paid her $14.00. worked about six weeks." On the same day "Mrs. Lord was paid for 21 1/2 skeins of blue yarn & 9 1/2 [skeins] of white [yarn] all coming to $5.25[.] Mrs. Volk paid her." *Maine Historical Society Collections.*

In her book Mrs. Albee took strong issue with the Sabatos methods, writing somewhat defensively:

> It has been urged by some that yarn can be used to better advantage than strips of cloth in making hooked rugs. I investigated yarn, and these are some of the objections that were conclusive to my mind. Using the same weight of wool in yarn and in strips of cloth, the yarn covered only five-eighths as much surface as the strips did. Again, using the heaviest yarn I could get, it had to be doubled and then trebled in the strands [the Sabatos rugs do have double strands in each loop] in order to make it thick enough to hold in the mesh of the burlap, and this doubling process made it so difficult to catch with the hook that it took three times as long to hook a square foot as it did to use the woolen strips. . . . The question has also been raised if one ought to use material at first hand and not after it has passed through the manufacturer's hands. I answer emphatically, no — if thereby a greater cost and less value is involved.
>
> Though an industry may be founded upon sentiment, this very sentiment for hand labor may become a snare and a hindrance if pushed too far; and this matter of using homespun yarn in order to say that all materials used are hand-made and furnished right in the vicinity offers an excellent example of the point in question . . . To add further to the difficulties, when the yarn is finally hooked and carefully sheared, if the pile is left long enough to hold firmly in the burlap, the surface, after a little wear, mats down and looks shabby; and if sheared short as a velvet carpet, the loops do not hold. [This problem was overcome in the Sabatos Industry with the special knot devised by Mrs. Volk to hold the loops firmly in place.][17]

Albee obviously would have been disturbed by a letter written to Mrs. Volk by Charles deKay, Managing Director of the National Arts Club, on April 23, 1901:

> I think you exaggerate the importance of having every part of your rugs handmade, so far as exhibiting them is concerned. It seems to me that you ought to show people what you are doing if only to encourage others. Mrs. John Albee has sent four rugs, and while they are good, yours are so much more attractive that we would be very unwilling to have them absent. I hope you will send them without fail sometime this week.[18]

The Sabatos rugs were included in the club's first exhibition.

Further on in her text Albee continued her complaints:

> There is a curious conviction prevailing in some quarters that beautiful durable colors are obtainable only from vegetable dyes. My first experiments were with barks, mosses, etc., but the difficulty of getting them, the enormous amount necessary to dye any quantity of goods, the tedious process in their use, and the fact that after all only a narrow range of colors is obtainable from them, compelled me to abandon them altogether.[19]

William Morris, one of the founders of the Arts and Crafts Movement, disagreed emphatically:

> The aniline dyes are reduced by a long process from the plants of the coal-measures. Of these dyes it must be enough to say that their discovery, while conferring the greatest honor on the abstract science of chemistry, and while doing great service to capitalists in their hunt for profits, has terribly injured the art of dyeing, and for the general public, has nearly destroyed it as an art. Henceforward there is an absolute divorce between the commercial process, and the art of dyeing. Anyone wanting to produce dyed textiles with any artistic quality in them must entirely forego the modern and commercial methods, in favor of those which are at least as old as Pliny.[20]

By using machine-made materials and chemical colors, Albee seemed willing to compromise some of her own artistic principles for the sake of facility, whereas the Volks, on the other hand, were willing to sacrifice facility for the sake of their art.

Despite Albee's contra-indications concerning the Sabatos rugs, an article in *The Magazine Antiques*, November 1922, [the period when folk art had come into prominence] contests her declarations of success:

> A few years ago a summer dweller from the city revived the industry in a New Hampshire town among the mountains. The resultant rugs were quite beautiful, and compared favorably with the products of famous looms; but they lacked the naïve charm of the old. Perhaps they were too artistic, aspiring to a something that was not inherent either in the material or in the mind of the worker. Certainly they lacked the domestic touch which made the old-timers so interesting. They were known as Abnáki rugs, an attractive

name, but not one entirely in keeping. The venture was not a success, as the women whom it was intended to benefit did not take kindly to it. The patterns and methods accordingly passed into the hands of the Art Institute of Manchester, New Hampshire.[21]

There is no record as to the total number of Sabatos rugs created, but it is highly doubtful that they were made in large numbers. The rug at the Maine Historical Society, is the best known example at this time.[22] It is in excellent condition and features the highly prized vat-dyed indigo. With the exception of the early, unsuccessful burlap-backed rug and mat in the recent estate auction, there were three others with the hand-woven foundation but only one survived with only minimal damage. The surprising thing is that they exist at all, having been used for many years as scatter rugs in summer rental cottages at Hewnoaks (the name later combined to become a one-word title), the Volk lakeside estate.

A possible explanation for this "abuse" is that they were likely "rejects," a suggestion kindled by the *Country Life in America* article:

> The Sebatos rugs of Center Lovell express various "motives," and such visions as the greenwood on a summer day of heavy yellow light, and a driveway down a channel of trees, are recorded in the arrangement and by-play of colors. And since the rug is the echo in wool of some out-door impression, it is tested on completion by being carried out of doors. If it bears the brightness and seems a natural thing in a world of sun and trees, then it is good. If it blinks, and hints of artificiality, then it is fit for nothing but to be put aside.[23]

Maybe the auctioned rugs "blinked" or they were excess inventory, although that seems doubtful considering the claims that the industry could not keep up with demands for the rugs.

Considered to be at least 100 years old, the rug now preserved at the Maine Historical Society adequately fulfills the terms of being "a marvel of velvety softness," a phrase once used to describe the Waldoboro rugs. One must hold or touch the rug to fully appreciate how the earliest rugs earned that distinction. It is exquisite in design, condition and coloring. The Society also purchased the very small mat made as an experimental project prior to the development of the wool webbing, as well as a lot of rug-related ephemera from the estate. The State Museum also purchased several articles including a segment of an unfinished rug and a box loom.

While no material has been found to indicate how long the Sabatos Industry endured, it seems more than likely that it never prospered fully because of the time and expense involved. Fortunately, efforts have been successful to preserve examples of these very special rugs created in, and now being preserved, in Maine.

shearing sheep

A photographic record of the industry was recorded in a 1906 article in *Country Life in America* magazine. The photographs also were included in a Maine State Museum album of Center Lovell. The rug-making started in the spring with the shearing of the sheep raised in the surrounding countryside. The old-fashioned shearing tool was also the preferred tool for shearing hooked rugs in the early days. *All photographs Maine State Museum.*

An interesting fragment created at the Sabatos Industry indicates an attempt to duplicate imported Persian rugs. It was a major goal of the period to provide a less expensive version of rugs being imported from the Middle East. It obviously was rejected early on. This example was hooked on a linen foundation with handspun, vegetable dyed wool yarn. The loops are knotted. The linen foundation (the potential size of the rug if it was completed) is 31.25" x 58.25". The hooked portion is 27.50" x 28.75" with the first six inches worked warp to warp. *Maine State Museum.*

raw wool bagged

The raw wool was bagged and taken to the carding mill for processing. Here it is being transferred by the side of the mill into a container for processing inside.

in carding mill

The carding process was the only segment done by machine. The raw wool was carded at the historic Oliver Hapgood Carding Mill at South Waterford, Maine. In 1963, the mill was disassembled and move to Old Sturbridge Village in Massachusetts where it can be visited today.

spinning wheel

The carded rolls of wool were spun into yarn on an old-fashioned spinning wheel. When the spindle was full, its contents were reeled off upon a clock reel to make a skein.

washing in brook

The large skeins were then washed and boiled to remove air and lanolin, which would interfere with the dyeing. This process alone stresses the tremendous amount of labor required to achieve the "hand-made" designation. Doing it by lakeside or brook may have improved the atmosphere, but did nothing to alleviate the physical aspects.

w/ clock reel

Once the wool was spun, carded, and dyed, an intricate web was made, a process involving a swift, a clock reel and spinning reel. The skeins of warp are wound upon a set of thirty or forty spools, shown spilling out of the basket.

preparing for loom

The spools were placed in the scarn or creel and the ends of warp gathered and tied, the whole banded together on the huge upright warping bars.

Young boys from the village would gather barks, berries and other organic materials to be made into dyes. "Barking Bees" were often held to add a note of entertainment to the process.

gathering bark

dying in vat

Another labor-intensive project was the dyeing, also done out-of-doors. The young Marion Volk dips the wool skeins into the dye bath. Her mother is seen over her right shoulder, hanging the dyed skeins for drying. This may well be a family portrait. It is believed that her brother Wendell is at the far left and it is likely that the young man seated on the ground at the right is her younger brother, Gerome. At the upper right is Douglas Volk. The elder gentleman could well be another family member.

at loom

Douglas Volk is seated at the indoor loom weaving the webbing for the rug foundation. When the webbing reached the desired length for a rug, it was taken from the loom ready for the rug-hooking frame.

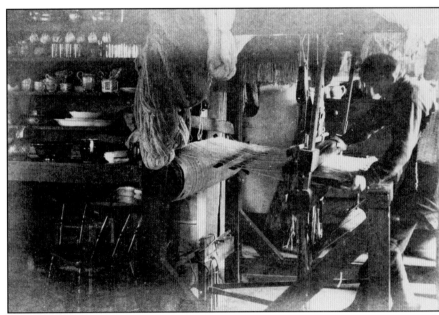

at hooking frame

Marion Volk is seen hooking a rug, comfortably ensconced indoors next to the fireplace with her skeins of dyed yarns hanging from the rug frame. She is using a very traditional rug hook.

Chapter X
The Cranberry Island Rugs

Contemporary with the Sabatos group another cottage industry was formed under a totally different concept on Cranberry Island just off the coast of Northeast Harbor, Maine. While the Sabatos group was a thoroughly "hands-on" involvement, the sponsoring organization at Cranberry Island chose to bring in a paid professional designer to fulfill their Ethical Culture responsibilities.

Nor was the industry undertaken for financial salvation, but rather to help quell the boredom of "cabin fever," the winter malady that affects many in colder climes. Adding an air of intrigue, as well as a barrier to in-depth research, it was developed under the aegis of a highly private, publicity-shunning organization of wealthy summer residents, The Cranberry Club of Northeast Harbor, Maine, a group still active today.

Although The Bureau of Labor *Bulletin* never defined this base of support, it outlined the history:

Of the various rug-making industries which have grown out of Mrs. Albee's pioneer efforts in New Hampshire, perhaps the most important is that established among the wives of fishermen on the Cranberry Isles, opposite Northeast Harbor, ME. Until the rug industry was introduced there these women, though intelligent and sufficiently well provided with the necessaries of life, had little to occupy their time during the winter and but little ready money. They were ambitious to raise money for church purposes and for building a wharf, etc., and when they heard of the success of the Abnákee rug industry a number of them were desirous of undertaking similar work. They were already familiar with the process of hooking rugs; and they were fortunate in having the benefit of the initiative, moral support, and financial backing of Mrs. Seth Low, Miss Miriam P. Reynolds, and one or two other New York women whose summer homes are at Northeast Harbor, [all members of The Cranberry Club].

The industry was started on a small scale in the autumn of 1901, under the supervision of Amy Mali Hicks, a designer [and author] identified with the Arts and Crafts movement in New York City, who designed the patterns and gave instructions in dyeing, etc.[1] A year later, Miss Hicks retired from the management of the enterprise and was succeeded by Miss Una A. Clarke of Cambridge, Massachusetts, also a designer who had some experience in making rugs. During the first winter six rugs were made which were exhibited the following summer at Northeast Harbor.

The next winter the industry was developed on a somewhat larger scale, twelve women working on the rugs regularly as their household duties allowed, averaging about two hours a day. In the summer comparatively little work is done. One woman stencils all the burlaps, while another dyes all the flannel. The dyestuffs are obtained from Mrs. Albee, and are identical with those used in the Abnákee rugs; but a somewhat firmer texture is obtained in the Cranberry Island rugs by using 2 yards of flannel to the square foot, instead of 1.25 or 1 yd. as at Pequaket. The use of vegetable dyes is now under consideration. [This may have been the result of consultations with the Center Lovell enterprise which offered to lend their expertise. Whatever the reason, the Cranberry Island women gave up the idea in favor of aniline dyes.]

The Cranberry Island rugs are distinguished by the monogram "CR" worked in one corner or on the selvage at the back. Several designs have been used with different arrangements of colors and from time to time new patterns are prepared. Most of the designs are original and striking, effective use being made of a somewhat conventionalized pine tree and other natural forms; but the patterns of old time samplers have also been adapted for use in bedroom rugs.

The rugs have been sold about as fast as they could be made, in most cases being made to order. They are used chiefly in summer cottages in Maine and in the vicinity of New York. An exhibit was sent to a New York City arts and crafts exhibition in the spring of 1903 [the Stickley exhibition], and all the rugs sent were sold. The industry is now firmly established on a self-supporting basis, but the committee of New York women still maintain an organization, Mrs. Charles Wesson having succeeded Mrs. Low as treasurer.

The stenciler receives 25 cents for each rug, and the dyer 6 cents per yard of material. The women who draw the flannel strips through the burlap receive 40 cents for each square foot, which is about three hours' work. The rugs are sold at $1.20 per square foot, of which 60 cents represents the cost of materials. This leaves a margin of a few cents a square foot, which is used for a sinking fund and to pay for the designing, etc. Most of the rugs made thus far have been small ones, selling from $7 to $32 and averaging about $10 apiece, [The Sabatos rugs were five times as expensive, selling for about $50 each] but orders have been received for at least two large rugs at $100 each. The small size of the fishermen's houses make it difficult for the women to handle the larger rugs."[2]

In a 1927 book author Ella Shannon Bowles gave a different description of the Cranberry Island rug designs. "Environment" she said, "influenced designers in their choice of subjects. The rugs made by the women of Cranberry Islands, Maine, were typical of seafaring life, their designs being suggested by lines left on the sand by the tide, by waves lapping on the beach, by seaweeds and shells, and the tips of distant sails at sea."[3] This outlook definitely fits the rug with the "crab" design illustrated in this chapter.

However, the description varies from others who claimed there was a Native American influence and the Labor Bureau *Bulletin* which mentions the stylized pine tree as a significant detail and other designs influenced by early samplers.

Gustav Stickley, famous as an Arts & Crafts entrepreneur, was known to have sold a few of the Cranberry Island rugs. His rug philosophy was expressed in a 1910 catalog stating that they should be "unobtrusive in design" and providing a "quiet and harmonious background to the furnishings"[4] Ms. Hicks, who was brought up from New York to become the manager and designer of the organizational effort at Cranberry Island, expressed her own philosophy in her book, *The Craft of Hand-Made Rugs."*

One of the greatest benefits which come from founding village industries is raising the standard of public taste. This influence comes directly through the individual worker, who in connection with rug-making begins to study a little design. So besides the benefit to the community, the individual worker has a keener interest in the work because of being able to plan it well.

This illustration shows undoubtedly the best surviving example of a known Cranberry Island rug. The crab, in shades of green and white, is an appropriate design for a Maine coastal rug. The Native American influence is seen in the triangular ornaments surrounding the crab hexagons. While it does not bear the CR monogram, the rug was owned by the family of Miss Mirriam P. Reynolds, one of the early founders of the industry, and descended in her family. This is a striking Arts and Crafts Movement design. c.1902-1905. Wool on burlap, 36" x 96". *Courtesy Great Cranberry Island Historical Society; gift of Victoria Murphy.*

The study of design is not a matter of technical complications. The workers are taught the application of decorative principles, learn line arrangement, placement of masses and the relation of tone and color values. They are also taught the use of reliable dyes which produce permanent and artistic colors. The workers themselves sometimes know of valuable dye recipes. These can be made serviceable by a systematic revision replacing the rule of thumb by exactness in chemical proportion . . ."[5]

There are no records to indicate the duration of the industry, but it is believed to have continued until World War I. Its demise undoubtedly resulted from concern about the war and not from a lack of success by the rug industry. The hookers' time could be better spent knitting stockings or rolling bandages for the troops. The islanders are said to have been extremely patriotic, perhaps more so than the average person for "The Hobo," a submarine hunter, was berthed near Little Cranberry and was crewed by island men. Its use by the sailors and fishermen of the islands hunting German submarines brought thoughts of the war very close to home. Hooking rugs was less important than helping out the war effort. [6]

Bowles credits the Cranberry Island project with inspiring the creation of the South End House Industry in Boston in 1923. One of the Boston directors, according to Bowles, had watched the successful growth of the Cranberry Island industry and when it ceased operation she saw the possibility of a similar project at South End House. Established in a lodging house district, it provided employment to women living there.[7]

The Cranberry Island industry was fortunate to be situated near Northeast Harbor, a rather "posh" community on Mt. Desert Island that did, and still does, attract a tight-knit colony of wealthy summer residents.

The cottage rug industry was the brainchild of a group of such women who had gathered together in a social organization known as The Cranberry Club. It was described by a former president as "the most unique club in the world."[8] Highly secretive and limited to a membership of 25 women, the club carefully guarded details of its activities from outsiders so its role in the development of the rug industry was little known. However, the founders listed in the Labor Bureau *Bulletin* were all members of the club.

Some light was shed on the industry history in 1926 when Mrs. Henry Parkman, president of the Club, read a paper, *Cranberryana,* at the annual luncheon at the clubhouse on July 28 and members voted to have the club history, preserved in a privately printed format.[9] It includes a description of their lives and summer activities:

The life was Arcadian in its simplicity, intimate with earth, sea, and sky. Boats, either sail boats or row boats, were our transportation. Often did we row ourselves over the sunset waters to take supper with some friend; and no place seemed too far to walk. An excursion to Bar Harbor by buckboard was a grand affair, taking a whole day. A little trail through the woods and tangle of raspberry bushes led to the modest village where the few shops were kept by our resident friends.

The islands in those seafaring days were familiar places of resort. Their inhabitants, retired captains with their little gardens of bright flowers, hardy lobstermen, and widows of the sea, became friends and supplied an interest which resulted among other things in the rug industry, now extinct. Samples of the rugs may be seen today on the clubhouse floor, and many of the summer people carried them away for their artistic designs to decorate winter homes. Miss Reynolds, a lady of ardent and impressive personality, sister in law of Dr. Huntington, was leader in the little group who frequented the islands and especially the cliffs of Great Cranberry, spending whole days watching the surf. After having been several times drenched by sudden showers and driven to board the one ox-cart of the island in search of refuge in the village, the idea of some sort of shelter or camp with a fireplace came naturally to these gentle ladies, and was taken up by the active mind of Miss Reynolds. Thus was born the Cranberry Club and many were the preliminary meetings held that winter in Grace Church [Episcopal] rectory to set it on its feet. Buying land in these islands where the title frequently runs back to Henry IV of France, is a problem in itself, necessitating recourse to what might be called the Law and the Prophets.

The club was officially incorporated on August 4, 1894, as "The Cranberry Club." At that time, the membership list was drawn up and a decision was made to organize "for social purposes." [It was only a brief span of time until the clubhouse was constructed and it remains in use today on Great Cranberry Island.]

Then the fun began. The one acre of land having been bought, a house costing six hundred dollars, later reduced to $575, was built

August 23d, 1894, and furnished by the united efforts of all the members. Table and chairs were brought over in sailboats. Miss Blodgett's taste was used in the selection of chintz and china. Members worked to mark the sheets and towels, and when all this was done, infinite difficulties were overcome in arranging for a water supply, proper plumbing, a landing at the Hamors (sic), and finally a float and slip at Fish Point . . .[10]

When the house was finished, various house-warmings were held including one for the Cranberry people "over the age of 18." This undoubtedly included all or most of the rug hookers.

The occasion was described in *Cranberryana:*

All the seats and benches in the house were filled with our good neighbors, the fishermen and their wives, and the captains of the little boats. At first it seemed a little hard to make conversation with them all, but by dint of plates plentifully loaded with cakes and sandwiches, and cups of tea, the ice was broken and we had very pleasant chats together. The minister of the church was among the guests. They all sang hymns to us, ending up with "God be with you till we meet again" and the party closed with a little address from the minister. Such pleasant parties were repeated two or three years in succession, so that we might become acquainted with the islanders.[11]

The Arts and Crafts influence is again seen in this very large room-size rug, one-third of which is shown here. Designed to fit under a large dining room table, the center field is plain. The four corner elements have identical designs and the border continues all the way around. The design has an over-all Egyptian-revival appearance, with the chief elements being dogs and the pine trees, the latter said to have been a popular motif among Cranberry Island rugs. Like the previous rug this one also came down through the Reynolds's family. c.1902-1905. Wool on burlap, 6'9" x 9'1". Courtesy *Great Cranberry Island Historical Society; gift of Victoria Murphy.*

Shown here is another view of the rug's corner to illustrate how the design was restricted to the corners and edges so nothing would be hidden when a large table was centered on it.

Unfortunately, as with Maine rugs in general, most left the state many years ago and that included the ones made by the island women and formerly used in the clubhouse. Much prized by collectors, Maine rugs, purported to be the best available, were sought by dealers and collectors. A few have ended up in museums in other states, as well as the Maine State Museum, but unfortunately any extensive effort on the part of Maine museums to preserve this segment of Maine's history has been seriously lacking. It is hoped that with the publication of this book, even local historical societies in all states will come to realize the value of collecting these rare historical artifacts. They offer a personal glimpse into the lives of America's women during periods when they had little opportunity for other forms of self-expression.

While earlier publications have stated the Cranberry Island rugs were marked with a "CR" as a means of identification, those found to date have no such designation. The two rugs that have returned to Maine and are now housed at the Great Cranberry Island Historical Society Museum are not so marked, but their provenance is virtually indisputable. They were donated by Victoria Murphy of Seal Harbor, having descended through the family of Miss Reynolds, one of the original founders of the industry.[12] It is believed that the rugs marked with the "CR" were those taken out-of-state for sale in New York City. Those ordered for local use or by local residents were not marked. These were private transactions between the maker and the buyer so the mark was unnecessary and perhaps unwanted.

Two flower pots dominate a rug probably produced by an island woman without the assistance of a professional designer. A large hint is the lack of duplication of the flowers on each side. It is obviously not a pre-planned rug with matching designs, but appears to be hand-drawn without the aid of professional oversight. c.1910-1915. Wool on burlap, 29.50" x 44.75". *Courtesy U. S. National Park Service, Acadia National Park's William Otis Sawtelle Collections & Research Center.*

Trying to track down specimens of these rugs to be photographed for inclusion in the book has been difficult but rewarding. It resulted in the return of the two rugs illustrated here to the Great Cranberry Island Historical Society Museum. However, the rugs once housed in the Cranberry Club, which were eventually given to the Islesford Museum, have gone astray. According to Robert Pyle, Librarian at the Northeast Harbor Library, Professor William Otis Sawtelle, his grandfather, had made an outstanding effort over a period of many years to preserve the history of the Cranberry Isles (Great Cranberry and Little Cranberry, the latter also called Islesford).[13]

In 1919 my grandfather Sawtelle, having an established interest in history, bought an old store on the beach at Islesford that had been built and owned by the Hadlock family. His objective was to gain a right of way to a wharf he had previously bought to provide public access to the island (imagine buying a dock without confirming that you could go anywhere from it other than back to sea! He was not a business man.) [Sawtelle was, however, a well-educated and highly intellectual man, having taught physics at the Massachusetts Institute of Technology, Harvard University, and Haverford College.]

In the store were a number of artifacts of the Hadlock family, accumulating to a ready made museum of local culture. He [Sawtelle] developed this museum and added to it until in 1926 he built with help a fireproof brick building. He died in 1939. In 1948 the [Acadia National] Park Service accepted the gift of the museum and property.

The National Park Service was not in the museum business, and put a naturalist in charge. The staff naturalist did not see a long future in the Sawtelle museum, regardless of the importance of its holdings. It was he who provided the rugs — and maybe a few more items — to the [Franklin D. Roosevelt] international site at Campobello.

Family members had lost track of the missing museum items until one day Mr. Pyle was visiting Campobello where he discovered his grandfather's label on a rug in the Campobello living room. He said, "A number of hooked and braided rugs had disappeared that Grandfather had used on the floors of his museum. We have no reason to think they went anywhere other than Campobello."

The William Otis Sawtelle Collections and Research Center is now housed in the National Park Service headquarters building at Acadia National Park, Bar Harbor. When questioned about these rugs, Brooke Childrey, museum curator, said the Cranberry Island rugs were sent to Campobello sometime in the 1960s or 1970s. When asked the rationale behind this transaction she responded: "I'm not sure why, other than the fact they requested them."[14] Clearly there was no formal deaccession and no records seem to have been kept of the transfer.

Campobello Island is in New Brunswick, Canada, reached by a short bridge from Lubec, Maine, where the Roosevelt family owned a summer residence, referred to as "Campobello."[15] The two-story Dutch Colonial-style frame structure was acquired by the Roosevelt family in 1910 and it was there in 1921 that the future president suffered a crippling attack of polio. In 1952 the house was sold to the Armand Hammer family by F.D.R.'s son, Elliott. Hammer attempted to furnish the house with articles contemporary to the period of the Roosevelt occupancy. The Cranberry Island

hooked rugs, of course, would be most appropriate for this purpose.

In 1962 the Franklin D. Roosevelt Memorial Bridge between Lubec, Maine, and Campobello Island, New Brunswick, was dedicated and the following year President John F. Kennedy suggested that the home be preserved as a memorial to President Roosevelt. The Canadian Prime Minister, Lester B. Pearson, agreed and today the property is administered by a joint commission made up of members from the two countries. It is not affiliated with the U.S. National Park Service although the rugs were provided by that Service.

Despite numerous e-mail attempts and a personal visit to the island, the personnel were unable to provide any information about the rugs.

After a lengthy conversation with the curator, it was finally determined that there were some rugs hooked on burlap, in storage and in need of repair. These might be the ones, she said, but no further information has been forthcoming. It is indeed sad to think that a significant portion of Maine's hooking history possibly lies unused and in storage at Campobello with no record available as to numbers or designs.

Here are additional stylized pine trees serving as a "forest" in which a handsome stag stands at attention. Flowers bloom under the trees to soften the scene and drama is provided by the swag-like border. Clearly an early rug designed while Ami Mali Hicks or Una A. Clarke were associated with the enterprise. c.1905. Wool on burlap. 17.50" x 29.50". *Courtesy Sawtelle Collections and Research Center.*

Chapter XI

The Sea Coast Mission Rugs

By 1920 America had "discovered" folk art. There was a sudden clamor to collect all things primitive, albeit "artistic."[1] This was fortunate for still another hooked rug industry was created as an adjunct to the Maine Sea Coast Mission housed at Bar Harbor on Mt. Desert Island. This was not far from the area where the Cranberry Island Industry had been successful prior to World War I. The Cranberry Islanders, in fact, may have provided impetus to the new group, whose major plan was modeled after the Grenfell Mission in Labrador. In fact, Dr. Wilfred T. Grenfell was contacted for advice about this program which developed more from chance than from any pre-planning.[2]

As opposed to the two groups previously discussed, the Maine Sea Coast Mission Rug Industry was initiated not by outsiders, but within a group of year-round Maine residents. Actually, it could not even be considered a "group," since its hookers were widely scattered among Maine's islands and headlands. With the exception of advice from Mrs. Leonard Kellogg, the hookers had no wealth supporting them, no professional designers and no summer residents involved in the organization. It was totally the brain child of Mrs. Alice M. Peasley, affectionately known as "Ma" Peasley.

The three cottage industries being studied in this book show a marked diversity. They were not just "rubber stamps" of the Abnákee Industry. The Sabatos group capitalized on the concept of the Abnákee, but went its own way to develop a "unique rug" that has likely never been faithfully duplicated by another organization. The Cranberry Island Industry, while it was a "step-child" of the Abnákee Industry, had a totally different initial concept inasmuch as it was not developed to supplement the income of the less fortunate, but to provide entertainment or amusement for a select group, while benefiting charity. The third was the Sea Coast Mission project; while it was indeed developed primarily to provide supplemental income for Maine coastal peoples, the whole organization was totally of its own making. It was not a consolidated group but individuals scattered among the islands serviced by the Mission, an organization still bringing religious, social and economic assistance to persons living in Maine's isolated coastal areas.

The Mission rug was defined by Peasley in the Society's annual report for 1929-30:

> A Maine Sea Coast Mission Rug is a rug made by a woman living either on the coast or an island of Maine, within the cruising radius of the *Sunbeam* [the organization's missionary vessel]. The characteristics of these rugs is a firm, close, velvety nap made entirely by hand. Types of work are the flat, the slightly raised and the low relief. Types of rugs are primitive florals, elegant florals, tapestries of typical Maine coast scenery; ship rugs, sea scapes, wild bird rugs, primitive animal rugs and geometrics. In artistic value they range from the beautiful to the grotesque; in color from the soft harmony to the screaming riot. Yet, there is a characteristic "something" which all these rugs have in common — a spiritual quality and individuality that marks them as the work of a homogeneous group, and under the same general influence. Whatever they may be, or whatever they may lack, they are sincere and very genuine.[3]

Having received approval from the Maine State Board of Charities and Corrections, the Maine Sea Coast Mission Society was incorporated in 1905.[3] A 1909 report listed its purpose — "to provide closer fellowship among scattered coast people who do not live within reach of an organized church." This included residents of remote Maine headlands as well as the islands which were serviced via the *Sunbeam*.

Peasley is first heard of when, in the thirteenth annual report published in 1918, it was announced that "Miss Douglass, the assistant missionary, supported by Mrs. Miles B. Carpenter, closed their labors in October. We were fortunate to secure the services of Mrs. Alice M. Peasley who, with her family, came to Crowley's Island, occupied the cottage and taught the public school in Mission Hall. The Town of Addison assisted in her support. It proved a great blessing to the island to have Mrs. Peasley and her family settled here."[4]

The 1924 report shows that Peasley "has been throughout the year located at South Gouldsboro and West Gouldsboro where she has shown exceptional ability in organizing the work and bringing forth good results." This was the year when Mrs. Leonard Kellogg sent two burlaps for hooked rugs, marking the start of the rug industry which continued until just before World War II, a period of just under 20 years.[5] [Mrs. Kellogg, as will be seen later, was a wealthy summer visitor to Mt. Desert, who supported the Mission's activities.]

The annual report for 1929-30 included a history of the rug endeavor written by Peasley herself. Recorded here in its entirety, it is a totally candid and intimate account of both the trials and rewards of such a program and is perhaps a unique document in the history of regional, cooperative rug-hooking in this country.

Written in the third person, this is her historical narrative:[6]

In 1923 Mrs. Peasley was sent to South Gouldsboro. She found the church in debt, and the people low in resources. Courage and a willingness to work were their assets. In canvassing the situation to discover some way of raising money that might be a genuine business venture, and not draw on the slender financial means of the community, Mrs. Peasley was impressed with the hook rug work. A few women could hook — that is, they had remembered from their mothers the mechanics of a hook rug. The designs were few and the colors awful. Hooked Rugs had begun to appear in some shops and there was promise that they might develop into a fad. [This is prime evidence that the folk art movement had begun.]

"Ma" Peasley, standing in the black dress, is seen with a group of women hooking a rug at their headquarters located at the time in South Gouldsboro. The initial organization took place there to raise funds for church repairs. Nine rugs were made the first summer and were sold at Bar Harbor and Hancock Point, both wealthy summer enclaves. Plans were immediately implemented to continue the project another summer. Unless otherwise noted all photographs and other materials are from the Sea Coast Mission Archives at their headquarters in Bar Harbor, Maine, and used with the permission of the Mission. *Courtesy Maine Sea Coast Mission.*

In talking with friends of the Mission we received definite encouragement from Mrs. Leonard Kellogg who urged the venture. Mr. [Alexander P.] MacDonald [head of the Mission] did not consider it as a serious development, but gave his consent to its development in a small way as a means of local relief. The first idea being that the rugs so made and marketed should be sold for the benefit of the local church. That first summer, nine rugs were offered by the South Gouldsboro ladies. These were bought [by the public] at Bar Harbor and at Hancock Point during the August fund raising campaign. The joy of the women reduced some of them to tears when the money came in that fall. The church debt was paid, new repairs were made and the women went to work with renewed zeal to have an offering the following summer that should be more adequate.

Many of the Mission supporters were delighted with the rugs and urged a continuance of the work. Again Mrs. Kellogg was our most definite inspiration. She copied some of her oldest rugs to furnish us with good burlaps, and all thro that year showered rug catalogs, descriptions and designs upon us

The year 1924 saw a group of women working up in the shed chamber of the S. Gouldsboro parsonage. They put in long hours and agonized humbly over the quality of their work. One of their number who had lost her home by fire was trying to pay for the new home. She asked if we would be willing to sell a few rugs for her, to go toward these payments. Her request was granted, and Mrs. Peasley lengthened her own working day to assist this new sister, with designs and color. We both felt that to take time from the regular day was not exactly honorable — so under great difficulties the work went on.

Mr. [C.W.] Turner, then Missionary Pastor, was enthusiastic about the rugs and forwarded the work in every way that he could. The circle at Frenchboro were eager to begin to hook and the fall of 1924 Mrs. Peasley was sent out there to start them. The simplest designs were used and the first fabrics were terrible. Rugs were turned out that were so uneven that their topography might well be taken for a study of the rugged coast that produced them. Material was scarce, the old clothes were inadequate, even that second summer, and we had nothing with which to buy. Mrs. Peasley did all the dyeing, all the marking and much of the rag cutting even for this year.

One spring day at Frenchboro work was being finished. Mrs. Peasley was with the women in the little parsonage on the hill. A tulip was unfinished and there was not a rag in the house that would do. One of the women suggested that Mrs. Peasley's stockings would be a good color. The stockings were at once removed, washed and dried on the oven door. In a few minutes the tulip was coming into being. This was not the only instance where clothing was sacrificed to meet an emergency. In fact one very unwise missionary went home that spring quite light of personal luggage. When these rugs were taken out of the frames, some of them refused to lie flat, others showed bumps and hollows. A nervous sister burst into tears over their obvious defects. But Mrs. Peasley took them all, and friends found something to desire in them for by fall not one remained in our possession.

At S. Gouldsboro the women worked feverishly to get a good roll of rugs done by July. One long floral, larger than any other yet attempted had so vexed the women with its ability to hang on and not get finished that it had been named "Methuselah." It was a torrid day the first of July when the women met early in the forenoon for an all day session to finish the rug. Afternoon found them still at work with much to do. The sky was overcast and the day breathless. The women gasped and sweated at their work but would not give up. At three o'clock it was almost too dark to see in the little loft and a terrible tempest burst over the town. Lightening seemed to dart thro the room and thunder to be tearing the roof over their heads, but still they worked. A hand lamp was finally lighted, and two of the more courageous sisters continued to ply the steel hooks, while others looked on gasping at such temerity. The rug was finished in almost total darkness. A prayer of thanksgiving to God for his mercies in guiding them in this new work and protecting them in the tempest, closed the hooking session of 1924

The summer of 1924 we started out in the first Sunbeam, with what seemed to us quite a roll of rugs. They were quickly disposed of in Bar Harbor, S W [Southwest] Harbor, Hancock Point and Brookline [all populated by wealthy summer visitors]. Thirty rugs were disposed of and orders taken for over one hundred more. The money was turned over to the women, who were delighted. We were all overwhelmed with importance at such an enormous increase in business.

Fall brought the problem, where was burlap, new rug material and postage to come from? No body had assumed the slightest responsibility. The women were pleased with the price of the rugs, but disinclined to cooperate in regard to expenses. They seemed to feel that a beneficent Mission or the opulent missionary should produce the needed material from "somewhere." The S. Gouldsboro group and individual hookers were appealed to. They generously bought burlap and $24 worth of new material.

The Sea Coast Mission published this special brochure outlining the cottage rug industry operation. Alice M. Peasley, known as "Ma" Peasley, founded the industry and remained as superintendent until World War II, when it was disbanded so the women could take on the more immediate necessity of canning fish to help feed the armed forces.

That year the work went forward as usual. Mrs. Peasley again did the marking, dyeing and sometimes the cutting. Facility was gained, and the rugs began to be less of a labor and more of a joy. When dye was needed Mrs. Peasley bought it and when a rug had to be mailed she mailed it. Thus unwisely long hours of labor and dribbles of money were given, where a more complete cooperation on the part of the women would have been the desirable thing. However, the exciting thing was that rugs were being produced that really were desirable. The workers prospered and many friends of the Mission were glad to be able to get genuine hand done rugs. That following summer two rolls of rugs were sold and a considerable order placed for more.

Peasley spent many hours studying the dyes and the color possibilities. Several large illustrated "dye books" she created are housed in the Mission Archives. She had taken each color and subjected it to various conditions, carefully documenting each trial. She would dye a portion of yarn, leave it on a sunny windowsill for one hour, noting the shade, then two hours and so on. Peasley did this with various dyes and under various conditions, indoor and outdoors. She studied her landscape and had color recipes to match the sky at various hours of the day, or the ocean or the trees. It is a tremendous encyclopedia of samples, each one carefully annotated.

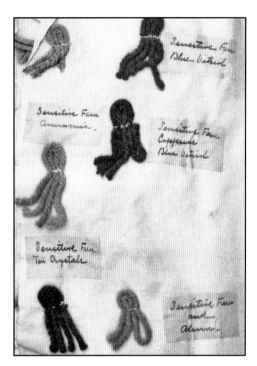

One of the many surviving dye books compiled by Peasley demonstrates the various shades of "sensitive fern" which resulted when different mordants were used.

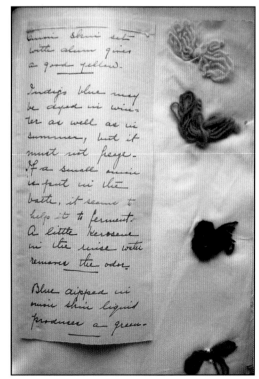

Still another page in the dye book shows Peasley experimenting with indigo. She wrote, "Indigo blue may be dyed in the winter as well as summer but it must not freeze. If a small onion is put in the bath it seems to help it ferment. A little kerosene in the rinse water removes the odor." The top sample color was created with onion skins and the lower sample shows the green shade resulting when the indigo dyed material was dipped in an onion skin bath.

Continuing Peasley's narrative:

Came fall, and Mr. Guptill.[7] The rugs did not appeal to him at first, as rugs, but as a means of advertising and of relief they did. He further saw the need of either dropping the work or of recognizing it and putting it on a more organized basis. It became a department. The rugs took a distinctive name and purchasers made checks out to this name. There was a check book and the hookers were all paid by the "Maine Sea Coast Mission Rugs." Addresses, sales, and all accounts were kept in a precious little loose leaf note book. There was really quite a bit to record.

It was at this time that a number of individuals asked for work, to better their own economic condition. Their entrance into the field caused some discussion, not all of it good natured, among the other hookers. These workers took the position that if the new worker did not join the circle, or independently work for the local church, she would be allowed no work by the Mission.

It was the feeling of the Missionary Pastor and the Sup't [Mrs. Peasley] that if there were to be financial gain from the rugs that it should go either to the hooker or to the Mission. If the local circles cared to work at stated intervals for the benefit of local work this was another matter. The independent hooker came into being, but the question still rankles in some breasts. This is an inevitable consequence of the way in which we started. To the coast mind, if a thing once was, it ever should be.

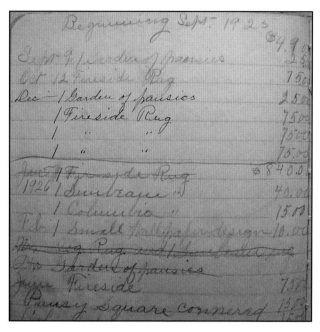

"Ma" Peasley kept meticulous records to account for every penny spent or received. Here is her book for the end of 1925 and beginning of 1926. In the fall of 1925 she sold two rugs with "garden of pansies" designs, each bringing in $25.00. In her reminiscences Mrs. Peasley mentioned how she looked at all sorts of printed material, not merely other rug catalogs, as inspiration for patterns. On Feb. 1 she recorded that a rug sold for $10.00 that had a "small wallpaper design."

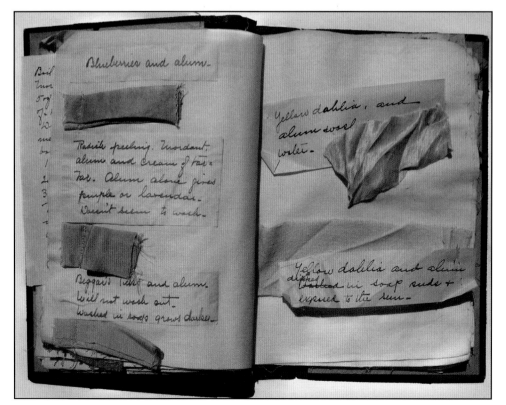

Although Peasley claimed that aniline dyes were used for dying wool, she obviously experimented to a great degree with vegetable dyes. One of her numerous dye book examples displays (top to bottom) blueberries with alum; radish peelings with alum mordant and cream of tarter with the note that alum alone gives purple or lavender; begger's tick and alum would not wash out and when washed in soda grew darker. On the right page, yellow dalia and alum washed in water; and yellow dalia and alum dipped in soap suds and exposed to the sun.

An unidentified island woman relaxes at her home, surrounded by at least three of her newly finished hooked rugs. It is also an interesting study of a Maine coastal home interior of the period.

This year produced more rugs than ever, and by winter there were nearly $800 worth on hand, with prospect of many more by summer. We began to wonder how we would market so many. True, the popularity of the hook rug was still growing, but we had a feeling that overnight the wind might change. That winter Mrs. Leonard Kellogg again came to our rescue. Sup't and rugs were invited to be guests of hers in New York for fifteen days. We went and found the time marvelously well organized. There was an engagement each day to meet some representative group. The way was made to show the work to dealers and finally at a reception and exhibition in her home over $500 worth of the rugs were sold.

Some dealers were interested, notably Mr. Hall, buyer for Altman.[8] He pronounced the rugs the most beautiful moderns that he had seen. He will take rugs from us at any time. The reason that we have never released to him is that the firm pay for rugs only a fraction of the selling price, which does not seem to us to be fair to the hooker.

The Needle and Bobbin Club were also willing to give our rugs space, but the expense of releasing in their shop was prohibitive. It was reassuring, however, to have them pronounce our work superior to any other they had seen. A few decorators saw and discussed the rugs. It was interesting to note that the discussion centered in the very oldest reproductions that we offered, or in the patterns that the sup't herself had put together. [Again, this is totally in keeping with the newfound admiration for the primitive and folk art craze] On the whole the trip was very reassuring.

The summer of 1927 was a most prosperous one. Nearly every rug offered was sold, and generous orders taken. Two groups and twenty individual hookers were working and the sup't was gaining skill in colors and design. She still did practically all the dyeing and made all the color schemes that went out to be done. This work was carried on in her own kitchen, with ordinary kitchen paraphernalia. For days and weeks at a time the air of the house was humid and acrid with dye and mordents. Water trickled on the floor and rags were everywhere. Rooms that should have been restful and placid were heaped with colors and old clothing. The odor of burlap became the atmosphere in which we all lived. At one time four rooms were given up to the stock, hooking and dyeing. It was impossible to achieve order or cleanliness. Still, there was great compensation. Women were being helped and occasionally a rug would come forth that was rewarding.

The following winter an unwise and over tired Sup't started for her vacation with books, correspondence and records, planning to catch up with her work and have things in perfect order when she returned in the spring. Fate willed otherwise. While she was on a short trip to Portland a fire wiped out the building and all her precious belongings. Not until she arrived back at Bar Harbor and reached out to take in her hand, that little book, her other self, did she realize that it was gone. The shock of this loss was decidedly upsetting. It wiped out all the tangible evidence of our beginnings.

The spring work was hard. Addresses were lost, orders hard to place and record of the individual hookers had to be made up from memory, or from their own word. That summer, in the midst of our most happy and successful campaign, a germ, more unkind than the fire laid the Sup't low. Everything stopped, and after recovering from the first phase of the malady, she had to creep home defeated, only to suffer relapse and complete disorganization. — The first work done was to sit up in bed, with perspiration pouring in streams down the face and a heart pounding at 130, and sort colors for a new rug.

At this time a beautiful fruit design that my daughter and I had worked on for weeks, was completed and its hooking begun. Hookers came silently in thro the door of the room and hung new rugs upon the wall for refreshment of the struggling spirit. Their love and devotion was a wonderful factor in recovery. The work, too, was a blessing, something materially definite and physically tiring to return to. But that next summer showed the work still much at loose ends. The following year work was again supervised and sent out. But it was a great effort, there was always a mountain ahead that could not quite be climbed. Records were poorly kept.

In 1929 we all began to find ourselves and do much better in every way. There were about thirty women at work. Some of the older hookers had dropped out and younger ones were beginning. This made more labor to instruct them, but kept us appreciative of the growth of the first hookers who remained to us. This summer we sold nearly every rug and found several dealers who would be glad to handle our rugs. This fall we found the work much less confusing, though still arduous and an insatiable time eater.

One of the S. Gouldsboro group, Mrs. Hilda Hammond, became our pattern maker. She works carefully and methodically, and will also receive and acknowledge rugs while the Sup't is away. A few of the women can be trusted with dyeing, and many have become not only proficient mechanically, but are developing a vision and imagination. We hope that the summer of 1930 will see us with the largest and most beautiful collection of rugs ever yet offered to our friends."

[Peasley's personal record book for 1929 cites several rugs including one very large rug which sold for $120.00; one Thatch Cottage, $50.00; one scroll and cacti-like conch shell; one autumn landscape with birches; and two small rugs of the sloop "Nancy Lee." Sales totaled $427.00 that year.[9]]

Record of Hookers:
South Gouldsboro, Circle of ten members — Lucy Cook, Mary R. Bunker, Hilda Hammond, Belle Norris, Etoile Earnst, Florence Hamond, Nettie Bunker, Annie Bunker, Christine Cook; Frenchboro Circle — Lyda Higgins, Tony Teel, Vera Van Norden, Mrs. Elizabeth Ross, Vera Dalzell, Lydia Dalzell, Sadie Lunt, Annie Lunt, Ella Lunt, Sarah Rice, Flora Rice, Mrs. Perkins, Mrs. Charles Wallace; McKinley [Circle] — Mrs. Lizzie Thurlow and youngest daughter work together, Mrs. Violet Davis; Loudville [Circle] — Mrs. Willard Carter; Little Deer Isle [Circle] — Mrs. Hattie Sawyer, Mrs. William Haskell, Mrs. Elsie Hendrick.

The amount of work produced by these people is at all times uncertain. If the mood is upon them and they are well they produce a reasonable amount. . . . it is perhaps an order which they took knowing that it should be delivered at a given time, weighs not an ounce with them. They are as calm as the sea and the tides, and as easy to impress.

A few have from the first been loyal to the department, and would not think of disposing of work elsewhere. Others have had to acquire loyalty, while still others are forced to be loyal by the fact that no other market pays them as well. Many of the newer hookers are extremely grateful for the work and are free to acknowledge that their work is only a part of the effort needed to produce the rug. Others imply to those who examine their work that is wholly the child of their own artistic gifts.

Hookers:
The list of hookers is not the original group that began with us. Only ten of them were with us at the beginning. Since then a few new hookers have come to us, making a small contribution, gaining skill, receiving instruction, and have gone their way, for various reasons. New ones have come in, making it necessary for each year to spend time with their initial instruction.

We have had hookers come to us who never produced more than two or three rugs. The greatest single achievement is one hooker who has hooked 140 rugs to date.

The department has never reached an output large enough to pay financial dividends to the Mission. This could hardly be expected of an industry lacking the equipment or place to take advantage of its work, lacking at all times a bulk of material from which to work, and capital sufficient to pay hookers when work comes in. Since the first days it has hung on by its teeth as it were. . . .

Peasley assembled an album of photographs of the various rug designs, annotated with a brief description and price. An interested customer could browse the album and select a rug of their choice. The cows was priced at $15.00 and the bird center with braided edge was priced at $18.00

"Ma" Peasley is seen aboard the *Sunbeam* displaying a hooked rug with two brightly plumaged birds (likely Blue Jays) perched on an ocean-side branch. Among many other obligations, the *Sunbeam* was the marine transportation facility not only for the Mission's pastor, but also for the delivery of hooking materials and the retrieval of the completed rugs.

To the Mission it has brought attention enough to pay very much indeed as a means of advertising.

Spiritually its harvest has been the richest. It has welded a group of women together drawn by comradeship of a common interest and labor. It has brought fulfillment to many who had almost ceased to hope that their individual lives might be productive of good and of beauty. It has quickened imagination, opened blind eyes to the beauty that lies around us, given a sense of line and color, and developed loyalties. . . .

The financial help to the hookers has brought comfort and safety in almost every instance. It has paid mortgages, repaired buildings and paid hospital bills, as well as adding a margin of safety and comfort to ordinary living.

taken years to educate a larger body of people in appreciation of the rug and its value.

In the first years the new rug had to compete with a mass of old rugs picked up all over the country and Canada and sold for as much or less than we were obliged to get for our rugs. This supply is almost exhausted. Its diminishing bulk is from time to time replenished from artificially antiqued hand made rugs and from machine made from both homes and factories.

But the discerning eye can often detect the difference, and the thinking customer knows that the genuine stock must be nearly gone. The only remaining way to get a hand hooked rug of beauty and desirability is to buy it from some reliable source. This has helped our rugs to at last come into their own.

Many dealers and decorators who were at first in favor of using only the rug softened by time are now frankly saying that the new hand hooked rug is of equal value with the old and will, of course, outlive it by many years. Dealers are also telling our customers that the rug they now buy of us will be much more valuable ten years from now and so it is a good investment.

Future of the industry:

From present indications it would seem that the industry is on a firmer foundation than when it was started and that its commercial future is more or less assured.

Prognosis:

The growing popularity of the hook[ed] rug has been a surprise. When the work was started it was thought to be a fad of perhaps two or three years. Double that time has passed and the rug [industry] is stronger in popularity than ever

From the first a few lovers of old New England things have appreciated the hand hook[ed] rug, such as we produce. [They have] realized the vast amount of labor necessary to finish the rug and so have understood why the price must be so high. Others did not understand and it has

Peasley's picture rests on one of the many work books she compiled, this one recording the rugs sold in 1929 with total sales amounting to $427.00. One large landscape rug sold for $120.00 and one cottage and garden pattern for $50.00. The remaining rugs sold for between $15.00 and $22.00.

One thing that is a source of anxiety is the fact that fewer bags of old material come to us than at first. [The advent of the Great Depression may have contributed to this lack.] So many are saving used material and making a rug or two for themselves. Then, too, the business as it increases calls for more material. This makes it imperative that we should buy material in larger quantities in the season previous to their being needed. The state of business has led some manufacturers to decide to sell no material. Others will sell only in quantities larger than we can handle. We are thus driven to buy thro brokers and at rapidly advancing prices. This adds materially to the cost of producing the rugs.

Burlaps and their marking:

It is hard to get a burlap with a close, even weave and a strong thread. The life of the rug depends absolutely upon the quality of the foundation used. We have bought in small quantities from year to year, getting the best we could find, but seldom finding the ideal foundation. This year we found that R. H. Burnham of Ipswich [Massachusetts] has both domestic and imported burlap in desirable grades. He generously offered to give us goods from whatever he has in stock at factory prices. We would have to buy in 200 yd lots, but the reduction in price would be at least 15¢ on the yard. We should have this amount on hand anyway if we are to continue our work, so that is no drawback. The only obstacle is to get money enough at one time to pay for the goods.

Most of our rugs are originals or reproductions from very old rugs, therefore we cannot use commercial burlaps. [This obviously refers to the commercially stamped patterns which, if used, would negate the claim of an "original" design.]

Some very bold or large patterns may be stenciled, but we have found that the average pattern gains in delicacy and beauty if done by hand. The process is very hard and very wearing, but if persisted in a rug of greater beauty is the result. We think it wise to continue this practice for a time at least adding, perhaps a few stencils to relieve the tedium of the rug marking.

Last winter a 45 ft. rug was ordered by a customer. It was to be a floral, tied in by a scroll. Both the Sup't and Mrs. Hammond worked 4 days making the pattern, transferring it to cloth, for a permanent record, and finally to the burlap to be hooked. The result was a rug of remarkable beauty and diversity of design. Not all burlaps take this amount of time, but all of them take enough time. It is not a process to be hurried.

Dyeing the rags:

Aniline dyes have been used with the simplest mordents, salt and vinegar. A few vegetable colors are used, like the clear yellow obtained from the onionskin. Vegetable dyes, while permanent, are more sharp and crude than the other. Their use is not to be recommended.

A great part of the coloring is still done by the sup't. This is desirable for many reasons. Where dyeing is done by individuals full instructions are always sent out. The worker is asked to let the goods boil at least 30 minutes and in some colors a full hour. To let the goods cool in the dye bath before removing to the first rinse. We can never be sure these instructions are carried out. If they are not the colors will soften too much and the rug will lose in value. On the other hand if more hookers were doing their dyeing we might get a desirable range of colors from the experiments of several people.

We are hampered in this work by lack of place and equipment. If the work is to continue we would feel more satisfied if we could buy our dyes in commercial blocks of pure color and use chemical mordents for permanency. This would necessitate the purchase of a copper boiler and allowing time for initial experiments to get formulas with the new mordents. The integrity of our color is a source of anxiety at present.

Rug Headquarters:

The finished rugs are first inspected and listed by the Sup't then sent to 24 Ledgelawn Ave. [then the Mission's headquarters in Bar Harbor] to be kept until sale time. Old garments and new stock is sent there and collected from time to time for the work. Burlap patterns, and some stock is at the Hammond Farm, South Gouldsboro, since they needs must be somewhere, and Mrs. Hammond assists in pattern making. Some stock is stored in a room loaned by Mrs. Nettie Bunker. Some stock has at times been left at outer stations [i.e., on the islands] where there were a number of hookers but this is not wise.

The little room at Mrs. Hammond's is needed for other purposes, and after a lot of work has been put up, the things have to be packed and stored until next time. This causes a great deal of futile labor and confusion as well. It is almost impossible to visualize future work without a place in which the stock is spread where one may see. The nervous strain and unhappiness caused by this disarrangement is considerable. It is doubtful if there can be much expansion of the business without a central place for keeping the property of the department.

There has been this advantage in mobility. Much of the heavy work and tedious preparation has been done in all parts of the coast while the sup't made social and spiritual contact with the group in that place. But the getting ready to go and the getting ready to come are like moving mountains of rags. It becomes after a time, almost an impossibility.

What the Supervisor Does:

In the general work of the Mission she has always tried to give a full year's work, aside from the rug work. In a sense this cannot be done. In another it can — the rugs have ever been the introduction to pastoral work — the material interpretation of spiritual things — a ministry in the name of the Master.

As general preparation for the work she remains at all times 'rug minded.' Sunset and sunrise alike yield their colors to study. Sea and sky as they ever change but always complement each other are fascinating in the range of exquisite color that they present. The Bar Harbor hills, whether seen from Gouldsboro or from the far off, lonely little parsonage at Frenchboro are at times the abiding place of all that is witching in nature. At other times they show forth a majesty that tells of the presence of God. Still again, especially in spring fairies and leprecorns [sic] inhabit them.

While in the fall the satyrs clothe them and then dance in their mysterious hollows. They challenge and baffle, but inspire. Evenings are given to poring over magazines, books and art gallery catalogs, wherever description or plates of rugs are found. Not only hook rugs but Orientals and Chinese rugs are studied. The leading plumbing firms in this country have kindly sent us glorious color plates of their latest offerings, and good wall paper people have done the same.

Wherever a rug is found it is studied. A large album, bristling with clippings shows hundreds of interiors and rugs. A drawer in the stock room is full of bits of choice color and scraps of lovely cretonne.

Whenever opportunity has offered we have visited other rug makers and rug menders, to see them at work. Beside the offerings of the Anderson Gallery in New York we keep in close touch with the stock of Altman, Wanamaker and Sloane in New York. In Boston, Paines, Jordan Marsh and R. H. White, at Ipswich, Mr. Burnham's interesting ménage. In Maine the Fuller Cobb-Davis stock, Warren Weston Creamer of Waldoboro and the Southern Mountain work wherever we find it. Mrs. Chilcott of Bangor is at all times in touch with the New York market and thro her kindness we learn much.[10]

New patterns or material for assembling new patterns are worked up in spare? time and so become rugs. She assists in the burlap marking and staining,

does the major part of all the coloring, decides on the color scheme or range for nearly every rug, puts material together, doing it up and getting it shipped, instructs new workers, guides experienced workers and inspects every rug, measures the rug and makes its record, has it marked, priced and tagged and sent to Headquarters ready for disposal, supervises the selling, attends to the correspondence and finally, weeps over a few tragedies and rejoices with great joy when a beautiful rug comes home.

To accomplish this decisions must be instant and almost the speed of a machine maintained to get such a bulk of work out in the time given to the work.

Methods of release:

Our output is small. If the industry continues it will probably remain comparatively small for the reason that it is a cottage industry. Much time is needed for instructing new hookers. The new hooker requires from three to six years to gain freedom and develop imagination, and the work is done entirely by hand. To radically change these methods might endanger the characteristic charm of the product, which is not desirable. The world is full of stock pattern rugs and rugs made by machine, enough for all who want this type of rug.

For the few who want the individual rug, produced by hand and as it were under special inspiration, the Maine Sea Coast Mission Rug will continue to appeal. These methods will never be able to produce a cheap rug, in price, for they are time and energy consuming. To be fair to the hooker and to the Mission the price must be the maximum or nearly the maximum in the rug market. Some of our best customers think the price very reasonable for the type of work offered. Given a small stock the release had better remain very exclusive.

Up to the present time the only really important release has been at our summer meetings and from the Sunbeam in August. A few sales are made from the Mission House.

Sales were made last year from the following places: Bar Harbor, Annual Meeting; S W Harbor at the Hotels Claremont and Dirigo; Sunset; Castine; Sargentville; Herricks; Haven; New Harbor; Christmas Cove (Holly Inn); Heron Island; Seal Harbor; Islesford; Hancock Point; Boothbay Harbor.[11] To these a few other places might be added provided the sales could be under the patronage of some well known club or individual.

It might be well to leave a small, representative collection at Islesford for the summer and at

Quite possibly the greatest rug produced by the Mission shows this stark, isolated house at West Quoddy Head. Its eloquent simplicity defines the true essence of isolation and the loneliness of island life in the 1920s and 1930s. The solitary dwelling looks out over an ocean endlessly expanding until it finally merges with the sky. There is no sign of life, no trees, no boats, no grass, merely total isolation. Referred to at the Mission as the "Sigma Kappa Rug," it was donated by Mrs. Mary Emerson Boudreau of Ocean Point whose grandmother was one of the founders of the sorority at Colby College in Waterville, Maine, in1874. Wool on burlap, 20" x 27".

Hancock Point, providing the use of the library could be obtained for this purpose. The Labie Shop at Boothbay Harbor and the Loomcraft at Bar Harbor have asked to handle our rugs and we would recommend that they be allowed to do so.

The Loomcraft is handling them at Longmeadow, Mass., during the year. Here they are in good surroundings and are slowly gaining ground. I doubt the advisability of allowing more than one dealer in a state handling the rugs, except on the coast of Maine in summer. Even then we will probably continue to dispose of the larger portion of the stock ourselves.

Once the industry was well established, Peasley provided a further history through the Mission's annual reports:

Report for 1925:[12]

This year 25 women from different parts of the coast worked during their spare time on rugs. In nearly all cases, designs, color scheme and material were furnished by the missionary [Mrs. Peasley]. The quality of the work and the artistic value of the rugs is ahead of that done last year.

The demand for the rugs still exceeds the supply.

This is a valuable form of relief work as it enables these women to help themselves. Three of the women working at present are using the money from their rugs to pay for improvements in their homes, making them more liveable.

If the work is to be continued and developed, time should be allowed a worker for adequate supervision. Also used material in quantity will be needed. Realized from sale last summer— $225.00; Sales during year — $875.00; On hand for summer sale — $1100.00 for a total of $2,200.00.

1926 Report:

The story of the rug industry the past year is quickly told but it is the summer of no little effort and thought on the part of the superintendent of this department of our work. In addition to many other cares and responsibilities, she has been indefatigable in her pursuit of the ideas of manufacture and sale and devoted to the work with her hookers. Some rugs of exceptional value have been produced and several women have added materially to the family purse. There has been, however, no great advance over last year in the amount of business and the number of workers has decreased rather than increased.

As a department of our work, this industry is a problem to be carefully studied. Market conditions are capricious and unstable. Rugs from other sections are to be had under conditions unfavorable to our competition, if there is anything to be left for the workers. Material of the right sort is difficult to obtain at prices which will allow the work to be remunerative. Except in very rare cases, those who do the work require the most careful superintendence and constant attention.

For the year ending 31st, 1926, sales have been amounting to $2,891 and there has been paid the workers a total of $2,700. There are now on hand for the summer sale a few rugs of exceptional value and some 50 others not so remarkable but worthwhile.

1927 Report:

Some 20 individual hookers and 2 organizations of women in the parish have been occupied this season producing the hooked rugs which are beginning to make a name for us. For the most part the work is remarkable for taste in design and excellence of workmanship. Each year, one or two really distinguished rugs are produced and the rugs of this year are even more remarkable than in the past.

Under the supervision of Mrs. A. M. Peasley the Mission is making a real contribution to the lives of these women who work, as well as helping them to make a better living. It calls for much labor on the part of the Superintendent of the industry and from year to year drains a bit on the Mission financially but it is worthwhile.

1928 Report:

Owing to the severe and continued illness of the Superintendent of this department very little has been accomplished the past year. Four of the hookers, including our most skilled workers, have also been unable to do anything for the same reason.

Notwithstanding this handicap, however, with some of the rugs left over from last year and a few choice rugs coming in, we shall have a very respectable offering by summertime. Those who own our rugs come back for more, and everywhere they are shown there is a special interest in all the work of the Mission.

Already plans are in the making for a busy fall and winter with new and interesting designs which give promise of the continuance of this work on the plane of excellence people have learned to expect from us.

The cooperation and interest of our friends is appreciated not only for the purchase of the rugs but that many of them think to gather material and old garments which they forward for our use in this department. Among many interesting letters received by the Superintendent was one from a Washington lady who said that she was collecting old stockings etc. for our rugs. "I am a Sigma mother," she said, "and it is a joy to me to have some part in the work which means so much to my daughter and her friends."

[The Maine Sea Coast Mission was selected as the national philanthropy project for the Sigma Kappa Sorority during its 1920 convention to honor the five Maine girls who founded the Sorority at Colby College in Waterville, Maine, in 1874.]

1929 Report

Includes a summation of the rug industry:

When the rug industry began, its present significance would not have been anticipated. It is not that large numbers have been employed — only 29 hookers have been active the past year. The output has not been amazingly large. It has, however, made a real contribution to the lives of the workers and through them to the communities in which they live.

The output this year is smaller than usual but the work is undoubtedly the best ever produced.

Further progress is to be seen, also, in the fact that some of the younger women have begun to hook and the men are increasingly interested.

An interesting folder has been prepared telling about this industry and with sales sheets is available for those who inquire at the Mission House. [13] The market is flooded with hooked rugs but we are assured by those who are informed, that Maine Sea Coast Mission Rugs equal or surpass any that they have seen. In material, workmanship and frequently in beauty and design they are unequalled.

The money that the hookers earn is no inconsiderable matter but there is added a new interest in life — the awakening of a love of beauty and not infrequently the life of the spirit — which becomes a by-product of the work.

1930 Report:

The Rug Industry provides work for some 30 individuals in five communities. The workers have increased steadily in skill, and the output, while not large, is of high quality. This year there will be on sale some pieces of exceptional worth.

This department has problems of organization, training of workers, providing raw material and the supervision necessary to secure the best results. The industry is of great value economically and socially.

Reports for 1929-1930:

This [year] shows a credit in materials and rugs to the dep't of $780, and to this as a part of the harvest from the materials bought, the rugs that will be coming in during the next 3 months. Of these rugs there should be 60 and there may be 100. It is hard to tell for there is no way of forecasting what the hooker will do. They are entirely independent and temperamental. Should at least 50 more come in it should give us a summer stock of over one thousand dollars more in value than we had last year.

We have over 300 pounds of goods on which to begin a new batch of work. We still have material on hand for making quite a few burlaps, but will soon need new burlap. If we order in a 200 yd lot we will be able to get this at manufacturer's price which will be a great saving.

A part of the cost of pattern making this year went into the permanent duplicate cloth patterns which we are preparing. One set is to be at headquarters and the other in the hands of the pattern maker. This will help to insure against the loss of original patterns by fire.

The Mission ship, the *Sunbeam,* still cruises the islands and headlands along the Maine coast ministering to the religious and social needs of isolated residents. There have been a series of vessels with the same name. In this rug it is the *Sunbeam II,* hooked by Henrietta Ames of Matinicus Island and donated to the Mission by the Rev. Neal Dousfield. Wool on burlap, 14" x 18".

Some dyeing should be done under the supervision of the sup't. this spring in order to have work ready early in the fall, so that hookers will not have to wait. In this way the output can be increased. Again some dyeing could be done early in fall to obviate dyeing in winter. This is not only hard on the one who does the work, but the extreme cold weather is not good for the colors.

This report carries a financial statement from May 1, 1929 to April 15, 1930:

Rugs sold	$2240.20
Paid hookers	58.00
Labor marking and coloring burlap and cloth patterns	65.50
Stamped patterns purchased	11.60
Carbon for tracing large patterns	7.54
Sheeting for making permanent patterns	6.35
Ink, stylus and burlap colors	11.44
Dyes and Mordents	24.22
Trade markers for rugs	2.40
Films and prints of new rugs	3.53
Postage and parcels post	26.81
Express	13.71
Tags, tying, office supplies and record book	6.71
Phone, taxi and trucking	2.95
Yarn, wool and other materials to hook	242.61
Total	$2,341.87

Stock on hand:
Cloth and wool for hooking $126.40
Patterns, dyes etc 81.00
Goods now assigned to hookers 199.00
Dyes 3.65
Burlaps 63.05
Goods to hook 132.40
Rugs out on memo 815.50
Rugs on hand 1134.00
Total $2355.90

Owed by the department:
Owed hookers on rugs
　　now coming in 680.39
Hilda Hammond –
　　work on patterns 33.39
Express unpaid 13.63
Dyes 7.00
Estelle Shoppe, white goods 124.90
Thomas and Hall, brokers,
　　for goods 35.30
Insurance 9.00
A. M. Peasley for cash
　　paid on small bills 72.46
Mission Loan unpaid 500.00
Total $1475.07

1931 Report:

Begins to show the strain caused by the Great Depression:

The Rug Industry has not been up to normal this last year. Sales were less than usual and the total paid the hookers has not been as large. For various reasons not so many have been employed, and the stock will be smaller this season. The high standards to which we have committed ourselves are being maintained and those employed find in the industry profit both economically and socially.

1932 Report:

Activity in this department has been limited by the fact that sales were few last summer. Many were eager for work but the market did not warrant a large output this year. Nearly all orders were cancelled and pay has been slow. The stock on hand contains little new work, but is said to be unusually desirable.

1933 Report:

Contains no mention of the Rug Industry.

1934 Report:

HOME INDUSTRIAL ARTS
Receives encouragement and active promotion as opportunity affords and our Rug Industry continues although haltingly on account of the condition of the market.

1938 Report:

Industrial and other social problems are faced constructively. A small rug industry and the manufacture of souvenirs receive encouragement and outlets. The staff is alert to cooperate in any venture which promises the development of talent and self.

The 1929 brochure published by the Mission, reprinted below, outlined the industry at the time the Rev. Orville J. Guptill was the missionary pastor and Peasley was superintendent of the Rug Industry.[14]

MAINE SEA COAST MISSION RUGS is an enterprise fostered by the Maine Sea Coast Missionary Society for the welfare of the women of the islands and isolated communities where The Sunbeam cruises. In workmanship, originality and beauty of design and durability of fabric, the rugs made under the auspices of the Mission are unsurpassed. A member of the staff, herself a coast woman, supervises the work watching every process and holding the standards high.
THE MATERIAL FROM WHICH THE RUGS ARE MADE comes from many sources. Much of it is new wool, direct from the factory. Friends of the Mission send discarded garments, silk stockings, old blankets and draperies of good or soft silk. The women themselves add their own small contribution.
From a pile of rags on the floor to the wonderful completed rug is a long process many of the steps of which are little realized by the uninitiated. The Director of the industry not only directs but has her fingers in things at every step of the way. The rags are sorted for color, quality of material and adaptability to the character of the rug. There is experimentation with dyes and dyeing, washing, boiling and drying. The pains taken in this particular makes a story by itself since fidelity to fact is ruthlessly demanded and not only must the color be true to the tree that is copied but true to the hour of the day.
The burlap is marked with the design and laced tight into a frame and the hooking begins but the experimentation is not done. And finally

the rug out of the frame, hemmed and finished passes a rigorous inspection before the trade mark MAINE SEA COAST MISSION RUG is sewed beneath the border, and it is marked for sale. The enterprise brings no profit to the Mission. It is not a money-making scheme. And while there is realized by the women a very comfortable sum of money each year, for them, also, it is not only a commercial venture but a spiritual experience as well.

All of the industry's rugs had a sewn-on label on the reverse identifying it as a Sea Coast Mission product.

Maine Sea Coast Mission Rugs are to be obtained from the headquarters of the mission:

The Mission House, 24 Ledgelawn Avenue, Bar Harbor, Maine; but are shown in the summer time at the summer colonies where the Sunbeam and the Missionary Pastor are welcomed to present the work of the Mission.

Officers: Rev. Henry Van Dyke, D.D., President; Rev. W. J. Houlton, D.D., Vice-president; Rev. J. Homer Nelson, secretary; Mr. Thomas Searles, Treasurer.

A listing of the designs and prices includes:

15" chair seat. Rose floral on tan ground. Shaded	$4.00
15" Floral mats. Rose wreath on cream ground	3.00
16" mat or chair seat. Black duck on sky ground	5.00
Black ducks, sea, and Bar Harbor Hills. 22x37"	15.00
Owl's Head entrance to Rockland Harbor. 27x38"	20.00
Autumn tapestry. Birch trees touched by frost	30.00
Cottage and floral garden. Choice. 33x55"	65.00
Tapestry. Meadow, marsh, hills and wild birds. 30x50"	60.00
2 horses at drinking trough. Primitive. 27x38"	15.00
Old floral on khaki ground. Primitive. 33x33"	18.00
Single floral spray on black ground. 33x33"	12.00
Floral with wild flower center on black. 26x36"	30.00
Parrot on green branch. Acorn border on tan. 24x35"	15.00
Welcome door mat. Rose floral on golden tan ground	12.00
Buffalo in pasture. Primitive. 24x36"	15.00
Red rose wreath in low relief on tan ground. 27x37"	25.00
Large shaded leaf wreath on soft red ground. 24x38	15.00
Oblong door mat. Browns with red and green florals	10.00
Brown dog on soft background. 4 ft. by 26" Quaint	20.00
Basket of pink roses on tan ground 20x36"	15.00
Small oblong door mat in browns	8.00
Carpet strip, patchwork pattern 3 ft. by 6 ft.	35.00
Carpet strip. Concentric circles with rose buds	25.00
Geometric design. Natural tints, like old carpet. 3 ft. by 4 ft.	12.00
Dust brown carpet strip. Autumn leaves. 3 by 6 ft.	25.00

In 1941, the year which saw the outbreak of World War II, Peasley was listed as 'Dean of the Staff." She continued in this role until 1956, when she was listed as "retired."[15]

Reminiscing several years after her retirement, Peasley summed up her impressions of the industry:[16]

The development of the rug industry was an effort to help the coast woman to help herself, using a medium with which she was already familiar and could develop in her own home. Beside her kitchen fire she could watch the dinner cook while she made a ship picture in rags.

All the sturdy coast character, all their sensitiveness to beauty came to life in this work and for some years these rugs were unique and precious possessions to those who were fortunate enough to have one.

Patterns were either traditional or original. Usually what she could see from her kitchen window was produced in rags. As the work developed it became evident that the financial return was secondary to the effect upon the hooker.

One woman stood in her doorway bidding me goodbye after a happy afternoon spent in rug planning. "You know," she said with a slow smile, "I never thought I'd live to see the day when I could do something somebody else would really want and value." Selenda and I were visiting in her back yard. She had done some lovely rugs for us the past winter and I was suggesting that they would be very interesting if instead of the unvarying green she had been using she should really reproduce her own back yard. 'There's a deep shadow under the pine tree and the path from your door is really a soft greenish tan—."

She looked in silence for a long time and then said, "Well, I reckon this is the first time I ever saw my own back yard. A body can't hook what she doesn't see."

The coming of the great war and the rush to get fish canned for the armed forces made it impossible for them to carry on, but in many an attic, the rag bag is still kept in hope that with peace will come leisure and she can again make lovely island pictures from that bag of rags plus her ability to see her own back yard.

A large, wide-eyed squirrel hesitates quizzically and stares at the viewer as it is about to climb a young tree in the yard of what appears to be a commercial or farm building. This rug is in keeping with Peasley's admonition to "hook what you see." Wool on burlap, 29" x 38".

One of the most charming of the primitive designs shows two horses about to drink from a large pail of water. Arching branches frame the scene. A similar Mission design depicts two cows eating or drinking from a central tub. Only one branch arches over the cow to the left. This rug was priced at $15.00. Wool on burlap, 26.50" x 38.75". *Sawtelle Collections and Research Center.*

Recently found in a private collection, a water scene shows ducks taking off from a lake fronted with realistic cat-o-nine tails. The realism is lost, however, when looking at the quaintly shaped mountain in the background. There is no label on the rug but the scene and colors are typical of a Mission rug, several of which featured ducks and geese. Wool on burlap, 38.50" x 72". *Courtesy Beverly BaRoss.*

Forest scenes with birds were popular subjects for the hookers. Partridge feed here among a bower of trees and wildflowers. Due to the erosion of time, it is difficult to make it out, but a deer peers out from behind the central tree. The dramatic sky and the tree colors give a hint of autumn. Wool on burlap, 30" x 53".

Peasley provided a rough, sketched outline for this rug and suggested that the hooker add the newborn calf in her pasture, and it was appropriately done. The next year it was suggested she add something new. Peasley was somewhat taken aback and embarrassed by the "inappropriate" buffalo that appeared. So she hid it deep in a pile of rugs being offered for sale. As one would expect, it turned out to be the first one sold and went on to become one of the most popular rug designs the Mission carried. It was hooked in at least three versions, the plain buffalo, this one with an added fence, and the third in a horizontal format. The rug originally sold for $15.00. Wool on burlap, 24" x 34".

Birch trees and bushes covered with frost hint at the approaching chill of winter in this autumn scene. The perspective here is especially good with the smaller tree suggesting distance and drawing the viewer inward toward the snow-capped mountains. In Peasley's price list this rug was called "Autumn Tapestry" and sold for $30.00. Wool on burlap, 30" x 39".

This extremely large rug is another in the series of landscape designs with birds or animals. At the right a group of energetic ducks splash in the pond, flap their wings and attempt to fly away. A densely wooded area at the left leads the eye to a mountain range and a bright blue sky with fleecy clouds. A large rug such as this was termed a "tapestry" by Mrs. Peasley. This design was available for $60.00. Wool on burlap, 30" x 50".

Seagulls were and are a common sight along the Maine coast. Termed in the Mission's rug catalog to be "A notable picture rug," it is a well constructed design with one gull devouring a fish while the other suggests a challenge is about to begin. The three versions illustrated here are a good indication of what happens to aniline dyes over time. They have faded to the point where the design is virtually invisible. To better appreciate the artistic value of the pattern, the black and white copy was taken from the original catalog. The two color illustrations show the faded front and also the reverse where the true, original colors are more identifiable. Wool on burlap, 20.25" x 26".

No example of this rug has been found, but it was advertised for sale in the rug catalog of the 1920s as a "typical rug of quaint design." The scale of the birds and animals is very naïve and folksy, the mule is totally dwarfed by the birds and chickens.

One of the most appropriate and more sophisticated designs by the Mission is that of a church. It is a free interpretation of the famous Congregational Church of 1846 in Ellsworth, designed by the master builder, Thomas M. Lord (1806-1880). It is a prominent Downeast landmark and still stands today in the town center.

The one-way design characterizes this rug out of the catalog as a hearth rug, with elaborate scroll designs at the top, the rug anchored at the lower edge with a much more compact scroll.

The floral design is derivative of other rugs of the period. The scroll is often referred to as "The Waldoboro Scroll," but it is also found in E. S. Frost & Company patterns. For example, see Frost Nos. 40, 47 and 44, especially the latter which is very close to this rug except for minor changes in the central medallion.

Although it has suffered damage, this rug has great charm with the parenting chicken and rooster attentively overseeing the two new additions to their family. The rug is beautifully framed with a vibrant and dramatic swag border. Wool on burlap, 28.50" x 40". *Sawtelle Collections and Research Center.*

An example of Yankee thrift. A damaged or otherwise unusable Sea Coast Mission rug has been cut up and used to turn a weighty object into a charming "make-do". The result is a perfectly serviceable doorstop. *Cyr Auction.*

Chapter XII
Marguerite Zorach

Contemporaneous with the activities surrounding the development of The Arts and Crafts-inspired cottage industries at the beginning of the twentieth century was the growing realization among those in the art world — notably painters and sculptors — that hooked rugs meshed into a philosophy that emphasized a purity and even simplicity of expression as the noblest manifestation of one's talents.

During this period, the superlative hooked rug was presided over by professional "designers" geared to the complementary ambience of the Mission Style furniture of Gustav Stickley, the "Prairie School" of Frank Lloyd Wright, and the bungalow style of houses popularized by Greene and Greene. Society was through with the "fussiness" of the Victorian era with all of its frills and tassels. In the continuing evolution of the lowly hooked rug, several of America's significant artists would seek a more honorable role for the rug by raising it to the level of a "fine" art.

One of a number of influential and key figures in the linkage of fine art with rug hooking was Marguerite (Thompson) Zorach (1887-1968), a pioneering American modernist artist, who would develop a close relationship with Maine.

At the start of the new century she was just one of numerous American artists traveling to France to imbibe the many currents affecting the French art world. The attraction was not only the quality and number of art schools, but the many artists working independently seeking new modes of expression, which would eventually include Marguerite's hooked rugs and embroidered tapestries. It was a time of revolt against the straitlaced, restrictive, uninspired art of the Salons and Academies of the late nineteenth century that "controlled" the art world and dictated what people should see. As has been said, "There was something for everyone, enough to prove any conceivable artist's point of view, and the artist found what he [and she] was prepared to find."[1]

France offered Marguerite Thompson a more liberating situation than that under which she had grown up in California. It allowed her to be "modern." At a time when women were fighting for the right to vote, to discard the restrictive clothing of their mothers, and, in general, to assert themselves in society, those who sought to become artists felt they could and should be as *au courant* as any male artist.[2]

When she arrived in Europe the continent was still very much influenced by Art Nouveau, and shortly thereafter, Art Deco. Both were, in a sense, "design" movements, which very much influenced Marguerite's later preoccupation with design and decoration. The experimentation of the Fauves, with their bold innovation and coloration, was also absorbed by Marguerite. New art in France in 1908 was based on first, creative spontaneity, second, the use of pure color, and third, simplification of form. It was this early love for fresh and original ideas that permitted Marguerite to view Paris with an open mind.[3]

In the period following her return to this country, her marriage to William Zorach and the establishment of a home in New York, Marguerite experimented with the common hooked rug as a creative outlet. Painting demanded one's full concentration and the arrival of small children demanded the same. The two were incompatible. Rug-hooking and embroidery, on the other hand, could be picked up and laid aside whenever the children needed her attention. Rug hooking, starting in 1917, was definitely experimentation for her, merely a variation, in her mind, of painting on a piece of artist's canvas. The new medium proved to be very successful for her. In an oral history recollection William Zorach acknowledged the important role the sale of Marguerite's embroideries and hooked rugs played in supporting the family. "When you ask me how we existed, I think it was probably through these hooked rugs and embroideries."[4]

Marguerite advanced the cause of early modern art among her peers and her husband also explored avant-garde painting. Post-Impressionism had taken hold in New York and both husband and wife were invited to participate in the ground-breaking 1913 Modernist exhibition, The Armory Show, in New York. In the following years the couple painted canvases that are Fauvist in color and motif and, in addition, had a new angularity and flatness of natural forms influenced by Cubist works they had viewed at The Armory Show.

Just as Picasso and other Cubists in France had been inspired by primitive African art forms, so American artists now realized that primitive art in this country, just beginning to be called "folk art," could be an inspirational and design source for the fine arts.

In the early part of the twentieth century museums and commercial galleries were mounting exhibitions of folk art of all sorts: furniture, painting, sculpture, and the numerous "decorative arts," including textiles. Modernist artists, such

Marguerite (Thompson) Zorach was photographed in the family's home in New York in 1923. She is working on her hooked rug, "Wild Horses," while her son, Tessim, looks on. *Courtesy Mrs. Dahlov (Zorach) Ipcar.*

as Elié Nadelman, Charles Sheeler, Robert Laurent, and others, as well as art patrons like Abby Aldrich Rockefeller, started their own personal collections of naïve art. A number of these artists established summer studios along the Maine coast, primarily in the Ogunquit area. It has been said, with considerable justification, that "this is where the collecting of American Folk Art had its humble beginnings."[5]

In 1913, Hamilton Easter Field commenced his Ogunquit (Maine) School of Painting and Sculpture, of which William Zorach was a member, as well as Marsden Hartley, Yasuo Kuniyoshi, Bernard Karfiol, Niles Spencer, and others. To decorate the artists' studios (converted rough fishing shacks), Field and his fellow painters went out into the countryside and found decoys, weathervanes, naïve paintings, hooked rugs, and samplers in junk shops and at auction.[6]

Not only did the buying and collecting of these pieces catch on with the artists but with many people who visited them throughout the summer. Much to the surprise and delight of the artists these primitive forms came to influence many of their paintings and sculptures.[7]

It is logical that the Zorachs, after they purchased property in Robinhood, Maine, in 1923 (on the rec-

ommendation of the sculptor, Gaston Lachaise and his wife) would appreciate the fledgling folk art collections being assembled by other members of the Maine summer art colonies and be inspired to collect folk art on their own. As far back as 1913 Marguerite was creating embroideries (or wall tapestries), struck by the brilliant colors available in woolen fabrics.

Without going into great detail on these famous embroideries, they burst on the art world with an immediacy that startled everyone.[8] Even the Rockefeller family commissioned a large one for their summer "cottage" in Seal Harbor, Maine, and other advanced collectors commissioned Marguerite to create embroideries. Foresighted critics realized that she had, indeed, pushed what had been a craft into the fine art category. The artist came to believe that rug hooking and embroidery were as creative as painting or sculpting since the technique involved permitted her to use her imagination throughout the length of time it took to finish a single work.

In 1917 Marguerite created what may be her first hooked rug, entitled "Eden." It was shown that year, together with a painting, *Maternity,* in the very first exhibition of the Society of Independent Artists at Grand Central Palace in New York City.[9] This was the golden opportunity for rug-hooking to be projected as a fine art. Normally an artist is "invited" to be among the exhibitors in a show and the works selected for inclusion are first approved by a jury comprised of art professionals.

The Society of Independent Artists, however, was formed to provide artists with an outlet in which they could exhibit, for an annual fee, articles of their own choosing regardless of style or subject-matter, not necessarily only those selected by a jury. The 1917 show was the largest and the most controversial exhibition ever held in this country. It was highly criticized for its "no-jury" policy and its alphabetical installation which placed each artist on an equal footing space-wise. Including about 2,500 paintings and sculptures by 1,200 artists, it was a show in which Marguerite could display a hooked rug as a work of art! And she did so successfully.

The rug entitled "Eden" was copied from her mural of the same title which was painted on the vestibule wall of the Zorachs' Tenth Street apartment in New York. So impressed were Mr. and Mrs. Lathrop Brown, noted art collectors, that they purchased the "Eden" rug and later became good patrons of the Zorachs.

While it is generally referred to as "Adam and Eve," Marguerite titled the rug, "Eden," as can be seen at its lower edge. It was hooked in 1917. William provided further insight into the design of the rug – and its two titles – in a description of the couple's early apartment in New York City:

> Our floors were red lead, our walls lemon yellow. We made our little hall into a garden of Eden with a [mural of a] life-sized Adam and Eve and a red and white snake draped around the trunk of a decorative tree, with tropical foliage surrounding it all. Critics and newspaper writers came around and wrote about us in the Sunday supplements and on art pages. The real miracle was that people came to these exhibitions and there was sometimes a sale.[10]

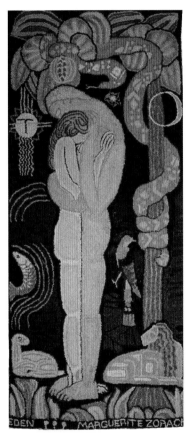

One of Marguerite's greatest rugs is entitled, "Eden," a complex and extraordinary design for a hooked rug that depicts the saga of Adam and Eve in the Garden of Eden. The symbolism throughout the rug is detailed and evocative. It has descended in the family of its original purchasers, Mr. and Mrs. Lathrop Brown, and is currently in the collection of Mrs. Pamela Grossman, the Browns's granddaughter. 1917. Wool on linen. 34" x 77.25". *Courtesy Pamela Grossman.*

The mural was the basis for the hooked rug that justifiably ranks among the country's all-time most artistic. It is owned today by Mrs. Pamela Grossman, granddaughter of the original collectors. Examining "Eden," it is difficult to deny it the "work of art" classification. Indeed, if she had taken the mural in her vestibule and used it to create another version in oil or watercolor, it obviously would be a work of art. Thus, creating a hooked rug version is likewise merely making another work of art in a different medium.

The Zorach scholar, Roberta Tarbell, said:

> The rugs were less complex designs based on paintings by the artist. The simple compositions were hooked with wool onto canvas [i.e., linen] and were often *created* for actual use by the family. In both her rugs and her embroideries the motivation was her fascination with the brilliancy and range of colors in woolen yarns which, according to Marguerite . . . "were beyond anything in paint."[11]

Examining the original mural of "Eden" and the hooked rug, however, it can hardly be said that the latter is "less complex." Considering it was her first foray into rug hooking "Eden" turned out to be a masterpiece. In terms of composition — a balancing of verticals, horizontal and circular motifs and images — the rug is without flaw. The entire rug exudes Art Deco design and the colors are purely Fauvist. The innocent couple in the Garden of Eden, lovingly entwined head to foot, dominates the rug; Adam slightly larger and taller with his right arm enfolding Eve to his bosom and his left caressing her hair.

Since she was a California native Marguerite well knew the cultural traditions of the Native Americans of the southwest. The Zia Pueblo symbol of their ancient Sun God appears over Eve's shoulder, counterbalanced by a conjoined partially eclipsed sun and crescent moon at the right, signifying night and day. The fish swimming amidst the curving waves of the ocean, the brightly plumaged bird, and large grasses at the bottom speak of the fecundity of the Eden that God had created, but the overwhelming aspect of the entire scene is darkened by a menacing snake slithering up a tree crowned with lush green foliage. It flicks its evil tongue at the innocent couple, drawing attention to the large, lush red apple hanging directly over their heads.

While the viewer knows from the biblical verses that the snake represented the devil, Marguerite has clothed it in a deceptive soft pink skin with gay geometric designs making it appear to Adam and Eve as non-threatening and benign. Although the couple will be cast out of Eden for succumbing to the devil's temptation, the picture for their future descendants is not all dim: as the bible prophesied, at some point all will not be sin and war and death, but the lion and the lamb will lay down together in peace. (Isaiah 11:16). How perfectly Marguerite has told the story of creation in such a complete and artistic manner.

During the 1920s and 1930s, the artist focused on embroideries, with hooked rugs interspersed. Thus, her needlework received much more exposure and critical attention than her paintings. Everyone noted that her work was marked by a superb sense of design and color. Clearly she was able to manifest her artistic expression in both the fine and decorative arts and to negotiate the boundaries between them. In a 1923 exhibition at the Montrose Gallery, which traveled to the Detroit Society of Arts and Crafts, she showed nine embroideries, two hooked rugs, and other textiles.[12]

These selections were obviously her choice, not that of the gallery director, because Marguerite throughout her career felt that her hooked rugs, embroideries, batiks and bedspreads, were also examples of fine art that deserved an equal place in art galleries with her paintings.

At the end of the Arts and Crafts period Marguerite Zorach joined others in attempting to elevate such crafts as embroidery and rug hooking into the realm of fine art. While her embroideries were undoubtedly more closely identified with the fine arts than other crafts, rug hooking still retained the stigma of a "craft" or old-fashioned folk art. It is the perennial question as to whether a craft can truly become a fine art when crafted beyond the normal aesthetic value of design and technique.

When Marguerite and other major American artists, such as Stuart Davis and Hans Moller, turned to designing hooked rugs in the first quarter of the twentieth century it was referred to as "rag painting" and recognized as a new medium of expression. One of Howard Pyle's students spent six years on three landscape hooked rugs of the Maine coast.[13]

After "Eden" there came a succession of rugs. The location of all of them is not known, some having been sold out of exhibitions and others done on commission for private collectors or friends.

Shortly after hooking Eden, Marguerite created a chair pad entitled "Cat." The original design of the black cat, green grass, and colorful leaves, was unsuitable as a chair pad, so the artist enlarged it by working in a black border and surrounding the entire composition with a swirling design of nautilus shells.

What had been an imperfect design now became a complete totality of color and composition. It demonstrated that in her mind a hooked rug, like a painting, was a work in progress that could be modified upon further reflection.

"The Nude and Flowers" probably is the most photographed and best known of Marguerite's rugs, dating to 1922. It shows a languid nude, posed in a classic manner, resting on a floral background. Long black hair flows down around her, highlighting her cream-colored skin. A riot of vaguely exotic flowers gives the nude a colorful forest bed on which to recline. Referred to at times simply as "Nude," Ann Wiseman, a hooking student of Marguerite's, claims otherwise. In her book *Rag Tapestries and Wool Mosaics,* she gives it a third title, "Eve," and claims it was William who preserved it "from the tread of muddy feet" by insisting that it be taken up and hung on the wall.[14]

"Wild Horses" is dated 1923 in the lower right corner. It can also be seen in Marguerite's lap in the illustration at the beginning of this chapter. The scene depicts a herd of wild, varied-colored and multi-striped horses romping through a Fauvist forest of trees in muted fall colors. The artist's playful nature and her love of striking colors combine to create horses that are fanciful beyond belief and trees and leaves that would do justice to an exotic South American jungle.

Marguerite created the design for "The Snake and Bird" in 1937 and it was hooked at the Crawford Shops of the New York Association for Improving Conditions of the Poor (an organization that later merged with the Charity Organization Society to become what is today's Community Service Organization). It was featured in an exhibition at the Museum of Modern Art consisting of rugs designed by well-known modern painters for commercial reproduction. They were not hooked by the artists themselves and the exhibit version was later sold at discount.

The rug, "Wild Horses," was given by the Zorach family to the Smithsonian Institution. Unfortunately a color photograph was not obtainable. Wool on linen. *Courtesy Dahlov Ipcar.*

Unhappy with the interpretation of her design, Marguerite made her own version in 1939 and it is this example which is shown here. A close examination reveals a black snake with white highlights moving through a forest carpeted with bright, primitive flowers. In the top corner a high flying, fanciful bird seemingly taunts the reptile so far below. The original version, titled "The Jungle," is now in the collection of the Museum of Modern Art in New York City.

The whimsical "The Black Pig" was made in 1944 for the Zorachs' daughter-in-law, Peggy Zorach, who had a collection of objects relating to pigs. Rugs made for family use show a special charm that is not as confining as the fine arts. It allowed Marguerite to "play" with her designs, liberating her from the necessity of pleasing the critics or a potential customer. The term "endearing" seems to be the most suitable adjective. Comparing this rug with "Eden" shows the complexity involved in her professional designs.[15]

The "Cat and Birds" rug, hooked in 1950, shows a reclining cat totally encircled by birds of all species and colors. The tricolored feline's dream-like demeanor is typical of Marguerite's talent for portraying the personality of her subject. Lazy and indolent, it is trying to sleep peacefully on its bed of soft green grass, but is distracted and has to squint up through the leaves into the bright sunlight at a flock of birds swirling about its head. It is a good example of the vibrancy of colors Marguerite found so appealing in woolen fabrics. According to Wiseman, Marguerite made this as a "bed-stepping" rug for her own personal use.[16]

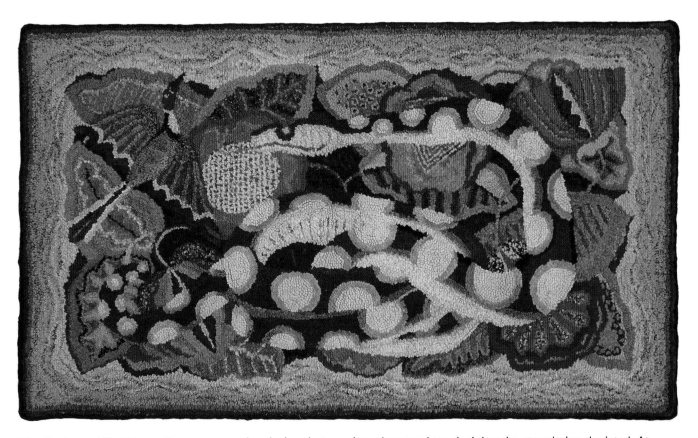

"The Snake and Bird" is another very complex design that requires close study to decipher the story being depicted. At top center can be seen the head of a black-and-white spotted snake entwining itself through a garden of lush flowers while observing a brightly plumaged bird at the upper left. Wool on linen, 34.25" x 59.50". *Private collection.*

The vibrant "Cat and Birds" is a rug Marguerite made for personal family use. A watchful tricolored cat keeps a close eye on a flock of birds circling in the sky above. Wool on linen, 35" x 42". *Private collection*

The various birds, horses, cats and flower motifs in Marguerite's rugs are reflected in the large murals painted on the four walls of the old keeping room of the 1810-1830 James Riggs homestead, where the Zorachs spent their summers. The artist, as did her husband, gloried in animal life and these motifs were often incorporated into their paintings and sculpture. It is also worth noting that if Marguerite's rugs are studied by decade the paintings in those periods are reflected in the artistic outlook that influenced each rug. In other words, as her painting style changed or was modified, so did the rugs.

Dahlov Ipcar, the Zorachs' daughter, has made her home in Maine for many years. Inspired by her mother's work, she also tried her hand at hooking and created what is probably the most copied and reproduced contemporary rug in America today. It has been widely featured in numerous books on hooked rugs and illustrated in many magazines and classes dealing with hooked rugs. Titled "Leopard and Tiger" it was hooked on a piece of Irish linen left over by her mother and even the rag wool strips had been prepared by Margue-

rite.[17] The colors in this rug clearly define why Marguerite was so enchanted with the wonderful tonal values available to her in woolen fabrics.

Made in 1974, this was the only rug Ipcar ever hooked, although, as a student at a private school in New York City, she participated in "The Year of the Rug" by making a punch-needle rug of a rooster. Ipcar has spent a lifetime in the field of art creating not only paintings but soft sculptures, as well as highly-regarded children's books. She is a noted artist with works included in the permanent collections of the Metropolitan Museum of Art, the Whitney Museum, and the Brooklyn Museum of Art, all in New York City. She is represented in all the leading art museums in Maine as well as corporate and private collections throughout the country.[18]

Like her mother, Ipcar has clearly created a rug that goes beyond the bounds of the traditional craft form. When the "Leopard and Tiger" was completed, Bates College, in Lewiston, Maine, mounted a special exhibit featuring unique rugs designed and worked by various Maine artists, thus validating a point that Marguerite had been trying to make fifty years earlier: that rugs could be fine art. The Ipcar rug was a centerpiece of the show. The Bicentennial Exhibition, which opened in October 1975, included 24 rugs, of which 18 were contemporary. Included were Marguerite's "The Black Pig," the "Cat and Birds," "Cat," "Nude and Flowers," and "Snake and Birds."[19]

While largely unheralded in the general craft of rug hooking, and yet strongly heralded in the field of art, Marguerite, forever changed the craft, elevating it to a new height of appreciation as a fine art where her work rightfully belongs. While it may still be considered a craft, it has raised the eternal question, "Just where is that magical point where a craft can be considered a work of art?" "Did Marguerite achieve that goal for which she strove?"

As an artistic duo, mother and daughter have left an indelible mark on the history of hooking, not only in Maine, but throughout the country.

This rug showing a black cat in a flower garden was the second piece hooked by Marguerite between 1918 and 1923. It very much reflects the period of her art influenced by the Fauvists. Originally created as a chair pad she reworked and enlarged it so it could be used as a small rug. Wool on burlap, 25.50" x 29.24". *Private collection.*

The well-known "Nude and Flowers" is probably the most reproduced of all of Marguerite's rugs, and certainly the one that is the most "painterly." It has been displayed both horizontally and vertically, but the latter is the way in which it is displayed by family members. Wool on linen, 49" x 29". *Courtesy Charles Ipcar.*

139

A large belted black pig complacently dominates this rug as it "snouts" through a treasure-trove of colorful fruits and vegetables. This also was made as a family piece. Wool on linen, 30" x 54". *Private collection.*

Dahlov Ipcar, the daughter of William and Marguerite Zorach, hooked only one rug later in her life. The "Rooster" was made using a punch needle machine while she was a young student at a private school in New York. The "Year of the Rug" designation by the school stressed the significance of the craft during the first quarter of the twentieth century. Wool yarn on burlap, 26" x 37.50". *Courtesy Robert Ipcar.*

Probably the most reproduced rug in contemporary times (often without authorization) is the "Lion and Tiger" hooked by Dahlov Ipcar. A well-known artist, she limited her rug-hooking to this one piece while also pursuing other artistic endeavors. Hooked in 1974 with remnants of her mother's linen backing and colorful wool fabrics, the rug remains in the artist's collection. 37" x 59". *Courtesy of Dahlov Ipcar.*

Chapter XIII

A Maine Sampler

While the various historical aspects of rug-making in Maine have dominated this presentation, the novice rug-maker continued, unheralded, to create rugs at his or her own level, be it primitive or sophisticated. This chapter recognizes, not only some of the more "elite" rugs generally featured in rug books, but provides a general overview of Maine rugs.

Unconditional provenance, however, is virtually impossible to determine, so, in addition to those with a documented provenance, many rugs in this chapter have been selected because of a Maine connection. Most are from known collections, while others offer an opportunity to glean what has been on the market through local auction sales. These are primarily from Maine-based estate auctions and are presumed to have been made in Maine.

In earlier days, and oftentimes even today, rugs were not looked upon as a significant asset. Made by women from rags, they were hardly worthy of inclusion in any will, and it would have been ostentatious to sign the rug. Many were eventually relegated to the woodshed having outlived their usefulness indoors. The anonymity continues even today for hookers rarely sign their rugs and only a handful are likely to keep any accurate records of their works of art. That is slowly beginning to change.

Leonard Burbank, writing in *The Magazine Antiques* in 1922, agreed:

> I have not chanced to find these rugs mentioned in the inventories of estates, of which so many have come down to us. In fact, almost the only mention of floor coverings in such documents refers to Turkey carpet, and that only in lists belonging to people of wealth, more especially those living in the more populous and affluent cities of the South. The hooked rug was of too lowly an origin to be considered of much value.[1]

Fortunately, some of the earlier Maine rugs have been saved and a precious few have been preserved in various museums throughout the country. They are included in such prestigious venues as the Metropolitan Museum of Art in New York City; Shelburne Museum in Vermont; Winterthur in Delaware, Old Sturbridge Village in Massachusetts, and even the New Hampshire Historical Society has several authenticated Maine rugs. The Detroit Art Institute has a wonderful reed-stitched Maine farm scene. The sad part is that so few have been saved in Maine. Through the years, Maine was, and still is, fertile ground for collectors and dealers who came to the state, traveled into rural areas for the sought-after gems, found them, and took them away.

Linen and burlap were the most common foundations in early hooking, but there were other fabrics. Fustian was a weave of linen and jute. Osnaburg was a cotton fabric used for grain bags, known as hopsacking when treated with a "finish." Crocus cloth was a coarse burlap-like material, used in early times to ship saffron, and more commonly known as gunnysack. Cotton also was used, but it was quite expensive in the early days.

Diary references to early rug-making are uncommon, but Barbara Copeland Wentworth of Cushing, Maine, left an extensive diary covering her life during the period from 1811-1890. Her book, *No Boughs on My Bonnet,* in an entry on January 1, 1869, noted:

> I have done more sewing this past year than I have done in any since I have been lame. I have made and made over and turned or flounced or trimed [*sic*] 25 dresses, I think besides other work to numerous to mention. Amongst these, bead cushions, and rugs some worked on [?] cloth.

In describing her bedroom she also mentioned "a rug, the design of a basket of flowers. . . ."[2]

In 1886, she wrote a letter to the *Farmer's Gazette,* describing her sitting room including the floor coverings:

> An oilcloth carpet has been used summer and winter for 15 years, quite good now. We wash it with milk and water, makes it look as if it was just varnished. Lots of rugs, some drawn through

with different coulers [*sic*] of rags in flowers. Mine was one of the first made in this [Knox] county. [Unfortunately, she gives no hint as to the date of that first rug.][3]

Tucked away in a private collection in Maine is a unique group of hooked rugs assembled during the second quarter of the twentieth century. For security reasons, the collector wishes to remain anonymous. The collection is a time capsule demonstrating how one person became fascinated and captivated by the colors and naïvete of design found in rummaging through the numerous antique shops dotting the Maine coast in the 1920-1930 era.

Two wide-eyed deer stare quizzically from this harvest-time scene. The use of strong autumn colors to define the deer accentuates the seasonal definition, while a covering of snow on the ground hints of winter. Branches from two oak trees bountifully laden with acorns add to the atmosphere and the subtlety of color delineates the antlers from the trees. A central fern provides depth. c.1880. Wool on burlap, 34" x 68".

This horse has personality plus, seemingly demanding "Look at Me. See how I prance." The raised foreleg and the extended, full tail add to that personality. The dark blue indigo background is rare, thus more desirable, in rugs. Alternating triangles form the border, interspersed at each corner with a stem of conventional leaves and star-shaped flowers. c.1880-90. Wool on burlap. 35" x 47.50".

142

This cat gives the appearance of wearing a rather smug clown-like mask, eyes filled with wonder or surprise. The long arched tail closely resembles what could easily be considered a fifth leg. The design is nicely centered within a trailing vine of blue and gold leaves and flowers contained within a second border of felt "tongues." c.1920. Wool on burlap, 44" x 47".

Dating to the Civil War era, the simplified version of the American flag was a testament to Northern patriotism. The flagpole, which extends into the border at top and bottom, is capped with a red arrow pointing upward. The flag's stars are exceptionally well delineated when considering the coarseness of the fabric strips. The "tongue" pattern, often seen as felt additions to border a rug, have been inverted here and hooked as an inner frame surrounding the flag. Three rows of straight hooking in different colors provide the final border. c.1880. Wool and cotton on burlap, 25" x 35".

Rug makers often looked to traditional sources for their designs. In the Victorian era, calling cards were commonly used and often featured a hand holding a bouquet of flowers, as seen in the accompanying example. The rug is a primitive version of that motif. While the design is lightly raised, the flowers lack the shading of more sophisticated designs. A single line of diamonds frames the rug with its mottled black ground. A true piece of folk art. Rug, c.1890-1910. Wool on burlap. 25" x 41". Card, c.1885.

One can readily discern where this design came from. A deck of cards provides the basic elements for a well-balanced and attractive rug. Simplicity reigns, but the hooker appropriately centered the rug with a ball made up of the two colors dominating the card deck. The border reflects two shades of the dark suits. c.1880-95. Wool on burlap, 23.25" x 39".

Geometrics were the easiest of the designs to draw, but the hooking and the organization of the components determined the artistry. This is an excellent example of geometric art. The placement of the red at the corners echoes the inner border and the central diamond which settles into a larger diamond amidst multi-colored striations. Softer red elongated triangles anchor the inner corners. While geometrics look easy to do, it takes a lot of patience and ability to keep the lines straight and even when working on the uneven mesh of burlap. c. 1910. Wool on burlap, 17.50" x 23.75".

Primitive in execution with a distorted sense of shading, this rug has quality in the overall design. Well balanced stalks of various flowers ascend from a single flower at the lower edge, and gracefully interlock at the upper center. The flower at the lower edge is repeated for the central focus. A very simple border of gold shaded clamshell motifs frames the design. c.1895. Wool on burlap, 27" x 41.50".

While Waldoboro women were busy creating rugs in Maine, they were not the only rug-makers. Hookers throughout the state were creating their own original designs. A sampling includes the following:

One of Maine's great early rugs is this shirred example from the 1810 Titcomb homestead in North Yarmouth. While the basic design is similar to a "lollipop" rug, the overall theme is much more fully developed than that term might suggest. Each of the scallops along the edge surrounds a set of "bunny ears." Adding depth and perspective is the double row of green and red stripes surrounding each scallop, the soft green repeated in a single row edging the entire rug. Dimensions and current whereabouts unknown. Shirred on linen. *Cyr Auction.*

Another one of Maine's great rugs was hooked in the mid-19th century by Julia Eastman Stubbs of Strong (1815-1887) and descended through several generations of the Stubbs family of Hallowell. Lacking such documentation, the rug likely would never have been attributed to Maine. A black man flailing his whip while leading a horse to water, was a highly unlikely scene for Maine; in fact highly unlikely for any rug of the period. Blacks were especially uncommon in Maine and rarely seen on any hooked rug. Otherwise, the rug fits comfortably within the Maine image, with the meandering cow trailed by a dog, the two being observed by a bird on a branch above. Tongues of black felt accent the strong border diagonals. It is obviously a hearth rug. c.1860. Wool on burlap, 24" x 84". *Maine State Museum, ex-Berdan collection.*

Found on an island in the mid-coast area of Maine, this is a yarn sewn and sheared reed stitch rug. The dimensions and design indicate it was likely a hearth rug with all vegetable dyes that have mellowed with age. The dark fringe of hand spun wool yarn provides a counterpoint to the overall light coloring. A lineal floral edge contains the double-tiered motif with its protruding branches. Half-circle floral wreaths at each end enclose spikes of inward branching floral stems. Another indication of age is the early hand-woven backing of blue and white checked linen gingham. c.1830-1840. Yarn-sewn wool on hand woven linen, 27.5" x 57.50". *MCP collection.*

An early rug from the Waterville area has replaced the traditional urn with a flower pot filled with gigantic flowers towering above a pair of birdhouses protruding into the rug from the lower edge at either side. Four diamonds fill up the empty spaces. The typical black frame shows the color changes seen in the fugitive black dyes used in early times. Boldness of design is greatly cherished in early rugs. c. 1875. Wool and cotton on burlap. Dimensions unavailable. *Julia Auction.*

Touches of the coveted indigo accentuate the brilliant red colors of an early rug from the Rockland area. Three large red and white flowers center this rug's bold design dominated with a quartet of multi-colored round balls at each side. The red in the fan-shaped corners is picked up again in the inner frame helping to contain the sharply contrasting dark tweed colors at the sides, c.1830-40. Homespun yarn and fabric on a hand woven foundation, 28.5" x 72". *Courtesy Jeff and Suzanne Good.*

A very simple design can become a great rug through a hooking technique that captures the sense of motion. Four feathery leaves set against a dark blue background are given life through the background undulations. They seem to be exploding out of a nighttime sky. Even more exciting is the frame which is totally filled with color and motion. Without the outstanding interpretation on the part of the hooker, this would be a very static and dull pattern. Hooking at its best! c.1910. Wool on burlap, 31" x 53". *Courtesy Lionel N. and Gerry Sterling.*

The gold highlights contrast well with the unusual deep maroon background color in this shirred rug. Cabbage roses dominate as a central motif and as corner spandrels. Each flower and leaf is clearly delineated with no overcrowding of the design. The rug was found in the Bucksport area of Maine. c.1880. Wool on linen, 32" x 65". *Courtesy Lionel N. and Gerry Sterling.*

148

Tulips form the center of a rug featuring two blue-banded cornucopias holding sprays of roses which serve as frames for the tulips. Obviously a hearth rug, the roses in the upper corners have pinwheel-like leaves. All the leaves are blue, contrasting with the bright red flowers in an almost mystical sense. Although the maker is unknown, it is signed "M C M." c.1890-1900. Wool and cotton on burlap, 32" x 70". *Courtesy Patricia Stauble.*

Hearts were one of the most significant design elements in early rugs as well as other decorative accents, especially the "heart-in-the-hand" symbol of the Odd Fellows. Here four central hearts point inward toward the rug center, while a heart in each corner points outward. The boldness of the pattern set against a solid bronze-colored ground gives the hearts a striking dominance. The hooker has carefully chosen a soft pink and a deep purple to contain the design without overwhelming it. c.1890. Wool on burlap, 28" x 52". *David Beane Auction.*

In striking contrast to the previous rug, this one is wild with color and motion. Two bright pink hearts are held in place by pale pink areas of undetermined shapes. They seem to be floating in a galaxy of explosive shapes that give rise to three pink stars at each end. The hour-glass frame is hooked in lighter shades allowing the central theme to dominate. c.1890. Cotton and wool, 28" x 52". *Courtesy Patricia Stauble.*

Autumn in Maine seems to be the theme of this rug centered with a bouquet of autumn leaves against a deep indigo sky. The maker of the rug has provided an excellent interpretation of the swirling motion of the riotous wind-driven leaves as they appear in the fall. c.1930. Wool on burlap, 38.75" x 57.5". *Courtesy Fred and Maureen Fenton.*

Intended as an all black rug interspersed with floral sprays and corner segmented pairing of leaves, this rug shows the dramatic change of the early black dyes. The reverse, not having been exposed to sunlight, retains its dark background. The rug is sculpted and hooked on linen and is of Waldoboro origin. c.1860. Wool on linen, 26.25" x 35.5". *MCP collection*

Lacking the confidence to create a design, the hooker simply inscribed her name, and the date, traced an oak leaf in each corner, and she was ready to hook. This rug-maker has artistically interpreted a very basic design concept. The brilliant red signature contrasts sharply with the indigo ground edged with a single row of dark brown. By using a darker indigo shade beneath the signature and date, she has enhanced its significance. Even the simple corner leaves have been sharply shaded and surrounded with rows of hooked material providing the motion of blowing in the wind. c.1876. Wool on burlap, 19.50" x 37". *MCP collection.*

151

Another inscribed rug bears the initials of the maker "S L D" within a gold-colored diamond. Floral sprays accent the central diamond, but the totally interesting and exciting concept here is the choice of ears of corn tumbling around the outer border as a major design component. c.1890. Wool on burlap, 31.5" x 52". *Courtesy Joseph Caputo.*

Since indigo is very special this rug-maker chose to use a minimum amount to dominate the design by placing one large flower in two shades of blue as the central design. The remaining flowers are much smaller to compensate for the use of brilliant red that would otherwise overwhelm the blue. Although it is not a one-way design, the size indicates that it was likely a hearth rug. c.1885. Wool on burlap, 20" x 61.50". *MCP collection.*

What better design as a summertime replacement for the winter fire. The rug itself is afire with color and "licking" flames. Even the border is burning. Great motion! c.1895. Wool on burlap, 29.5" x 55.50". *Courtesy Joseph Caputo.*

Quilt patterns were a popular design choice and simplified the task of creativity. Two examples were all that were found from an elusive industry labeled the "Hatch Industries" of Oceanville, Maine. Everett and Frances Hatch were listed as the makers of the rugs, but evidence suggests that the rugs were made by Mrs. Hatch, while Everett may have made other saleable articles included under the "industries" title. Frances was born May 1, 1886, in Danbury, Connecticut, and Everett was born in Oceanville on November 5, 1878, and except for a few winters in Connecticut had always resided in Oceanville, which includes "Hatch Cove."

Frances was graduated from Wilbraham Academy in Connecticut, Wesleyan University, and Smith College, and for a number of years worked as a librarian in New Haven and Bridgeport, Connecticut. She married Everett at some unknown date but there is no record of the marriage in Maine. Everett was listed as a lobsterman as well as a "yachtsman." Since many Stonington-area men served as sailors for the wealthy summer visitors, sailing the New England Coast, he may have met Frances in this manner.[4]

The couple operated "Hatch Haven," a tourist home for summer guests and may well have formed "Hatch Industries" to provide saleable articles to their summer guests. No record of any such industry was found, however.

An article in the local paper, *Island Ad-Vantages*, on March 27, 1947, announced "Considerable interest has been aroused in Oceanville by the big hooked rug recently completed by Mrs. Everett Hatch. Mrs. Hatch has worked all winter on the all-wool 10x11 [feet] floor piece. She plans to ship it away in April, but will welcome visitors who care to inspect it before that time."[5]

Everett died in August 1956 and Frances in November 1962. Two rugs, one bearing the label, with identical quilt patterns are the only ones known to date.

This rug bears a professional-looking label attributing it to "Hatch Industries" of Oceanville, Maine, but extensive research has failed to find any references to such an industry. Everett, a lobsterman and yachtsman, and Frances Hatch, listed on the label as the rug makers, operated a tourist home "Hatch Haven" for summer guests in Oceanville, located on a peninsula in the Deer Isle-Stonington area. The geometric rug has the quilt pattern "Sunshine and Shadows" as the design. A larger companion rug, lacking the label but with the same design, was sold separately. No other rug bearing the Hatch label is known. c.1940. Wool on burlap, 29.25" x 58.25". *Maine Historical Society Collections. 2007.163.*

The Hatch rugs were not unique in using a quilt pattern. Another hooker adapted a quilt pattern for this rug in vivid contrasting tones carefully arranged to create strong diagonal rows. The log cabin pattern has numerous variations. This one is known as the "Straight Furrow." c.1920. Wool on burlap, 25.75" x 32.50". *Private collection.*

Some rug-makers preferred to experiment with new methods or new ways of dealing with an earlier form.

Although positive attribution was not possible, this rug is believed to be of Maine Shaker origin (either the communities at Alfred or Sabbathday Lake) because of its crocheted netting-type foundation. Its stunning simplicity (a Shaker hallmark) is best manifested in the arrangement of stripes and colors contrasted with the multifaceted central motif. It has achieved an unusual harmony of colors in an unusually large rug. c.1920. Wool on cotton twine, 39" x 92.50". *Courtesy Fred and Maureen Fenton collection.*

Some rug-makers would qualify as what would be considered avant-garde at the time, willing to experiment with different techniques or combinations. An excellent example is a braided rug with penny or button shirring used as a filler inside the outer braided circles. It was an effective way of enlarging the rug while adding substantially to an otherwise traditional rendition. c.1860. Wool on coarse blue and white homespun, 36.75" x 38.50". *Courtesy Suzanne and Jeff Good collection.*

The dots of color are an outstanding achievement in this primitive bias-shirred rug. The simple striped design belies its complexity in a shirred technique. c.1890. Wool on early ticking, 29.50" diameter. *Courtesy Joseph Caputo.*

Animals were a favorite topic including farm animals, pets and wild life, but cats, tame or wild, predominated:

A pair of cats appear to be resting on the ledge of a cave, the depth suggested by the shadowy-colored background framed with a garland of flowers. Single flowers are seen in the scalloped corner spandrels, and a rust-colored ground and colorful diamond motifs add a splash of color. The rug is edged with a row of braided fabric. This was seen fairly often and was a good reinforcement for the fragile edges. c.1910-20. Wool on burlap, 29" x 45.25". *Courtesy Joseph Caputo.*

What was likely intended to be a heart-shaped locket has been placed around the neck of this pet, obviously meant as an expression of love for the animal. The cat stares out at the viewer while birds fly in the background and bees sniff the flowers in the corners at the right. Another note of endearment is the numerous touches of indigo, the coveted color. c.1920-30. Wool on burlap, 29.5" x 44.50". *Courtesy Fred and Maureen Fenton.*

156

A very simple cat design has been personalized with the addition of the initials "M P" and the date 1889, both given added emphasis through the use of red dye. Multi-colored striped fans share the corners while simple floral boughs enclose the upper and lower edges. c.1889. Wool on burlap, 30.25" x 38.75". *Courtesy Jeff and Suzanne Good.*

The family pet is comfortably seated atop a scalloped footstool. A ribbon or collar has been placed around the animal's neck as a sign of affection. Red is a vibrant background for the white cat. c.1885. Wool on burlap,14" diameter. *Cyr Auction, ex-Berdan collection.*

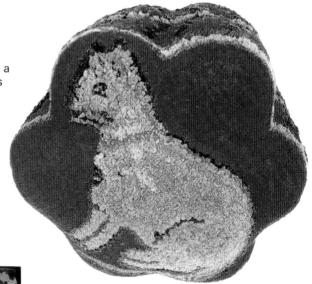

The ferocity associated with the lion has been successfully captured in this animal with teeth bared and claws extended. The demeanor has been further exaggerated with a single staring eye and a crouching position. In sharp contrast is the gentle floral spray framing the animal. Each corner has been "tied up" with bow ties. c.1890. Wool on burlap, 36" x 60". *Cyr Auction, ex-Curtin Collection..*

The wide-eyed lion appears to have been created with the punch-needle method. The precise
straight rows and even loops are a good indication of the punch-needle technique. Corner ferns
help to soften the staid background and the tail
protruding into the border frame is a nice personal
touch. Changes in the black dye help to identify it
as an early rug. c.1885. Wool on burlap, 30" x 59".
Cyr Auction.

Far more whimsical is this lion with its
"pasted on" face filled with awe or curiosity.
Giving an animal personality is a challenge to
the designer who has succeeded, albeit in a
primitive fashion. A bird, a few flowers and a
couple of butterflies add complexity. c.1900.
Wool on burlap, 29" x 53". *Cyr Auction.*

Two bunnies have been startled in their
resting place beneath a single flower stalk
bearing two flowers; certainly a fantasy
world, but well organized to accommodate all the design elements. The dramatic frame contrasts starkly to the pastel
shades of the central motif. c. 1930. Wool
on burlap, 23" x 33". *Cyr Auction.*

As expected, Maine has a rich heritage in maritime rugs, usually hooked by men of the sea. It seems likely the majority were hooked by the ship captains since it would have been necessary to carry on board all the necessary equipment and supplies needed to make the rug.

According to material found with the rug, this view of Portland Head Light was hooked in 1898 by a Captain Pierce on his last voyage out of Portland. Since there were several Captain Pierces, a more definitive attribution could not be determined. As expected from a man of the sea, there is a striking capacity for capturing the turbulence of both sea and sky with Maine's "rockbound coast" clearly delineated. However, as in many folk art rugs, the would-be artist lacks the courage to "create" without the need for black outlines adding definition to the design components. This rug is important for several reasons. While there has been significant mention of men hooking, documentation is quite rare. Secondly, the rug is unused and clearly shows an early transition to a mechanical stripper in the wool used for sea and sky. Many original rugs of this era still featured the wider hand-cut strips. c.1898. Wool and cotton on burlap. 22.5" x 28". *Courtesy Maine Maritime Museum, ex-Burden collection.*

Without the signature, this lighthouse rug could have been made by the same hands as the preceding rug. It is signed by a Captain Rumple, master of the *Commodore Hull,* a brig from Bangor. On December 13, 1853, on a voyage to Boston, the vessel was wrecked when she went aground on Adam's Ledge in the Bucksport Narrows at the mouth of the Penobscot River. The rug obviously was made somewhat later. The same black outline technique was employed here to sharpen the image, but the sea and sky are in a calmer mood surrounding Portland Head Light, which can be identified by the red roof, a rarity among lighthouses. Of added interest is the far-away ship seen on the horizon at the center right. c. 1880. Wool and cotton on burlap, 24" x 36". *Courtesy Lionel N. and Gerry Sterling.*

The ship dominates the scene in this rug, but Nubble lighthouse with its red roof shares the dominance. The rope border provides an appropriate nautical frame, but the sea and sky are lackluster without any turbulence or other sign of motion. This is characteristic of a punch-needle rug which does not allow for any intricate variety of color changes. Compare the green yarn of the sea with the seas in the following two rugs and the static colors of a punch-needle rug are immediately apparent. In this technique, the needle punches the yarn through the burlap from the reverse and is pre-set to create loops of a specific height obviating the need to shear the rugs, an important economy factor. Late nineteenth century. Wool and cotton yarn on burlap, 20" x 35". *Maine Maritime Museum, ex-Burden collection.*

160

This is a virtual duplicate of the ship seen in the previous rug. This time it is heading west toward the setting sun which has nearly faded into oblivion at the horizon next to the land mass at the left. The standard hooking technique is employed using wool strips as opposed to the yarn of the previous rug. The colorful floral border arches over the design typical of welcome mats. c.1875. Wool on burlap, 24" x 33". *Courtesy Patricia Stauble.*

Surprisingly a third rug featuring the same ship, with minimal alteration, was seen again, this time at auction. It is the same design as the previous rug lacking the floral border and an added change in the lower "Welcome" legend with two fish swimming toward the greeting. It definitely was made by the same person as the earlier punch-needle version. This one, also a punch-needle, used identical colors and yarns as the earlier version. Unfortunately the maker remains unidentified. Late nineteenth century, wool yarn on burlap. Dimensions unavailable. *Cyr Auction.*

A nice change from the characteristic ship/lighthouse nautical theme is this nicely balanced design of a pair of spouting whales floating on a rippling sea. According to the central compass rose, the ship is heading east. The four red stars encircled with rope extending around the central motif adds an art-deco note. The use of cotton yarn is a strong indication that the rug is worked with a punch needle. c.1910. Cotton and wool on burlap. 27" x 45". *Courtesy Maine Maritime Museum, ex-Burden collection.*

Multiple strands of wool yarn make up a rug hooked by Captain Charles H. Reed aboard the *Storm King* out of Woolwich. Family legend indicates it was made aboard ship while Reed was captain in the late nineteenth century. The mariner's star is raised against the background in which different shades of wool yarn are combined to create a "tweed" effect. c.1874-86. Wool yarn on burlap, 18.5" x 37.5". *Courtesy Maine Maritime Museum.*

Made by the same Captain Reed as in the previous rug, the eagle and shield are hooked in yarn on hand-woven linen. The eagle, shield, and banner designs are all raised as are the 26 stars surrounding the inner frame. The colors and materials are the same in both rugs. c.1874-1886. Wool yarn on hand-woven linen, 25" x 47". *Courtesy Maine Maritime Museum.*

With the harvesting of so many of Maine's native rugs by out-of-state dealers and collectors, the search expanded into the Maritime Provinces of Canada. Transporting them across the border saw them suddenly become Maine rugs. While provenance is important, point of origin sometimes takes precedence over quality and should not be the only determining factor in purchasing rugs.

While making no claims to be an expert on Canadian rugs, this author has seen many highly desirable and wonderful rugs from the Provinces. In the process, some observations have been noted which are offered here, not as a professional assessment, but as an homage to Canadian rug-hookers who share Maine's history in the craft.

An early article in *The Antiquarian* offered a description, "Canadian rugs, which were as a rule tight hooked and made in larger sizes than the New England type, favored geometrical patterns. Also the emblematic maple leaf in many variations of shade and size marks a rug of Canadian manufacture or descent."[6]

Burbank, writing in *The Magazine Antiques*, had a different opinion:

Many of the Nova Scotia rugs now coming to the United States are made of wool, are low in tone, being black or gray or dark green, with a small amount of brilliant red or yellow. The designs are attractive and harmonize with modern furnishings, but the drawing-in so regular and the loops so far apart as to give the appearance of machine work. The rugs too often lack the body that the old ones possessed.[7]

Traditional garb in the Maritimes was black or dark grays and browns, lending a plausible explanation as to why the hooked rugs of the area tend to have sober colors with only occasional bright color highlights. This is especially true of rugs from Newfoundland. Lack of access to any great variety of berries and other organic materials for dyes prohibited the stronger, more pluralistic shading seen in other Maritime provinces and New England.

An article by Robert Jackman in *The Antiques Journal* explained that Newfoundland hookers were working with scraps of clothing, limiting their array of colors. A second distinction was the extensive use of white.[8]

A brilliantly conceived maritime rug is centered with a rotating propeller stirring up the blue ocean water in a circular foamy spray. The multiple hooked segments in the background are an artistic atttempt to display the sea in its "choppy" mood. An anchor lies on the ocean floor and the moon and stars are reflected on the surface. The ocean is landbound at each corner with floral sprays. Here and there can be seen depictions of such land mases as an isthmus or cape as well as creatures of the sea, such as a snail and a sand dollar. Dated 1887. Wool on burlap. 31.75" x 60.25". *Courtesy Jeff and Suzanne Good Collection.*

Lacking actual provenance, this lion with its smug countenance, adequately fits the description of a Newfoundland rug. Here we see drab colors of black and browns with extensive use of white and small touches of bright red. The tassel at the end of the tail appears to be a modified heart shape. Although not identified as such, it could well be a stamped pattern. c.1920. Wool on burlap, 28" x 43.75". *Private Collection.*

The similarity of this rug with the previous lion rug suggests they may have been made by the same person. Again, there is extensive use of white in the central urn motif, set against a ground of dark browns with red highlights. c.1920. Wool on burlap, 29" x 45.5". *Private Collection.*

The checkerboard corners tend to identify this rug as of Nova Scotia origin. Cubed corners are referred to as "Nova Scotia Corners." While there are more colors than in most Newfoundland rugs, they remain rather drab and there is a total lack of any shading. A multi-colored braided edge makes a dramatic frame. c.1900. Wool on burlap, 29" x 45.50". *Private collection.*

164

Many Canadian rugs are identifiable by the design elements. The beaver, a national symbol in Canada, is a broad hint that the rug is Canadian. This outstanding design depicts a pair of beavers, each one working on the tree branches that will be used to make the dams and houses for which they are so famous. c. 1900. Wool and cotton on burlap. Dimensions and current location unavailable. *Cyr Auction.*

Another beaver rug dramatizes the same activity, but here the singular flat tail is dominant and a scalloped frame is set off by a wide dark gray border. Once again, the colors tend toward the drab shades. c.1895. Wool yarn and fabric on burlap, 36.50" x 24.75". *MCP collection.*

Foxes are rarely seen in any rugs of U.S.A. origin. They were a much maligned animal, despised for their affinity for killing chickens. However, foxes with silver-tipped tails were raised on special farms in Prince Edward Island starting around 1900 and fur farming became a big industry, spreading to Nova Scotia in the following decades. The motif of a silver tip fox is seen in a number of rugs from that province. This rug relates the age old legend of the fox searching for a meal in the yard of the chicken house while the chickens roost in the tree far above the animal's head. The chickens are given added importance by their huge size. c.1900. Wool and cotton on burlap, 20.75" x 35". *MCP collection.*

This rug was easy to identify as Canadian. The flag flying from the roof is the French National flag suggesting a strong tie with Canada. Added evidence is the yarn used for the background, tree trunks and roof. It is of a special twist, not usually seen in this country. The same type of yarn was used in the single beaver rug's background. Another Canadian consideration is the lace curtains at the windows. A special touch is the unusual dominance of the cellar windows. c.1885. Wool yarn and fabric on burlap, 20.5" x 35". *MCP collection.*

This rug is an interesting combination of cotton and jute on a burlap base. The c. 1920-1930 period house is hooked with cotton strips, while the trees, grass, steps and porch elements are made with unraveled burlap or "brin" as it is commonly referred to in Canada. The brin areas appear to have been "punched," while the house is hooked in the traditional manner. The fringe at each end is attached with a double folded strip of green-dyed burlap the outer 3 inches raveled to create the fringe. c.1925. Wool and burlap on burlap, 21.5" x 35". *Courtesy C. Gardner Lane, Jr.*

This hooker obviously was a snowshoe devotee, dedicated enough to the sport to feature it in a hooked rug. It could have been made in Maine, but the addition of the pompoms along the edges is of French Canadian origin, probably Quebec. Again the drab colors are seen in a delightfully whimsical rug that demands a chuckle from the viewer. c.1900. Wool on burlap, 27.5" x 41.50". *Courtesy Lionel N. and Gerry Sterling.*

A raised design adds a touch of elegance to a rug made entirely of raveled burlap in both natural and dyed colors. In earlier times rugs of raveled burlap were considered inferior to those made of rags, but there is a new and well-deserved appreciation for them today. c.1920. Burlap on burlap, 27" x 49". *Courtesy Joseph Caputo.*

Just when a rule has been established, something interferes. While raveled burlap or brin-made rugs are considered a Canadian art form, a rug found in Northern Maine, home to many French-Canadians and Acadians, was made from raveled burlap, again using a raised design technique. c.1920s. Raveled burlap or brin and cotton on burlap. 28" x 47". *Courtesy Jeff and Suzanne Good.*

Poverty did not deter our Canadian neighbors from expressing their creativity through rug-hooking. When rags and brin were unavailable they turned to corn husks, an otherwise wasted product. Their determination is obvious when one realizes that to make a corn husk rug, the husks were first steamed in hot water until pliable, then used while the husks were still hot. Rugs of this type are very rare. In this case, some of the husks first had to be dyed to create the design. A rug in the New Brunswick Museum, hooked entirely of corn husks, was made by Mary Ann Toole at Kars, King's County, in 1841. Husks were dyed green to create the leaf design. c.1850. Corn husk on burlap. 20.50" x 31.50". *Courtesy Joseph Caputo.*

FOOTNOTES

Chapter I

[1]*The Bay Boy* is an unfinished autobiographical novel by Royall Tyler (1757-1826), American dramatist, author, poet and jurist. Never published, it survived in manuscript and is included in Marius B. Péladeau, *The Prose of Royall Tyler.* The quote is from Chap. 2, p. 52. (See Bibliography for full citations of all books and periodicals cited in the footnotes.)

[2]William Winthrop Kent, a Bangor, ME, native (1860-1955), authored three books on the subject: *The Hooked Rug; Rare Hooked Rugs;* and *Hooked Rug Design.* His brother, Edward A. Kent, who was a noted Buffalo, N.Y., architect, was lost with the sinking of the *Titanic* in 1912.

[3]A description of the Fair, including the Premiums awarded is in: *First Exhibition and Fair of the Maine Charitable Mechanic Association Held at City Hall in the City of Portland From Sept. 24 to Oct. 6, 1838.* A rare copy of this booklet is in the library of the Maine Historical Society, Portland, Maine. There was an advertisement for the Fair, with ticket information, in the *Eastern Argus.* Sept. 24, 1838. p. 3; a review in *ibid,* Oct. 1, 1838, p. 2; and a more detailed report in *ibid.,* Sept. 28, 1838, p. 2. The Mechanic Association still exists.

[4]The Burbank article is cited and discussed in William L. Warren, *Bed Ruggs/1772-1833,* p. 20, footnote 15.

[5]There was only one married female Barnard in Waldoboro at this time: Mrs. John Barnard. See U.S. Census for 1840, Waldoboro, Lincoln County, Maine, at the Maine State Archives, Reel No. 144. John Barnard, sixth generation from the original Thomas Barnard who arrived in the New World in 1640, had come from Amesbury, MA, to live with his uncle, Ezekial Barnard, a prominent Waldoboro merchant. John learned the shipbuilding trade and later moved his family to nearby Thomaston, ME.

All the quotations referring to the different rug prize categories in this and the following five paragraphs are taken from the 1838 Premium Booklet cited in footnote 3.

[6]The theories on the origins of hooked rugs put forward by Kent – which have been contradicted by modern scholars – are contained in Kent's *The Hooked Rug*, pp. 5ff.

[7]The *Boston Merchantile Journal* review is quoted in the Portland (Me), *Eastern Argus*, Sept. 28, 1818, p. 2. The Wilton carpets mentioned below in the text originated in England. They were the standard by which other carpet weaving was compared. The company, The Wilton Carpet Factory, Ltd., still exists.

[8]*Ibid.*

[9]See *Exhibition and Fair of the Maine Charitable Mechanic Association, at Lancaster and City Hall in the City of Portland. September 1854.* Hearth rugs have also been variously called "bedside rugs" or "hallway runners" (see Kent, *Rare Hooked Rugs,* p. 17, plate 19).

[10]See *Fourth Exhibition and Fair of the Maine Charitable Mechanic Association at The New City Hall in the City of Portland, October, 1859.*

[11]The newspaper article on the Bristol, ME, Farmer's Festival is contained in the *Lincoln County News,* Oct. 9, 1874, p. 2. The paper was published in Waldoboro. There are other mentions of award-winning hooked rugs at the Lincoln County Fair, *ibid.,* Oct. 16, 1874, p. 2; at the Boothbay Farmer's Festival, *ibid.,* Oct. 23, 1874, p. 2; and the Boothbay Agricultural Fair, *ibid.,* Oct. 18, 1877, p. 2

[12]Péladeau, *The Prose of Royall Tyler,* pp. 52-53.

[13]*Ibid.*

Chapter II

[1]For a good, concise history of Waldoboro and the surrounding area see Jasper J. Stahl, *History of Old Broad Bay and Waldoboro,* especially Vol. II, pp. 140, 363. See also, Samuel L. Miller, *History of the Town of Waldoboro, Maine.* Waldoboro was one of the largest towns in Lincoln County. In 1840 its population included 1,852 males and 1,809 females for a total of 3,661. See: U.S. Census for 1840, Waldoboro, Lincoln County, Maine, at the Maine State Archives, Reel No. 144.

²A rare, priced copy of the original auction catalog is in the collection of Samuel Pennington of Waldoboro, publisher of the *Maine Antique Digest.* It is used here with his kind permission. The title is: *Early American Furniture . . . Including Many Heirlooms of the Reed Family, Waldoboro. . . . Hooked Rugs, Including a group of the rare Waldoboro Type, now practically unobtainable.* The auction was conducted by H. H. Parke and O. Benet, who later formed the famous auction house, Parke-Benet, which merged into Sotheby's. At the time the auction's consignor, Warren Weston Creamer, lived in the beautiful home of Col. Isaac G. Reed, an early settler and leading citizen of Waldoboro (See Stahl, pp. 91-93). The house, which still survives, is on the National Register of Historic Places.

³ See citations for footnotes 3 and 5, Chap. I.

⁴Stahl, *op. cit.*

⁵Mary Johnson Carey, "Hooked Rugs," *The Antiquarian,* May 1925, p. 6.

⁶Katherine Q. Holway, "American Hooked Rugs and Other Rugs," *The Antiquarian,* Aug. 1929, pp. 32, 72.

⁷Holway, *op. cit.*

⁸ See *Lincoln County News,* Waldoboro, ME, Oct. 9, 1874, p. 2. Other mentions of prize-winning rugs in rural fairs in the Waldoboro area at this time can be found in the same newspaper: for the Lincoln County Fair, Oct. 16, 1874, p. 2; the Boothbay Farmer's Festival, Oct. 23, 1874, p. 3; at the Lincoln County Fair, Oct. 23, 1875, p. 2; and at the Boothbay Agricultural Fair, Oct. 18, 1877, p. 2. A good run of the newspaper can be found at the Lincoln County Courthouse, Wiscasset.

⁹*Ibid.*

¹⁰*Lincoln County News,* Oct. 11, 1877, p. 2.

¹¹*Ibid.*

¹²*Ibid.*

¹³Sam E. Connor, "Waldoboro Had Fine Examples of Early Hooked Rugs," *Lewiston* [ME] *Evening Journal,* May 9, 1941.

¹⁴*The Magazine Antiques*, July 1923, p. 40.

¹⁵*Ibid.,* May 1925, p. 293.

¹⁶See footnote 2.

¹⁷See Kent, *The Hooked Rug*, p. 8.

¹⁸See footnote 2 above.

¹⁹*The Magazine Antiques,* July 1930, p. 59.

²⁰*Ibid.,* April 1931, p. 243.

²¹Likely E. S. Frost & Co. pattern No. 7. Information in this and the following two chapters from 1931 auction catalog cited in footnote 2.

²²Appears to be a variant of Frost No. 80; also Gibbs Mfg. Co. pattern of the same number.

²³*The Magazine Antiques,* April 1938, p. 287. Also conversation between Mrs. Marjorie Freeman of Waldoboro and the author, July 23, 2002.

²⁴Quoted in Kent, *The Hooked Rug,* pp. 178-79.

²⁵For further in-depth research on the Waldoboro Rug see Mildred Cole Péladeau, *Art Underfoot: The Story of the Waldoboro Rug.* This monograph accompanied an exhibition curated by the author at the American Textile History Museum, Lowell, MA, in 1999 and at the Maine State Museum in the following year.

²⁶The documentation for 1817 date is in the *Day Book of William Ryan, Belfast, Maine,* in the Old Sturbridge Village Archives.

²⁷The mill, which predated the Civil War, became the Georges River Woolen Mill in 1868, the time when Waldoboro rugs were first mentioned in local fair accounts. The mill continued to operate until the late 1950s. See: Ellis Spear, *A Walking Tour of Warren Village,* p. 4; and *Warren History: Census, History, Statistics, Businesses,* pp. 6, 8.

²⁸Conversation by the author with an anonymous rug hooker from Waldoboro, Aug. 15, 1999.

²⁹Elizabeth Coatsworth Beston, "Tea at Chimney Farm," *Down East,* March, 1978, p. 54. The author also received the same information from Mrs. Beston in a personal interview, January 10, 1978. Attempts to contact Mrs. Beston's daughter have been unsuccessful.

Chapter III

¹Elizabeth Waugh & Edith Foley, *Collecting Hooked Rugs,* p. 13.

²Holway, *op. cit.*

³Waugh/Foley, p. 14.

⁴For a good discussion of the Chetticamp rug industry see: Fr. Anselme Chiasson & Annie-Rose Deveau, *L'Histoire des Tapis "Hookés" de Chetticamp et Leur Artisans.* For further details and citations see: Kent, *Rare Hooked Rugs,* p. 31.

⁵Waugh/Foley, p. 97.

⁶Data on Elizabeth Waugh is contained in George R. Havens, *Frederick J. Waugh: American Marine Painter*, pp. 123, 185. Waugh went to paint in the Boothbay Harbor region of the Maine coast for several years. The family, including Elizabeth, would have been within a short drive of Waldoboro.

⁷See: *An Extensive and Exceptionally Interesting Collection of Early American Hooked Rugs Formed by Mr. James M. Shoemaker of Manhasset, L.I.* The catalog for the second session was titled, *Rare Early American Hooked Rugs Collected by James M. Shoemaker of Manhasset, Long Island Second and Last Afternoon Sale, Tuesday, May 1, 1924.* All following data in this paragraph taken from these publications.

[8]Reed stitched rugs featured the use of a reed or length of rattan laid on the drawn pattern and over this reed the wool yarn was sewn. The reed, which was pliable when new or soaked in water, was bent to conform to the design. When a few inches of the reed had been covered by the yarn, or when, in its curving, it became unmanageable, the tops of the stitched loops were cut through with a sharp knife or pointed scissors. This freed the rattan and produced from the upstanding yarn a pile similar to that of a velvet or moquette carpet.

For more on this subject see the author's "Reed-Stitched Rugs Rediscovered," *Maine Antique Digest*, Oct. 2000, p. 10-C.

[9]For an example see: Kent, *The Hooked Rug*, p. 71.

[10]See: *Hooked Rugs, Footstools With Hooked Rug Coverings and Bedspreads Collected by Mrs. Edward O. Schernikow, New York City.* All citations in this paragraph from this catalog. The American Art Assn./Anderson Galleries placed an ad for this auction in *The Magazine Antiques*, Feb. 1930, p. 111. It illustrates an early floral rug "on canvas," and calls Mrs. Schernikow "a connoisseur of hooked rugs" with an "enviable reputation."

In the magazine's next issue (March 1930, p. 276) there is an ad for Mrs. Schernikow as a dealer in hooked rugs, indicating she was selling rugs even after disposing of her personal collection. Her shop was at Madison Avenue and 74th St., New York. Another well-known dealer was the New England Antique Shop, 75 Charles St., Boston. Their ad in *The Magazine Antiques,* July 1930, p. 6, said they carried "Old Hooked Rugs of the Better Grade" that could be "sent on consignment to Reliable Antique Dealers."

In the same periodical (Dec. 1930, p. 475) the Plaza Art Galleries at 9-11 13 E. 59th St., New York, announced they would be auctioning the "Magnificent Collection of Antique New England Hooked Rugs" owned by Fred. Wellington Ayer, Esq., Bangor, Maine" on Nov. 30.

[11]Kent, *The Hooked Rug,* pp. 71, 89.

[12]Kent, *Rare Hooked Rugs,* p. 30.

[13]For another statement of this mistaken belief see Kent, *Hooked Rug Design,* p. 35.

[14]Dr. Marius Barbeau, "The Origin of the Hooked Rug," *The Magazine Antiques,* Aug., 1947, pp. 110-113. Dr. Barbeau (1883-1969), collected Canadian art and decorative arts from his youth. He was on the staff of the National Museum of Canada (now the Museum of Civilization) from 1911 to 1949.

[15]Correspondence from Mr. Robson to the author, May 30, 2003, and June 26, 2003.

[16]*Ibid.* Robson authored the chapter on textiles in Richard H. Field, *The Spirit of Nova Scotia: Traditional Decorative Folk Art, 1780-1930.* This excellent text is on pp. 32-34.

[17]See: *France and New England; Being a Further Account of the Connecting Links Between That Country and New England,* Vol. II, pp. 8, 59.

Another scholarly work worth mentioning is Prof. William Otis Sawtelle's "Acadia: The Pre-Loyalist Migration and the Philadelphia Plantation." Sawtelle, in providing a history of the French and English claims to Maine and the Maritimes, correctly points to wording in the Treaty of Utrecht of 1713 (ending Queen Anne's War) that leads to all the later confusion as to what was Acadia. The Treaty said that "Acadia **or** Nova Scotia" was ceded to the English while what the treaty commissioners really meant was "Acadia **and** Nova Scotia." In other words, it confused everyone to thinking Acadia and Nova Scotia where the same while, in reality the misplaced conjunction should have specified the two were different entities.

Later in the Treaty it is correctly pointed out that Acadia was that part of Maine from the Kennebec River eastward to the St. Croix River (including the area where, centuries later, Waugh and Kent found "Acadian" rugs"). Interesting, Prof. Sawtelle, on the faculty at Haverford College in Pennsylvania, summered in Maine on Little Cranberry Island off Mt. Desert and his name will appear in Chap. IX in relation to Cranberry Island rugs.

[18]There are numerous road signs from Waldoboro eastward on Route 1 placed by the Maine Department of Transportation and the Maine Publicity Bureau touting the highway as "The Acadian Trail."

[19]Kent, *Hooked Rug Design*, p. 64.

Chapter IV

[1]Among those who have passed on this and other facts and traditions about Minnie Light are Mrs. Muriel Kenoyer of Windsor; her mother, Mrs. Gladys Cunningham of Burkettville, both of whom knew Minnie; Mrs. Margery Freeman of Waldoboro; and Mrs. Barbara Calderwood of Union (Minnie's cousin). All were interviewed by the author several times between 1995 and 2006.

The name is a corruption of the German name Leigher or Leghr and the family can be traced all the way back to the original settlers of "Old Broad Bay" [Waldoboro] who were Germans brought over by General Samuel Waldo in 1753 to inhabit the virgin lands. See also Stahl, *op. cit.*

[2]Minnie's birth date is in the Appleton Vital Records, Town Hall, Appleton, ME. The "first rug"

by Minnie is illustrated in Kent, *Rare Hooked Rugs,* p. 76, plate 90. The caption describes the rug as "exquisite flower designs, field of neutral gray, scrolls of deep red, outer border a dull brown, worked on old, heavy, white cotton cloth." This is also repeated in the interview by Mary C. Kelley with Mrs. Bullard about Minnie Light in the *Maine Sunday Telegram,* Jan. 31, 1940, entitled "Never Took Lessons But Minnie Light of Burkettville Has Designed Beautiful Rugs." When Kent's book was published in 1941 the rug was in the possession of Mrs. Hazel Bullard who had just purchased Minnie's patterns.

In Kent, p. 85, plate 112, there is pictured an adaptation by Mrs. Bullard of an old Minnie Light design. Another obvious Minnie Light rug, with the inward curving scroll border, is illustrated but not attributed on p. 39, plate 41. See also conversations by the author with Mrs. Cunningham, Sept. 24 and Oct. 8, 1985; Mrs. Freeman Oct. 10 and Nov. 23, 1998, and Feb. 6 and March 11, 1999; and other Waldoboro area historians and residents over the past three decades. Creamer was quoted in Kent, *The Hooked Rug,* p. 178.

[3]Mrs. Bullard's recollections are in Allen H. Eaton, *Handicrafts of New England,* pp. 122-23. It also mentions she owned the original patterns of another "early" rug designer, Mrs. Lila Bumps of Thomaston, Maine. Their current location is unknown. Mrs. Bullard's mother, Clara Wigfall Wallace, had also hooked rugs (Kent, *Rare Hooked Rugs,* p. 88).

[4]The Fraser firm has been most helpful in the author's research. Special thanks are due to Jeanette Szatkowski for her assistance and cooperation. After Mrs. Bullard went out of business it appears that Mrs. Fraser came into possession of the Minnie Light patterns, although the exact line of descent has been forgotten. They were used for years by the Harry M. Fraser Company of Stoneville, N.C., which has since presented to the author the remaining 24 original designs. Copies of some of the Light patterns are still in the firm's current catalog. The Fraser company is an active printer of burlap rug patterns for contemporary hookers under the "Keepsake Patterns" brand name.

[5]The original Minnie Light pattern of the elk, drawn in charcoal on cotton sheeting, was viewed and photographed by the author in a private collection in the Waldoboro area in 1994. It is now at the Waldoborough Hist. Soc.

[6]See 1940 *Maine Sunday Telegram* article cited in footnote 2.

[7]This information was gathered by the author from an examination of a Light rug in her own collection and others she has examined in private collections over the previous decades.

[8]Ross's patent application for the 1891 "turfing machine" was granted by the U.S. Patent Office on Nov. 17, and given No. 463,548. The quote is from p. 2 of the specifications. The 1881 patent will be discussed in Chap. V.

[9]Mrs. Kenoyer's recollections of rug hooking by her mother and Minnie are from interviews by the author.

[10]The quotes are from Elmer E. Light, *History of Burkettville,* pp. 5, 7-9, 11, 17, 21. Gen. Waldo ran his survey northward from Waldoboro into what is now Appleton/Burkettville in 1768. It was known as the "Black Rock District" due to the presence of labradorite found only here, in Oklahoma, upper New York State and, naturally, Labrador.

The first settlers started to arrive in the first decade of the 19th century. The area of Burkettville where Minnie's parents settled was at what was known as Luce's Corner. The first trail cut – which became the first road – ran past the Light homestead.

[11]This article is cited in footnotes 2 and 7.

[12]Ben Ames Williams (1889-1953), from neighboring Union, was one of the many fine regionalist writers that flourished in the early part of the 20th century. His most famous work, set in the Union/Appleton area, was *Come Spring* (Boston: Houghton Mifflin, 1940).

[13]Mrs. Bullard's home at Governor's Corner, where she also had her studio, still stands north of Alfred. The author thanks Frank Wood of Alfred for his kindness in filling out Mrs. Bullard's background. An adaptation of one of Minnie's patterns by Mrs. Bullard is in Kent, *Rare Hooked Rugs,* p. 85, Plate 112.

[14]*Handicrafts of New England,* p. 122.

[15]Kent, *Hooked Rug Design* , p. [32], plate 22.

[16]Taped interview by the author with the late Mr. Hall, one-time Dover-Foxcroft, ME, antiques dealer, in Aug. 5, 1975.

[17]"Esancy" is another German name that was spelled several different ways, i.e., Esansa. For more on Esancy and the direct descent of his family to Minnie's mother see: Light, *History of Burkettville,* pp. 20-21. The ten-acre parcel that Esancy gave to his oldest daughter, Margaret, became Minnie Light's residence.

[18]*Ibid.,* p. 20.

[19]*Ibid.* See also the U.S. Census, Appleton, Knox County, ME, at the Maine State Archives for the years 1860, 1870, 1880, 1910, 1920, respectively reels numbers 443, 548, 482, 542 and 684. In the Vital Records at the Appleton Town Office

there is an intention of marriage for Joseph M. Light and Sarah Grinnell of Appleton on May 26, 1849, and record of their marriage in Appleton June 11, 1849, witnessed not by a minister but a town official.

The 1860 census gives Joseph's age as 35 and Sarah's as 28. He had real estate valued at $2,100 and personal property of $865. Minnie's birth date of June 22, 1864, is in the Appleton Vital Records. It is confirmed in: *The Appleton Register, 1903,* p. 35. See also: *Appleton Records: Census, History, Statistics, Business . . . Directory, Etc.*

The record that she was away "at school" at age 15 is in the 1880 Census. Her brother's attendance at the school in Castine is in Light, p. 2. Royce W. Miller has done a number of vital records compilations all published by the Appleton Hist. Soc. See his *The New Appleton Register,1888,* 3rd edit., vol. 2; *The 1900 Appleton Register*; and *The 1920 Appleton Register*. Miller also authored *Register of Deaths, Appleton, Maine*, 8th edit.

[20]Light, p. 3.

[21]See 1920 U.S. Census. Her death date is also in the Appleton Vital Records. Since she died in the winter while the ground was still frozen the coffin was placed in the nearby Union burial vault and interred the following spring in Appleton.

[22]Alice Van Leer Carrick, "Just Old Rugs," *Good Housekeeping,* Oct. 1918, 40, 117-20.

Chapter V

[1]See: Helene von Rosenstiel, *American Rugs and Carpets,* p. 42.

[2]*Handicrafts of New England,* p. 115

[3]The original Maine Adjutant General's records for the 1st Maine Cavalry are at the Maine State Archives in Augusta. The information on Frost is taken from an individual's consolidated record card compiled by the AG after the war. It too is at the State Archives. The information is repeated in McGown, pp. 59-60, and, in part, in Kent, *Rare Hooked Rugs,* pp. 177-79.

[4]See U.S. Census for Biddeford, York County, Maine, 1860, on microfilm at the Maine State Archives. Additional information is in *Greenough's Directory of . . . Biddeford and Saco* for 1860. This city directory, issued with minor changes in title, was published during the last half of the 19th century by W. A. Greenough of Boston. This information is also published in Kent, "A Yankee Rug Designer," *The Magazine Antiques,* Aug. 1940, pp. 72-73.

[5]See Greenough's city directory for 1870. The 1870 U.S. Census for Biddeford notes Edward is age 27 and a "Peddler." Also in the household were his wife, Ellen, age 28, and a son, George, age 1.

[6]Kent, "A Yankee Rug Designer," *The Magazine Antiques,* Aug. 1940, pp. 72-73.

[7]*The Maine Year-Book,* 1871. This publication was edited and published by Edward Hoyt of Portland. It was later retitled *The Maine Register* and issued annually and biennially at different periods. It continues to this day.

[8]The peddler's lifestyle flourished just before and after the Civil War, reaching its peak in the 1870s (which incidentally, was the most prosperous times for the rug pattern firms who employed "agents"). See William H. Bunting, *A Day's Work. Part II,* p. 128.

For a concise discussion of peddlers see: Margaret Coffin, *The History & Folklore of American Country Tinware, 1700-1900,* pp. 68-72. Most men who sold on the road stocked tinware as their basic merchandise. There is a good surviving example of a peddler's wagon at The Farmers Museum, New York State Historical Assn., Cooperstown.

[9]*Ibid.,* p. 71.

[10]*Ibid.,* 72.

[11]The extremely informative chart is reproduced in *Ibid.,* p. 94.

[12]Frost was interviewed about his life and career by a *Biddeford Times* reporter in 1888. It has been reprinted several times and is most easily found in McGown, pp. 60-65, and Kent, *Rare Hooked Rugs,* pp. 174-79. Unfortunately, there is no known complete file of the original newspaper for 1888 and the few surviving individual copies do not contain the Frost article.

[13]Gibbs & Warren was a partnership of Alvin Gibbs and Samuel Warren. According to the Boston city directories of the period they were located at 22 Tremont Row and listed as retailers of "rug patterns." Further details on this business will be presented in the following chapter.

[14]As noted by Frost himself, he sold his business to Strout and Shaw in 1876. Both men are neglected in other discussions of hooked rug pattern manufacturers. The 1880 U.S. Census for Biddeford shows Strout was a New Hampshire native, age 37. At the time of his purchase of E. S. Frost & Co. he was mayor of Biddeford. He must have parleyed E. S. Frost & Co. into some profit to be able to become financially involved in E. Ross & Co. with Ebenezer Ross of Toledo, Ohio. However, by 1902 the city directory shows he had fallen in his social and economic position and was a mere "edge setter" (an operative who used a machine to put a sharp bevel on a cutting tool, such as a chisel or saw blade.)

Shaw, in the same 1880 U.S. Census, appears to have been the junior partner. By 1902 the city directory says he was an agent for the York Light & Heat Co. Further details on the Strout/Shaw ownership of E.S. Frost & Co. are given in the next chapter.

[15]See *The Maine State Year-Book* and the W.A. Greenough city directories for these years to plot the name and address changes of the firm. The data on the change of street address is from *Greenough's Directory of . . . Biddeford and Saco for 1880* (Boston: Greenough & Co., 1880), p. 41. The home addresses of Strout and Shaw are on p. 80 and 75, respectively.

[16]*Ibid*

[17]The information on the awarding of the medal and diploma is from the E. S. Frost & Co. catalog cited in the following chapter.

[18]The descent of the Frost rug stencils is to Whiting in Lowell, Mass., to Mrs. Stratton in Montpelier VT, and then Greenfield, Mass., to Deerfield Village at the Henry Ford Museum, Dearborn, Mich., and finally to the Maine State Museum, Augusta. This is discussed in further detail in a following chapter.

Chapter VI

[1]For the transitional listings between Edward Sands Frost's sale of his firm in 1876 and the first listing for the new E. S. Frost & Co. owned by Strout and Shaw see the *Maine Year-Book* for 1876, 1877 and 1878, with the former year being the last listing for Edward Sands Frost and the latter the first for E. S. Frost & Co. The same data is found in the Biddeford-Saco directories for the same period. Pearl McGowen, in her book, *The Dreams Beneath the Designs,* pp. 70, 73, suggests that Frost's daughter carried on a portion of the business in New York City until at least 1879.

[2]*Maine Year-Book* for 1878.

[3]See: *Descriptive Circular: E. S. Frost & Co's Turkish Rug Patterns* [and] *Colored Rug or Mat Patterns.* (Biddeford ?: [E. S. Frost & Co.], 1882). This date is assigned for the publication's first printing because of the inside text dated in January of that year. There were apparently other printings in 1883 and 1885.

[4]The quotation above is taken from a section entitled, "A Card to Agents" in this unpaginated booklet. The back cover touts the new punch needle machine which it states was patented Dec. 27, 1881. The "A Card to Agents" is dated Jan. 10, 1882, indicating the pamphlet was apparently ready to be printed a few days after notice that the patent had been approved by the U.S. Patent Office.

[5]This rare catalog is in a private collection.

[6]See Chapter VII for details.

[7]Ebenezer Ross's patent was given No. 251,381 by the Patent Office on Dec. 27, 1881. Ross's three claims for his new invention, as outlined in the patent were: 1 – two wooden blocks with a reciprocating needle sliding against each other; 2 – the needle with a flattened shank designed to engage a spring to feed the yarn or other filler; and 3 – the spool attached to the entire unit.

[8]See the illustration of the Novelty Rug machine taken from the American Rug Pattern Co. catalog discussed in Chap. VII.

[9]See *Circular, op. cit.*

[10]The American Life Foundation Study Institute was located at Watkins Glen, N.Y. in 1972. The son of the director, L. Goodman, is still alive but efforts to contact him have not succeeded. It should be noted that the Foundation possessed illustrations of stencil patterns that are not found in later catalogs by Greenfield Village and Charlotte K. Stratton. The Foundation published its own (now uncommon) catalog of Frost patterns.

[11]In a circular advertising his Turkish patterns published by Ross about the time he started his business in 1883, the "Novelty Rug Machine" is mentioned but there is no record he took out a new patent to supplement the original 1881 patent. In fact, the instrument he was selling looks suspiciously similar to the American Rug Pattern Co. machine of the same name, without a reel.

[12] From an examination of U. S. Patent Office records.

[13]The 1883 date for the start of Ross's business is confirmed in *Leading Manufacturers and Merchants of Ohio* , p. 83. The quotation in the following paragraph is taken from this volume.

[14]From the specifications page for Deal's patent,

[15]*Ibid.*

[16]*Ibid.*

[17]Ayer and his American Rug Pattern Co. are discussed in Chap. VII. His patent is No. 409,900.

[18]The Ross patent of 1891 was given No. 463,548.

[19]See both the alphabetical listing of residents and the section naming "manufacturers and merchants" in the *Boston Directory for the Year 1871.*

[20]The 1875 date for Gibbs's establishment of his business in Chicago is taken from the title page of the catalog of rug patterns issued by the Gibbs Manufacturing Co. Since it contains material dated 1887, the catalog obviously was not published un-

til twelve years after the business was established. The full title is: *Descriptive Catalogue and Price List of Turkish Rug Patterns, Rug Machines, Rug Yarn, Hooks and Clamps.* The cover also carried the statement *"Established 1875."* A rare copy of this publication is at the Winterthur Library in Delaware and is reprinted in *Trade Catalogues at the Winterthur Museum, Part 2.*

[21]See: *The Lakeside Annual Directory of the City of Chicago* for 1881 through 1886 (the listings for Gibbs as an individual businessman, not as a "company."). There are no entries for 1887 and 1888, but the reconstituted Gibbs Mfg. Co. reappears in 1889 through 1893.

[22]*Ibid.*

[23]*Ibid.*

[24]*Lakeside Directory, op. cit.* The full title of the second catalog is: *The Gibbs Manufacturing Co./ Manufacturers and Sole Owners of the Celebrated/* [illus. of rug machine]/ *Jewell Fabric Tufting Machine. 88 and 90 State Street, Chicago.* This Gibbs Mfg. Co. catalog has been recently reprinted by a firm that would not allow reproduction of any material contained therein.

A comparison of the two Gibbs catalogs with the E. S. Frost & Co. pamphlet of the mid-1880s is interesting. As noted elsewhere the Frost patterns go as high as 182. In the first Gibbs catalog there are a total of 47 patterns and in the second one, one is dropped and six are added for a total of 52. Clearly the Gibbs offerings are nowhere as extensive as Frost & Co.

Because of the relationship between Edward Sands Frost and Alvin Gibbs that went back to 1870 in Boston (see Chap. V), it would be logical to discover a linkage between the rug patterns issued by Gibbs after he moved to Chicago and started his own business. A close examination of the catalogs issued by the two firms shows that of the 47 in the first catalog 20, or nearly half, are identical to the Frost originals or have their main design element (the center) taken from Frost. If one adds two more identical designs in the second Gibbs catalog, a total of 22 are Frost look-alikes.

Every company, including Frost, used certain center designs and interchanged different borders to come up with different patterns. To give merely one example, the reclining lamb (Nos. 88 and 89) is found with two totally different borders. Likewise Gibbs could copy a Frost cat or dog and, by cutting a new stencil for the border, come up with a pattern that was not a direct infringement on Frost. It is clear, however, that Gibbs was greatly inspired by the Frost designs he had dealt with in Boston years earlier and probably took with him to

Chicago examples of many burlap patterns from which he could make new stencils.

[25]The last listing for the Gibbs Mfg. Co. in the Chicago directories as dealers in rug patterns and associated goods is in 1891, although it apparently remained in business as retailers of "fancy goods" from 1891 to 1893. In 1894 it was reformed as Bratt & Pruden, dealers in fancy goods.

[26]The 1904 Toledo directory states Ebenezer Ross died Jan. 12 of that year. The news story on the death of Parks is in the *Toledo Blade* of March 8. 1916.

[27]In the catalog cited in footnote 3 above. It is unpaginated.

[28]Four of the cards, in the author's collection, are illustrated in this chapter's text. The quotation is from the circular cited in footnote 3 above.

[29]*Circular, op. cit.* Numerous scholars have pointed out that the practice of firms engaging "agents" to sell everything from bibles, rug patterns, and patent medicines ended at the close of the 19th century. "By 1900, however, the traveling salesman was losing ground to catalogs and Rural Free Delivery," according to Bunting, *op. cit.,* p. 128.

[30]*Ibid.* The "chromo business" refers to the craze for inexpensively printed chromolithographs. The business sprang to popularity after the Civil War. Louis Prang of Boston brought it to high state of development but his numerous competitors debased the product and flooded the market with cheap images. See Larry Freeman, *Louis Prang: Color Lithographer — Giant of a Man.*

[31]*Ibid.*

[32]The descent of the Frost rug stencils to Whiting and finally to Greenfield Village at the Henry Ford Museum, Dearborn, Mi., is recounted in *Edward Sands Frost's Hooked Rug Patterns,* p. [5]. Vital in researching the original Frost patterns are two rare catalogs. One was produced by Mrs. Stratton after she had acquired the stencils. See: *Old New England Hooked Rug Craft Presents the Original Frost Hooked Rug Patterns . . .* (Montpelier, VT.: Old New England Hooked Rug Craft Studio, 1939). (Copy in the author's collection.) There was a revised printing of the catalog in 1952 when Mrs. Stratton moved her studio to Greenfield, MA.

The most important, however, is the catalog issued by The American Life Foundation in 1972 entitled: *Choice Hooked Rugs and the Original Frost's Hooked Rug Patterns.* The cover text indicates the patterns in the catalog were "from the original hand cut printing plates made by the E.S.

Frost Co. . . ." The catalog contains some Frost patterns not available in any other contemporary publication.

For the donation of the stencils to the Maine State Museum see: Jane Radcliffe, "Rugs All Marked Out," *Maine Antique Digest,* Nov. 2004, p. 22-23-C, and Radcliffe, "New Burlap Patterns by Frost Featured in Maine State Museum Exhibit. *Maine Antique Digest,* Feb. 2006, pp. 18-19-B.

[33] See previous footnote for data on The American Life Foundation.

[34] The continuation of an E. S. Frost & Co. retail store at 247 Main St., Biddeford, is confirmed in the Biddeford-Saco city directory for that year. The next surviving directory in 1907 is silent on the company. In 1911 Strout had become secretary and treasurer of the York Loan & Building Assn.

[35] Borrows is listed in the *Portland City Directory* for 1903 as a "junk dealer" – no address given – but renting rooms at 133 Sheridan St. This gives the impression he was a peddler with no fixed business address. In 1904 he is recorded as in the "antiques" business at 46 Portland Pier and now owns a home at 34 Hancock St. He moved again in 1906 to 43 Huntress St., and in 1912 was a "traveling salesman" living at 931 Forest Ave.

[36] *Portland City Directory* for 1924. All 19th century buildings on Union St. were razed for 20th century urban renewal and so Borrows's 67 Union St. no longer exists. According to the city directory it appears to have been a two-story building with up to four firms on both levels.

[37] See the *Portland City Directory* for 1924, 1925, 1926 and 1927. *The Maine Register* for the same years confirms the directory information but adds the notation Borrows was a "mat and rug manufacturer."

[38] *Ibid.*

Chapter VII

[1] For data on Bennett see S.B. Brackett, *Portland Directory and Reference Book for 1863-4.* This indicates that what became the Bennett firm had its roots in the stencil cutting business of E. Fairfield in 1863. He took on Bennett as a junior partner in 1871. For information on the company's later history see *The Maine Year-Book* and the *Maine Business Directory* from 1873 to 1881.

[2] See footnotes 5 and 11, Chap. V. Over the years the *Year-Book, Register* and city directory all underwent minor changes in titles. For example some years the latter is called *Greenough Directory . . . of Biddeford and Saco* while at other times it is titled *Greenough's . . . Biddeford and Saco Directory.* See also: *Maine State Year-Book,* 1870.

The listing is for "E. S. Fogg," clearly a typographical error for E. S. Frost. Pond was born in 1816 but no death date has been found.

When the *Maine State Year-Book* went from annual to biennial the actual date of publication was always in the first of the two years encompassed on the title page. Thus, if a person or firm is noted in the 1870-71 edition it referred to information gathered in 1870 and the data may no longer be accurate by 1871.

[3] See *Greenough's . . . Directory of Biddeford and Saco* and the *Maine State Year-Book* for 1870 through 1880 inclusive.

[4] *Greenough's . . . Directory of Biddeford and Saco,* 1882.

[5] *Ibid.,* 1884 through 1890. Kent said he was told that Pond had reestablished himself in Waterville, ME, after closing his business in Biddeford, but no *Maine Register* nor city directory entry confirms this information. See Kent, *Rare Hooked Rugs,* p. 180, and *A Yankee Rug Designer,* p. 73.

[6] The data in the above paragraph is taken from the *Maine Year-Book* and *Maine Register*, 1881 to 1893. With Frost at 245-47 Main St. and American Rug Pattern Co. at 227 Main St., the firms were located fairly close to each other. In *Greenough's . . . Biddeford and Saco Directory* for 1888 John S. Grant is listed as the "proprietor" of The American Rug Pattern Co., residing at 3 Union St. The partner, Melville C. Ayer, resided at 10 Center St. By 1890 Grant had dropped out of the business and the city directory states Ayer was the proprietor. After the failure of the company Ayer became an electrician and Grant was employed as a grocer. (See the *Biddeford and Saco Directory* for 1902.)

[7] The catalog is now in the author's collection.

[8] See Bibliography for full citation of the *Leading Manufacturers* publication. The illustration is reproduced therein.

[9] U.S. Patent Office, Patent No. 251,381; copy in the author's possession.

[10] Quoted from the specification page for Patent No. 251,381

[11] The author has studied all applicable patent applications and this invention cannot be found.

[12] See footnote 5 above.

[13] McGown, p. 73. Apparently she did not know that Pond's first name was Daniel and she did not connect Ayer to the American Rug Pattern Co., of which she was unaware.

[14] The illustrations are on pp. [2-3].

[15] The Sears Roebuck machine, in its original box, is in the author's collection.

[16]For more on the technique of Grenfell mats see: Laverty, *Silk Stocking Mats: Hooked Mats of the Grenfell Mission.*

Chapter VIII
[1]This reprint of an early 1900 article, "Rug Weaving in the United States," is found in Old and Sold Antiques Digest at www.oldandsold.com/articles/rugs-35.shtml.

[2]The entire Arts and Crafts Movement is so thoroughly covered in many sources it is not further documented here.

[3]For more on Adler see his *An Ethical Philosophy of Life in its Main Outlines;* and Horace L. Friess, *Felix Adler and Ethical Culture: Memories and Studies.*

[4]The Ethical Culture Movement is further discussed in: "A Brief History of the Ethical Culture Movement," http://www.org/hist1.html.

[5]For a general discussion of the Sante Fe's publicity campaign around the area's Native American heritage see Don Ball Jr., & Rogers E.M. Whitaker, *Decade of the Trains: the 1940s,* pp. 185-86. There are numerous works on Fred Harvey and his railroad restaurants. A good overview is in John Kelley, "Meals by Fred Harvey," *Trains,* April 2006, pp. 60-61.

[6]The following paragraphs are from Max West, "The Revival of Handicrafts in America," *Bulletin of Bureau of Labor*, pp. 1597-98.

[7]The *Tribune* article is in a scrapbook of newspaper clippings and manuscript documents relating to the Sabatos rug industry kept by either Douglas or Marion Volk. Now in the Smithsonian Institution, Washington, D.C., a copy was kindly made available to the author by Mr. John Mayer, curator of the Maine Hist. Soc. Hereafter cited as "Scrapbook," it is invaluable for intimate details of the rug business. Many of the newspaper clippings are undated or unattributed.

[8]The data on the Abnákee rugs is taken from Helen R. Albee, *Abnákee Rugs: A Manual Describing the Abnákee Industry, the Methods Used, With Instructions for Dyeing*, 2nd edit., pp. 6-7. Albee made it very clear that she drew many of her designs from Native American sources. When she revised the second edition of her book in 1903 Albee said she had started her industry a little "more than six years" previously (p. 22). See also West, *op. cit.,* p. 1587.

[9] West, *op cit.,* p. 7.

[10]Alice Frost Lord, "At the Home of the Volks in Lovell: A Center of Art and Handicraft, *Lewiston Journal Illustrated Magazine,* Lewiston, ME, Sept. 10-14, 1904, p. [1].

[11]Arthur H. Gleason, "A Rug-Making Community," *Country Life in America,* Feb. 1906, p. 412. The entire article is on pp. 412-14. The photographs that illustrate the article, some of which are reproduced in the following chapter, were taken in 1903. Some are presently at the Maine State Museum and others, not duplicates, are in the author's collection.

An article in the *New York Press* of Jan. 13, 1901, about the Sabatos rug industry typified Center Lovell as a "remote Down East locality." The reporter made no apology that the prices of the rugs were designed to appeal primarily "to the tastes and purses of the cultivated and rich."

[12]*N.Y. Press* article in "Scrapbook."

[13]Quoted from a letter by Mrs. Volk to the *N. Y. Herald* on Nov. 26, 1900, p. [1]. in Maine Hist. Soc. collection.

[14]*Herald* letter, p. [3].

[15]*Ibid.*

[16]The patriarch of the family was Leonard Volk (1828-1895) who, as a sculptor, became famous for making a life mask of Abraham Lincoln. The mask, made in 1860, was praised as "the most reliable document of Lincoln's face and far more valuable than photographs, for it is the actual form." Volk also did a sculpture of Stephen Douglas, which was highly praised, and of Elihu B. Washburn, one of the famous seven brothers who played key roles in the development of the Republican Party as well as the administrations of presidents Lincoln and U.S. Grant. The Washburn home, "The Norlands," is on the National Register of Historic Places and maintained as a living history center in Livermore, ME. For more on Leonard Volk see: *Who Was Who in American Art,* Vol. III, p. 3415.

[17]For additional data on Douglas Volk (1856-1935) see *ibid.*

[18]Marion and Douglas Volk themselves gave different dates for the commencement of the industry, depending on whether they were talking of the first organizational meeting, the completion of the first rug, or other landmarks.

Chief Sabattus was called variously the head of the Andoscoggin (Anasagunticook) tribe of the Abnaki Confederation, or "the last of the Norridgewocks." Although much of his life is undocumented, it is recorded that he served as a spy/guide on Benedict Arnold's famous 1775 attack on Quebec City. Overlooking Center Lovell is Sabattus (Sabatos) Mountain, which appears to be one huge block of micaceous rock. The town of Sabattus (a village in the town of Webster), Sabattus Pond, Sabattus Stream, Sabattus River and another Sabattus mountain in Wales are all located east of Lewiston. There are numerous spellings of the name.

[19]The auction of Mrs. Wendell (Jessie) Volk's estate was conducted by Cyr Auction Co., July 19, 2006, at Gray, ME. The illustrated auction brochure contains information on the estate.

[20]"The Centre Lovell Art Colony" article in "Scrapbook."

[21]Townsend Ludington, edit., *The Autobiography of an American Artist,* p. 43.

[22]Marsden Hartley, *Somehow A Portrait: The Autobiography of Marsden Hartley,* pp. 184-85.

[23]Quoted in Lord, *op. cit.,* p. [1]

[24]Ludington., pp. 42-43.

[25]See: *The Official Catalogue of Exhibitors, Universal Exposition, St. Louis, U.S.A., 1904....* See especially "Group 14 – Original objects of art workmanship." See also the St. Louis World's Fair webpage at http://ftp.apci.net/~truax/1904wf.

[26]*Ibid.* Wendell was the son of Douglas and Marion Volk.

[27]David R. Francis, *The Universal Exposition of 1904*, pp. 556-57. Francis had been the president of the Louisiana Purchase Exposition Co. Mrs. Volk's certificate awarding her the silver medal and correspondence relating to her entry between herself and the Fair Exhibition Committee were in the Volk family material auctioned in 2006. An ephemera lot containing material on Sabatos Industry crafts – especially the rugs – was purchased by the Maine Hist. Soc. Hereafter cited as MHS ephemera. The silver medal itself was not found at Hewnoaks when the estate went to auction.

[28]*Evening Journal* article, *op.cit.*

[29]"Among the World's Workers: A Village Industry in Fine Rug-Making" in "Scrapbook."

[30]Lord, *op. cit.,* p. 2.

[31]Whiting/Volk letter, *ibid.*

Chapter IX
[1]Copies of this rare pamphlet are in the collections of the Lovell Hist. Soc. and the author.

[2]*Making Rugs Again* in "Scrapbook."

[3]*Ibid.*

[4]*Ibid..*

[5]John K. Mumford published his book, *Oriental Rugs*, in 1902. A copy of this volume from the Volk library at Hewnoaks was in the estate sale at the Cyr Auction Co. See also Gleason, *op. cit.,* p. 412.

[6]*Lewiston Journal* article dated Feb. 16, 1915.

[7]In Me Hist. Soc. Scrapbook. See also *Making Rugs Again* in "Scrapbook." In the same source there is also a typescript of a long article from *Cur-*

rent Literature, March 1901, entitled "The Crafts: Hand-Made Rugs and Fabrics." It also contains important details on Mrs. Volk's dying of yarns from aniline dyes. For more detail on the subject of indigo see: "Dyeing with Indigo – Natural Fermentation Vat," http://www.auorasilk.com/info/indigo_tutorial.shtml.

[8]Interviews and correspondence with Mrs. Tufts, 2004-05. Samples of Sabatos yarns dyed by using different herbs and barks are in MHS ephemera lot.

[9]*Lewiston Journal, op.cit,* and Lord, *op. cit.,* p. 2.

[10]*Oxford County Advertiser* clipping in "Scrapbook."

[11]Hewnbeam Press item from MHS ephemera lot. All information in this paragraph from it.

[12]Ms. in "Scrapbook."

[13]Gleason, *op. cit.,* p. 412.

[14]The letterhead stationary in MHS ephemera.

[15]*Ibid.*

[16]Gleason, *op. cit.,* p. 412.

[17]Albee, pp. 30-32.

[18]The deKay correspondence in "Scrapbook." DeKay (1848-1935), a noted painter, especially of marine subjects, is best remembered as the founder of both the National Arts Club and the National Sculpture Society. In the "Scrapbook" there is an article entitled "Some Arts and Crafts Happenings in New York" by Sophia A. Walker from an unnamed periodical. It reports on the first exhibition held at the new National Arts Club that featured Sabatos rugs submitted by Mrs. Volk.

[19]Albee, pp. 50-51.

[20]Gleason, *op. cit.,* p. 413.

[21]Leonard F. Burbank, "More About Hooked Rugs," *The Magazine Antiques,* Nov. 1922, pp. 213-18. The Art Institute of Manchester is now the Currier Museum of Art.

[22]The family of Mavis Chubb Gallie also donated in her memory two woven Sabatos pillow covers (one signed) and an ash basket by basketmaker Albra Lord, also a member of the Sabatos Industry group of craftsmen.

[23]Gleason, *op. cit.,* p. 414.

Chapter X
[1]See: Ami Mali Hicks, *The Craft of Hand-Made Rugs,* pp. 103-37 (Chap. VII) This section outlines the author's views on how to make hooked rugs, including the dying of the fabric and stenciling the patterns. She specifically mentions the Cranberry Island endeavor on p. 103. The book was so popular that it went through a second edition in 1936.

[2]Max West, "The Revival of Handicrafts in America," *Bulletin of Bureau of Labor, U.S. Dept. of Commerce and Labor,* Nov. 1904, pp. 1590-91.

[3]See: Ella S. Bowles, *Handmade Rugs,* p. 27; also second edit. of 1937, pp. 191-92.

[4]Gustav Stickley's involvement with the Arts and Crafts Movement is well documented elsewhere. See: http://en.wikipedia.org/wiki/Gustav_Stickley.

[5]Hicks, p. 105.

[6]Information on the "Hobo" and the island's involvement in watching for German submarines off the Maine coast during World War I is in: Hugh L. Dwelley, *A History of Little Cranberry Island, Maine,* pp. 158-58.

The biggest newsmaker of the period on Mount Desert Island was the arrival of the German liner *Kronprincessin Cecilie* only a few days after World War I was declared. After leaving New York the ship's captain was told by his government to return quickly to the nearest U.S. port since British destroyers were looking for the vessel, which carried eleven million dollars of gold bullion. The island residents entertained the German crew and passengers for weeks until the *Cecilie* was returned to Boston and appropriated by the U.S. as a troop ship.

[7]Bowles, *op. cit.,* pp. 191-92.

[8]Liz Roman Gallese, "Down East in Maine, The Cranberry Club Is for Brahmins Only," *Wall Street Journal,* Dec. 24, 1975. See also: an article from the *Ellsworth* (ME) *American,* "Cranberry Club Isn't Even for the Locals," available online at: http://www.ellsworthamerican.com/ourtown.cranisle/ot_cranisle2_06-13-02.html.

[9]The Northeast Harbor Public Library has a copy of this uncommon pamphlet about the formation of the Club: Mary F. Parkman, *Cranberryana.* (Northeast Hbr.: Cranberry Club, 1926). The paragraphs quoted here below are from that booklet. There is also a vertical clipping file at the library which proved most helpful. So restrictive was the Club membership that a new member could not be proposed until someone had died.

[10]*Ibid.*

[11]*Ibid.*

[12]See an e-mail to the author from Bruce Komusin, director of the Great Cranberry Historical Soc., Oct. 20, 2005, and a personal visit to the island by the author, Sept. 20, 2005.

[13]The following material on Mr. Sawtelle is gained primarily from an e-mail from his grandson, Mr. Robert R. Pyle, librarian of the Northeast Harbor Library, June 20, 2006, and an interview by the author Sept. 20, 2005.

[14]Interviews and correspondence with Ms. Brooke Childrey, museum curator, National Park Service, Bar Harbor, ME, June 6, Sept. 15, Sept. 20, Sept. 28, and Oct. 18, 2005. See also a letter from Hugh L. Dwelley, president, Islesford Hist. Soc., to the author, June 27, 2004.

[15]Much has been written about F.D.R. and Campobello. A quick synopsis is available on the National Park Service website: http:/www.cr.nps.gov/history/online_books/presidents/site2.htm.

Chapter XI

[1]The first recorded exhibition of American Folk Art was at the Whitney Studio Club in New York City in February 1924. The initial museum in this country to mount a major exhibition of folk art was The Newark Museum in New Jersey from October 1931 to January 1932, almost simultaneously with one at the Museum of Modern Art

[2]For an excellent examination of the famous Grenfell rugs see Laverty, *Silk Stocking Mats: Hooked Mats of the Grenfell Mission.*

[3]*Report of the Maine Sea Coast Missionary Society . . .1929-30.*

[4]The history of the Maine Sea Coast Mission is taken from its various annual reports on file at its headquarters in Bar Harbor. The author thanks the Mission staff, especially Archivist Marianne Barnicle, for allowing her to do research in their annual reports and other documents. At its peak the Mission ministered to the needs of 10,000 persons living in isolated communities along the Maine coast and its offshore islands. It had more than one hundred ports of call along the 300 miles of indented shoreline which, if stretched out, would total 2,500 miles. All further quotes from annual reports and other documents are from copies in the Mission's Archives. The 50th annual report of 1955 is especially useful for facts and dates of the Mission's first half century. (*Fiftieth Annual Report of the Maine Sea Coast Missionary Society – 1955)*

[5] *Report of the Maine Sea Coast Missionary Society. . . 1924.*

[6]Mrs. Peasley's typewritten history of the rug-hooking industry is in the files of the Mission. Page 1 is missing. This could be due to a fire which destroyed some of the Mission's records. The account ends with p. 14.

[7]This marks the arrival of the Rev. Orville J. Guptill as missionary pastor. He served from 1925 to 1928.

[8]B. Altman, a select New York department store of the period, is no longer in business. It is interesting, however, that John S. Burk, vice president of

the company, collected antique hooked rugs (see Kent, *Rare Hooked Rugs,* p. [10], plate 11).

[9]This financial statement is on a separate sheet of paper but is inserted here as appropriate to the flow of the narrative.

[10]Wanamaker and Sloane in New York, and Paine's, Jordan Marsh, and R.H. White in Boston were all "high-end" department stores at the time but all have now been gobbled up by mergers or closed. Fuller Cobb-Davis, Creamer, and Mrs. Chilcott were all Maine antique dealers. The Southern Mountain Workers, a group of craftspeople around Asheville, NC, was formed in 1928 although its origins can be traced back to 1895. The organization survives to this day as the Folk Art Center.

[11]These were all famous summer resorts frequented by the rich and famous. Many of them were destroyed in the great Mt. Desert fire of 1947.

[12]*Report of the Maine Sea Coast Missionary Society. . . 1925.* All the following yearly synopses are taken from the annual reports in the Mission's Archives.

[13]This brochure is reprinted below.

[14]From a copy in the Sea Coast Mission files. One of the early benefactors of the Mission was the Sigma Kappa Sorority, starting in 1920. This gesture was made to honor the five Maine girls who founded the sorority at Colby College in Waterville, ME, in 1874. There is a photograph in the Mission's Archives of "Ma" Peasley holding a hooked rug with the sorority's Greek letters as the central design.

[15]*Annual Reports,* 1941-56. From 1941 through 1945 she was listed as Dean of the Staff, disappears in 1947, reappears in 1948 as Dean of the Staff until 1956 when she was noted as retired.

[16]The following paragraphs are from a typed letter by Mrs. Peasley in the Mission's Archives.

Chapter XII

[1]Jessica Nichols, *Marguerite and William Zorach: Harmonies and Contrasts,* p. 34.

[2]For more on Marguerite's formative decades see Roberta Tarbell, *Marguerite Zorach: The Early Years, 1908-1920* (hereafter cited as *Early Years*). For a discussion of both William and Marguerite's careers see Tarbell, *William and Marguerite Zorach: The Maine Years* (to be cited as *Maine Years*); and Nichols, *Marguerite and William Zorach: Harmonies and Contrasts.*

[3]Among the Fauvists were Henri Matisse, André Derain, Albert Marquet, and John Fergusson [sic]. Shortly Fergusson, Paul Gauguin, Vincent Van Gogh, Paul Cezanne, and George Seurat became known as "Post-Impressionists." Both Marguerite and her future husband, William Zorach, studied under Fergusson at LaPallette. Marguerite also went to Munich where she viewed the works of the Blaue Reiter artists, especially Wassily Kandinsky, Gabriele Munter, and Alexey von Jawensky. Ms. Munter, also exhibited in Paris while Marguerite was in the city. Similarities between Marguerite's paintings and those of the German Expressionists can be attributed to their common relationship with the French Fauvists.

[4]Columbia Univ. Oral History Project (1958), p. 148. In 1910 Zorach, a young art student from Cleveland, arrived in France. On seeing Marguerite at her easel at LaPallette William went over and introduced himself. She was painting a pink and yellow nude with a bold blue outline. His first reaction was to say, "Do you know what you are doing . . . And why are you doing it." He later wrote: "But I just couldn't understand why such a nice girl would paint such wild pictures." (William Zorach, *Art is My Life,* p. 23.) The couple married on their return to this country in 1912.

[5]Kenneth and Ida Manko, *Maine Antique Digest,* Aug. 2005, p. 33-A. See also Cynthia Fowler, *Early American Modern: The Embroideries of Marguerite Zorach,* pp. 79-80, for a discussion of the Zorachs and others collecting Folk Art in Maine.

[6]Field was also a collector, patron of the arts and editor of *The Arts* magazine. The Zorachs and Field were very close, the latter having lent the couple a farm in Randolph, NH, during the summer of 1915 so that they could get away from New York City and paint in a rural setting, which they preferred.

[7]Manko, *op. cit.*

[8]A complete discussion of Marguerite's embroideries is contained in Fowler, *op. cit.* The dating of the first yarn wall tapestries is on p. 75. Marguerite taught embroidery at the Modern Art School in New York during 1915-16, in the latter year at the artists' summer colony in Provincetown, MA, and at Columbia Univ. in the 1940s. The last sentence is a paraphrase of Fowler, p. 66.

[9]See *Early Years,* pp. 47-48. The papers of the Society of Independent Artists are deposited in the John Sloan Collection at the Delaware Art Museum, Wilmington. The organization is still a legal entity. For data on the S.I.A. see *The Grove Dictionary of Art* (www.groveart.com). Realizing the inadequacies of burlap, from the very the beginning Marguerite always hooked her rugs on fine linen and made her strips of wool rags.

[10]Zorach, *Art is My Life,* p. 37.

[11]*Maine Years*, p. 24.

[12]Fowler, p. 96.

[13]*Hooked Rug Design,* p. 40. There were numerous attempts at this period to exhibit woven and hooked rugs as works of art. An example is: *Rugs Designed by Artists of the Americas and Executed, Interpreted and Supervised by Gloria Finn.*

[14]Ann Wiseman, *Tapestries and Wool Mosaics*, p. 82. The rug is currently owned by Marguerite's grandson, Charles Ipcar.

[15]In the summer of 1917 the Zorachs spent the summer season on a farm near Plainfield, NH. They raised a vegetable garden and fattened up a pig which they ate before they returned to New York late in the fall.

[16]Data from an interview between the author and Ann Wiseman, Oct. 24, 2005.

[17]The information on "Leopard and Tiger" is from conversations with Mrs. Ipcar, May 23 and July 5, 2005, and is repeated in the exhibition brochure published by Bates College where it was exhibited in 1975. The catalog is entitled *Hooked Rugs in Maine*: *A Bicentennial Exhibition, Treat Gallery, Bates College, 17 October – 21 November.* The college also mounted another excellent exhibition of antique hooked rugs in 1980. That catalog was entitled, *19ᵗʰ Century Maine Rugs.*

[18]The citations on Ipcar's artistic career are numerous. A good basic volume is: Patricia Davidson Reef, *Dahlov Ipcar, Artist.*

[19]The other artists in the exhibition (listed in *Hooked Rugs in Maine*) were all well known in the Maine art world (and beyond). They included: Jeana Dale Bearce, "Boris as a Four Month Old Unicorn;" Chenoweth Hall and Miriam Colwell, Unitled; Dahlov Ipcar, "Rooster" and "Leopard and Tiger;" Bernard Langlais, "Lions" (1975); Martin Leifer and Margaret Wilson, "Herring Gull;" Ben Mildwolff and Margaret Wilson, Unitled; Stell Shevis, "Carnival;" Barbara Rackovan, "Russia Czardom;" and Judy Zorach, "Alligator."

Chapter XIII

[1]Burbank, *op. cit.*

[2]Barbara Copeland Wentworth, *No Boughs On My Bonnet,* pp. 43, 90, 91.

[3]*Ibid.*

[4]Information on Mr. and Mrs. Hatch is in the clipping and newspaper files of the Deer Isle-Stonington Historical Soc. The author thanks the society for its assistance in her research.

[5]*Ibid.*

[6] Holway, *op. cit.,* p. 72.

[7]Burbank, *op. cit.*

[8]Robert Jackman, "Newfoundland Hooked Rugs," *The Antiques Journal,* April 1996, p. 43. For more on rugs from Québec Province see Barbeau, *op. cit.*

BIBLIOGRAPHY

Adler, Felix. *An Ethical Philosophy of Life in its Main Outlines.* New York, New York: D. Appleton, 1920.

Albee, Helen R. *Abnákee Rugs. A Manual Describing the Abnákee Industry, the Methods Used, With Instructions for Dyeing.* Cambridge, Massachusetts: Riverside Press, 1903. 2nd edit.

Appleton Records: Census, History, Statistics, Business . . . Directory, Etc. Union, Maine: Union Publishing, 1888.

Appleton Register, 1903. Appleton, Maine: Harry C. Pease, 1903.

Ball, Don, Jr., and Rogers E.M. Whitaker. *Decade of the Trains: the 1940s.* Boston, Massachusetts: New York Graphic, 1972.

Barbeau, Dr. Marius. "The Origin of the Hooked Rug," *The Magazine Antiques,* August 1947, pp. 110-13.

_____. "The Hooked Rug – Its Origins," *The Transactions of the Royal Society of Canada,* 3rd Series, Section 11, Vol. 36, 1942.

Beston, Elizabeth Coatsworth. "Tea at Chimney Farm," *Down East,* March 1978, pp. 50-54.

Boston Directory for the Year . . . Commencing July 1, 1871. Boston. Massachusetts: Sampson, Davenport & Co., 1871. *Ibid.,* for 1872-76.

Bowles, Ellen Shannon. *Handmade Rugs.* Boston, Massachusetts: Little, Brown, 1927, and 2nd edit. Garden City, New York: Garden City Publishing, 1937.

Brackett, S. B., *Portland Directory and Reference Book for 1863-4.* Portland, Maine: S. B. Brackett, 1863.

Bunting, William H. *A Day's Work, Part I.* Gardiner, Maine: Tilbury House, 2000.

Burbank, Leonard F. "More About Hooked Rugs," *The Magazine Antiques,* November 1922, pp. 213-18.

Carey, Mary Johnson. "Hooked Rugs," *The Antiquarian,* May 1925, pp. [5]-9.

Carlisle, Nancy. *19th Century Maine Rugs: February 8 – March 17, 1980.* Lewiston, Maine: Bates College, 1980. [Exhibition catalog.]

Carpenter, Mary C. "Never Took Lessons but Minnie Light of Burkettville Designed Beautiful Rugs," *Maine Sunday Telegram,* January 31, 1940.

Carrick, Alice Van Leer. "Drawn In Rugs," *Country Life in America,* June 1920, pp. 69-71.

_____. "Just Old Rugs," *Good Housekeeping,* October 1918, pp. 40, 117-20.

Chaissom, Anselme and Annie-Rose Deveau. *L'Histoire des Tapes "Hookés" de Chetticamp et Leur Artisans.* Yarmouth, Nova Scotia, Canada: Les Éditions Lescarbot, 1985. There is a 1988 edition in English.

Coffin, Margaret. *The History and Folklore of American Country Painted Tinware, 1700-1900.* New York, New York: T. Nelson, 1968.

Connor, Sam E. "Waldoboro Had Fine Examples of Early Hooked Rugs," *Lewiston Evening Journal,* Lewiston, Maine, May 21, 1941.

"Cranberry Club Isn't Even for the Locals." *The Ellsworth American,* Ellsworth, Maine, n.d.

Cyr Auction Co., Gray, Maine. Various auction catalogs, 1982-2007.

Dwelley, Hugh L. *A History of Little Cranberry Island, Maine.* Frenchboro, Maine: Islandport Press, 2000.

Early American Furniture . . . Including Many Heirlooms of the Reed Family, Waldoboro. . . . Hooked Rugs, Including a Group of the Rare Waldoboro Type, Now Practically Unobtainable . . . New York, New York: American Art Association, 1930. [auction catalog.]

Eastern Argus [newspaper], Portland, Maine, for 1834-38.

Eaton, Allen H. *Handicrafts of New England.* New York, New York: Harper & Bros., 1949.

Edward Sands Frost's Hooked Rug Patterns. Dearborn, Michigan: Edison Institute for Henry Ford Museum, 1970. [rug pattern catalog.]

Fennelly, Catherine. *Textiles in New England, 1790-1840.* Sturbridge, Massachusetts: Old Sturbridge Village, 1961.

Field, Richard Henning. *Spirit of Nova Scotia.* Toronto, Ontario, Canada: Dundurn Press for Art Gallery of Nova Scotia, 1985.

Finn, Gloria. *Rugs Designed by Artists of the Americas and Executed, Interpreted and Supervised by Gloria Finn.* Washington, District of Columbia: Pan American Union, 1962.

Fitzpatrick, Deanne. *Hook Me A Story. The History and Method of Rug Hooking in Atlantic Canada.* Halifax, Nova Scotia, Canada: Nimbus Publishing, 1999.

Forbes, Allan, and Paul F. Cadman. *France and New England: Being a Further Account of the Connecting Links Between That Country and New England.* Boston, Massachusetts: State Street Trust Co., 1927. Vol. II.

Fowler, Cynthia. *Early American Modern: The Embroideries of Marguerite Zorach.* Dover, Delaware: University of Delaware, 2002. [thesis.]

Francis, David R. *The Universal Exposition of 1904.* St. Louis, Missouri: Louisiana Purchase Exposition Co., 1913.

Fraser, Harry M., Company. *Keepsake Rug Patterns.* Stoneville, North Carolina: For the company, c. 2000. [hooked rug patterns.]

Freeman, Larry. *Louis Prang: Color Lithographer – Giant of a Man.* Watkins Glen, New York: Century House, 1971.

Friess, Horace L. *Felix Adler and Ethical Culture: Memories and Studies.* New York, New York: Columbia University, 1981.

[Frost, E. S., & Company]*Descriptive Circular: E. S. Frost & Co.'s Turkish Rug Patterns* [and] *Colored Rug or Mat Patterns.* Biddeford, Maine: [E. S. Frost & Co.], c.1882. There is a later printing with an internal date of 1885.

Gallese, Liz Roman. "Down East in Maine, The Cranberry Club Is For Brahmins Only," *Wall Street Journal,* December 24, 1975.

[Gibbs Manufacturing Company,] *Descriptive Catalogue and Price List of Turkish Rug Patterns, Rug Machines, Rug Yarn, Hooks and Clamps.* Chicago: Gibbs Manufacturing Co., c. 1887. [hooked rug pattern catalog.]

_____. *The Gibbs Manufacturing Co. Jewel Fabric Tufting Machine, 88 and 90 State Street, Chicago.* Chicago, Illinois: Gibbs Manufacturing Co., c.1891. [hooked rug pattern catalog.]

Gleason, Arthur Huntington. "A Rug Making Community," *Country Life in America,* February 1906, pp. 411-14.

Goodman, L. *Choice Hooked Rugs: and the Original Frost's Hooked Rug Patterns.* Watkins Glen, New York: The American Life Foundation, 1972.

Greenough's Directory of . . . Biddeford and Saco. . . . Boston, Massachusetts: W.A. Greenough, various dates, 1860-1911.

Gross, Esther, edit. *Waldoborough Anniversary, 1773-1973. A Pictorial History.* Waldoboro, Maine: Bicentennial Book Committee, 1973.

Harris, Mary Ann H. *A Spirit in the Hills: Alice Van Leer Carrick at Dartmouth, 1901-1930.*

Hanover, New Hampshire: Dartmouth College, 1982. [thesis]

Hartley, Marsden, *Somehow A Past: The Autobiography of Marsden Hartley*, edit. Susan E. Ryan. Cambridge, Massachusetts: Massachusetts Institute of Technology Press, 1997.

Haven, George R. *Frederick J. Waugh: American Marine Painter.* Orono, Maine: University of Maine Press, 1969.

Hicks, Amy Mali. *The Craft of Hand-made Rugs.* New York, New York: Empire State Book, 1936. [2nd edit. of 1914 printing.]

Holway, Katherine Q. "American Hooked Rugs and Other Rugs," *The Antiquarian,* August 1929, pp. 32, 72.

Hooked Mats of Newfoundland and Labrador: Beauty Born of Necessity. St. John's, Newfoundland, Canada: The Rug Hooking Guild of Newfoundland and Labrador, 2006.

Hooked Rugs in the Folk Art Tradition. New York, New York: Museum of American Folk Art, 1974.

Hooked Rugs in Maine: A Bicentennial Exhibition: Treat Gallery, Bates College, 17 October – 21 November. Lewiston, Maine: Bates College, 1975.

Jackman, Robert. "Newfoundland Hooked Rugs," *The Antiques Journal,* April, 1996, p. 43.

Kelly, John. "Meals by Fred Harvey," *Trains,* April 2006, pp. 60-61.

Kent, William Winthrop, "A Yankee Rug Designer," *The Magazine Antiques,* Aug. 1940, pp. 72-73. [Re: Edward Sands Frost]

_____. *Hooked Rug Design.* Springfield, Massachusetts: Pond-Ekberg, 1949.

_____. *Rare Hooked Rugs.* Springfield, Massachusetts: Pond-Ekberg. 1941.

_____. *The Hooked Rug.* New York, New York: Tudor Publishing, 1930, rev. edit., 1937.

Ketchum, William C., Jr. *Hooked Rugs. A Historical and Collector's Guide.* New York, New York: Harcourt Brace Jovanovich, 1976.

Kopp, Joel and Kate. *American Hooked and Sewn Rugs. Folk Art Underfoot.* New York, New York.: E.P. Dutton, 1975.

Landreau, Anthony N. *America Underfoot. A History of Floor Coverings from Colonial Times to the Present.* Washington, District of Columbia: Smithsonian Institution Press, 1976.

Laurette, Patrick Condon. *Ellen Gould Sullivan. Hooked Mats.* Halifax, Nova Scotia, Canada: Art Gallery of Nova Scotia, 1979.

Laverty, Paula. *Silk Stocking Mats: Hooked Mats of the Grenfell Mission.* Montreal, Québec, Canada: McGill-Queens Univ., 2005.

Leading Manufacturers and Merchants of Ohio. . . . Toledo, Ohio: International Publishing Co.,1886.

Light, Elmer. *History of Burkettville.* Gloucester, Massachusetts: R.W. Miller, 1996.

Lincoln County News [newspaper]. Wiscasset, Maine, for 1872-1882.

Lord, Alice Frost. "At the Home of the Volks in Lovell," *Lewiston Journal Illustrated Magazine Section,* Lewiston, Maine, Sept, 10-14, 1904, pp. [1]-2.

Ludington, Townsend. *Marsden Hartley: The Biography of an American Artist.* Boston, Massachusetts: Little, Brown & Co., 1992.

Mahnke, Susan, and Don L. Snyder. "Hooked Rug Renaissance." *Yankee,* Dublin, New Hampshire, Yankee, Inc., Nov. 1981, pp. 132-137, [Re: Mildred Cole Péladeau and Joan Moshimer.]

The Maine Business Directory. Boston, Massachusetts: Briggs & Company, 1869ff.

[Maine Charitable Mechanic Association]. *Exhibition and Fair of the Maine Charitable Mechanic Association, at Lancaster and City Hall in the City of Portland, September 1834.* Portland, Maine: for the Assn., 1834.

_____. *Exhibition and Fair of the Maine Charitable Mechanic Association, at Lancaster Hall and City Hall in the City of Portland September 1854.* Portland, Maine: Ira Berry, 1855.

_____. *First Exhibition and Fair of the Maine Charitable Mechanic Association Held at City Hall in the City of Portland From Sept. 24 to Oct. 6, 1838.* Portland, Maine: By the Board of Managers, 1838.

_____. *Fourth Exhibition and Fair of the Maine Charitable Mechanic Association at the New City Hall in the City of Portland, October, 1859.* Portland, Maine: Ira Berry, 1859.

The Maine Register, and Business Directory. So. Berwick, Maine: Edward C. Parks, 1856ff.

Maine Seacoast Mission Society. *Annual Reports, 1918-1956.* Bar Harbor, Maine: For the Society, various dates.

The Maine State Year-Book. Portland, Maine: Tower Publishing, 1871-1905.

McGowen, Pearl. *The Dreams Beneath the Design.* N.P.: By the author, 1949.

Miller, Royce W. *The 1850 Appleton Register. An Alphabetized Version of the 1850 Census.* Gloucester, Massachusetts: R.W. Miller, 2000.

_____. *The New Appleton Register, 1888.* Gloucester, Massachusetts: R.W. Miller, 2000. [A reprint.]

_____. *The 1900 Appleton Register.* Gloucester, Massachusetts: R.W. Miller, 2000. [A reprint.]

_____. *The 1920 Appleton Register.* Gloucester, Massachusetts: R.W. Miller, 2000. [A reprint.]

_____. *Register of Deaths from the Beginning Until 1950, Appleton, Maine.* Gloucester, Massachusetts: R.W. Miller, 1959.

Miller, Samuel L. *History of the Town of Waldoboro, Maine.* Wiscasset, Maine: Emerson Print, 1910. Reprint: Newcastle, Maine: Lincoln County Publishing Co. for Waldoborough Historical Museum, 1987.

Morton, Sabra. "Beauty on the Floor," *Down East,* March 1980, pp. 32-36.

Moshimer, Joan. *The Complete Rug Hooker.* Kennebunkport, Maine: Leith Publications, 1986.

Mumford, John K. *Oriental Rugs.* New York, New York: Scribner's, 1902.

Nichols, Jessica. *Marguerite and William Zorach: Harmonies and Contrasts.* Portland, Maine: Portland Museum of Art, 2001.

Nolan, Emily M. *Hooked Rugs. A Bit of History. Origin and Modern Methods.* N.P.: Fireside Industries, 1926. [subtitled, *Lesson One.*]

_____. *Hooked Rugs. A Bit of History. Stories and Anecdotes.* N.P.: Fireside Industries, 1926. [subtitled *Lesson Two.*]

_____. *Hooked Rugs. Rudiments & Mechanics.* N.P.: Fireside Industries, 1926. [subtitled *Lesson Three;* see Gabriel André Petit for citation to *Lesson Four.*]

Parkman, Mary F. *Cranberryana.,* Northeast Harbor, Maine: Cranberry Club, 1926.

Péladeau, Marius B., edit. *The Prose of Royall Tyler.* Montpelier, Vermont: Vermont Historical Society and Charles E. Tuttle Co., 1972.

Péladeau, Mildred Cole. *Art Underfoot: The Story of the Waldoboro Rug.* Lowell, Massachusetts: American Textile History Museum, 1999. [exhibition catalog.]

_____. "Reed-Stitched Rugs Rediscovered," *Maine Antique Digest,* October 2000, p. 10-C.

Petit, Gabriel André. *Hooked Rugs. Color Appreciation.* N.P.: Fireside Industries, 1926. [Subtitled *Lesson Four.*]

Pitman, Joseph A. *The Story of Appleton, Maine. Historical Address Delivered at the Celebration of the One Hundredth Anniversary of the Incorporation of the Town of Appleton, Maine,*

Aug. 21, 1927. Rockland, Maine: Courier-Gazette, 1929.

Portland City Directory. Various publishers between 1865-1927.

Radcliffe, Jane. "New Burlap Patterns by Frost Featured in Maine State Museum Exhibit," *Maine Antique Digest,* February 2006, pp. 18-19-B

_____. "Rugs All Marked Out," *Maine Antique Digest,* November 2004, pp. 22-23-C.

Ramsay, John. "A Note on the Geography of Hooked Rugs," *The Magazine Antiques,* December 1930, pp. 510-12.

Reef, Patricia Davidson. *Dahlov Ipcar, Artist.* Falmouth, Maine: Kennebec River Press, 1987.

Ries, Estelle H. *American Rugs.* Cleveland, Ohio: World Publishing, 1950. [The American Art Library Series.]

Ross, E[benezer]., & Co. *Manufacturers of Rug Patterns and Machines Catalogue.* Toledo, Ohio: E. Ross & Co., 1889. [rug pattern catalog.]

Ryan, Nanette, and Doreen Wright. *Garretts and The Bluenose Rugs of Nova Scotia.* Mahone Bay, Nova Scotia, Canada: Spruce Top Rug Hooking Studio, 1995.

Sawtelle, William Otis. "Acadia: The Pre-Loyalist Migration and the Philadelphia Plantation," *A Paper Read at a Meeting of the Historical Society of Pennsylvania,* Dec. 13, 1926.

[Schernikow, Mrs. Edward]. *Hooked Rugs, Footstools With Hooked Rug Coverings & Bedspreads. Collected by Mrs. Edward Schemikow, New York City.* New York, New York: Anderson Galleries, 1928. [auction catalog.]

[Shoemaker, James M.]. *An Extensive and Exceptionally Interesting Collection of Early American Hooked Rugs. Formed by Mr. James M. Shoemaker of Manhasset, L.I.* New York, New York: Anderson Galleries, 1923. [auction catalog.]

_____. *Rare Early American Hook Rugs Collected by James M. Shoemaker of Manhasset, Long Island. Second and Last Afternoon's*

Sale. New York, New York: Anderson Galleries, 1924.

Skinner, Inc. Auction catalogs, 1982-2007, especially Sale No. 2056, February 25, 2001: The Peter Brams collection. Bolton, Massachusetts: Skinner, Inc., various dates.

Spear, Ellis. *A Walking Tour of Warren Village.* Warren, Maine: Warren Historical Society, n.d.

Stahl, Jasper J. *History of Old Broad Bay and Waldoboro.* Portland, Maine: Bond Wheelwright, 1956.

Stratton, Charlotte K. *Old New England Hooked Rug Craft Presents the Original Frost Hooked Rug Patterns Hand Colored From the Original Metal Stencils.* Montpelier, Vermont: C.K. Stratton, 1939.

_____. *Rug Hooking Made Easy.* New York, New York: Harpers, 1955.

Tarbell, Roberta. *Marguerite Zorach: The Early Years, 1908-1920.* Washington District of Columbia: Smithsonian Institution for the National Collection of Fine Arts, 1973.

_____. *William and Marguerite Zorach: The Maine Years.* Rockland, Maine: Wm. A. Farnsworth Art Museum, 1980.

The Lakeside Annual Directory of the City of Chicago. Chicago. Illinois: Chicago Directory Co., for the years 1881-1891.

The Maine Year-Book. Portland, Maine: Edward Hoyt [and successors], 1845-1920. [Followed in sequence by *The Maine Register.*]

The Official Catalogue of Exhibitors, Universal Exposition, St. Louis, U.S.A., 1904 . . . Department of Art. St. Louis, Missouri: For the Committee on Press & Publicity by the Official Catalogue Co., 1904, rev. ed.

Thompson, Eleanor McD., comp. *Trade Catalogues at the Winterthur Museum.* Bethesda, Maryland: University Publications, 1990. Part 2.

Traguair, Ramsey. "Hooked Rugs in Canada," *Canadian Geographical Journal,* Vol. XXVI, No. 5, May 1943.

United States Census for Waldoboro, Knox County; Appleton, Knox County; Biddeford, York County; and Portland, Cumberland County; for various years between 1850 and 1940.

Volk, Marion L. "Scrapbook." [This accumulation of clippings and newspaper articles relates primarily to the rug making industry at Center Lovell, Maine.] The original is at the Smithsonian Institution, with a copy at the Maine Historical Society, Portland, Maine.. [The numerous references to the contents of this volume are noted individually in the appropriate footnotes].

Von Rosenstiel, Helene. *American Rugs and Carpets: From the Seventeenth Century to Modern Times.* New York, New York: Wm. Morrow, 1978.

Warren History: Census, History, Statistics, Businesses . . . Union, Maine: Union Publishing, 1888.

Warren, William L. *Bed Ruggs/1722-1833.* Hartford, Connecticut: Wadsworth Atheneum, 1972.

Waugh, Elizabeth and Edith Foley. *Collecting Hooked Rugs.* New York, New York: Century Co., 1927.

Waugh, Elizabeth. "Distinguishing Good Hooked Rugs," *The Magazine Antiques,* January 1927, pp. 47-50.

Wentworth, Barbara Copeland. *No Boughs On My Bonnet: The Journal of the Times of Barbara Copeland Wentworth of Cushing, Maine, 1811-1890.* Augusta, Maine: Maine Historic Preservation Comm, 1983; edit. Ruth M.J. Aiken.

West, Max. "The Revival of Handicrafts in America," *Bulletin of the Department of Labor.* Washington, District of Columbia: GPO for the Department of Commerce, 1906.

Who Was Who in American Art. Madison, Connecticut: Sound View Press, 1999. Vol. III.

Wiseman, Ann. *Tapestries and Wool Mosaics.* New York, New York: Van Nostrand Reinhold, 1969.

Zeiser, Louise Hunter. *Heirloom Rugs. Designs of Louise Hunter Zeiser.* Rumford, Rhode Island: Heirloom Rugs, 1979.

Zorach, William. *Art is My Life.* New York, New York: World Publishing, 1967.

INDEX